TRUTH AND CONSEQUENCES
How Colleges and Universities Meet Public Crises

Jerrold K. Footlick

AMERICAN COUNCIL ON EDUCATION ★
ORYX PRESS ★
Series on Higher Education
1997

© 1997 by American Council on Education and The Oryx Press
Published by The Oryx Press
4041 North Central at Indian School Road
Phoenix, Arizona 85012-3397

Published simultaneously in Canada
Printed and bound in the United States of America

∞ The paper used in this publication meets the minimum requirements of the
American National Standard for Information Sciences—Permanence of Paper
for Printed Library Materials, ANSI Z39.48-1984.

Library of Congress Cataloging-in-Publication Data

Footlick, Jerrold K.
    Truth and consequences : how colleges and universities meet public
crises / Jerrold K. Footlick.
        p. cm. — (American Council on Education/Oryx Press series on
higher education)
    Includes bibliographical references and index.
    ISBN 0-89774-970-7 (alk. paper)
    1. Public relations—Universities and colleges—United States–
–Case studes. 2. Education in mass media—United States—Case
studies. I. Title. II. Series.
LB2342.8.F66 1997
659.2'97873—dc21   97-24508
                                                                        CIP

For Ceil and Robbyn and Jill
Strength and Beauty

CONTENTS

PREFACE

I have observed higher education as a journalist for more than three decades. I have also attempted to contribute to higher education both professionally and personally: in 14 week-long visits to colleges as a visiting fellow of the Woodrow Wilson National Fellowship Foundation; in three years as journalist-in-residence at Queens College in New York; as a trustee and a member of advisory boards and visiting committees at several colleges and universities; and in countless talks to organizations of university presidents and university news officers. I bring to this book an appreciation for the complexities faced by leaders of higher education.

In the following chapters, I deal with cases that have affected the lives of people I know. I am pleased that so many leaders were willing to trust me with candid recollections about issues sometimes painful to recall. In particular, I mention two friends of a quarter-century, Robert A. Reichley, who was until recently executive vice president of Brown University, and Edwin M. Crawford, who has served as vice president at four major universities, one of which, The Ohio State University, is the subject of a chapter in this book. Most particularly, I note that my wife, Ceil Cleveland, served as vice president for institutional relations at Queens College during the period described in the chapter concerning Queens College.

Edwin Crawford first encouraged me to do this book. Robert Barnett, a Washington, D.C., lawyer and friend of writers, worked to bring it to a wide audience. James Murray, director of publications—and a lot more—at the American Council on Education, was my principal sponsor during its preparation, dealing steadfastly with publishers, foundations, and others to bring it to fruition. A number of foundation executives were helpful; I want to thank publicly President David P. Gardner and Raymond Baccetti, higher education program officer, of the Hewlett Foundation. I would also like to thank Susan Slesinger, senior vice president, and Anne Thompson, vice president and managing editor, of the Oryx Press for their help and patience. Hugh Tipping is my invaluable mentor in the mystical world of computers.

My daughters, Robbyn and Jill, validate my personal theory about higher education: Give your children the best, and they will take good care of themselves.

My chief support through all this has been Ceil, as creative a writer and thoughtful an editor as anyone I know. I would not trust any chapter to anyone until she had first offered her wise, imaginative counsel.

Jerrold K. Footlick
Centerport, New York
January 15, 1997

FOREWORD

A Failure to Communicate
Higher Education and the Media

The first response I received from almost everyone to whom I mentioned this book was, "Oh, you're going to do a chapter on X, of course." Or, maybe Y. Or Z. Mention a book on crises at colleges and universities, and anyone who knows anything about American higher education has a nomination, or two, or six. It's not as if we didn't have a lot of choices.

Surely American higher education is the best in the world by any reasonable measure, whether it be the number of Nobel Prizes won, the number of international students who choose to attend institutions in the United States, the percentage of our citizens effectively prepared for professions, or technological contributions to the economy. Yet state legislatures and the U.S. Congress have become less enthusiastic in their support of higher education and its students. And no one, from scholars to know-nothings, seems reluctant to criticize. Why do we see such a surprising level of dissatisfaction with one of the things in this country that works best?

Answers are plentiful. Tuition is too high, professors who are tenured for life don't work hard enough, undergraduates are given short shrift, administrations are too fat; the list is almost endless, and the relative significance of any one of them can be argued almost endlessly. What frustrates educators is how little the public understands about why these circumstances exist. Educators often think of their critics as incapable or unwilling to understand complex conditions, and, without fail, they blame unthinking or incompetent media. Less frequently do they consider how they get themselves into trouble, often unnecessarily, or how they fail to tell their own side of the story.

The nine cases in this book describe public crises in higher education: what the institutions did wrong, what they did right, and what changes they made in their methods of operation. To say *public* crises is inevitably to invoke the prickly relationship of these institutions with the media. It is surprising how relatively little even leading educators understand about the way the media function and how little leading journalists understand about the way education operates. So it is appropriate to begin with a discussion of this critical interface between higher education and the public.

The masterful system of higher education in the United States comprises large research universities; small liberal arts colleges; community colleges; postsecondary vocational schools; private colleges and universities, large and small; and public colleges and universities, large and small. These institutions vary in countless ways; they have different aspirations and serve different needs. How can anyone reasonably equate tuition prices or research and teaching assignments among them? Yet consider how often the media report on higher education as if it were one huge, monolithic entity.

Talk to educators, on the other hand, and hear them refer casually to "the media" as if it were one huge, monolithic entity. But the mass media are, to name a few examples, *Time* and *Business Week*, ABC News and CNN, the *Wall Street Journal* and the *Washington Post*, *Nightline* and *Face the Nation*, MSNBC and Bloomberg News Service, *People* and *Vanity Fair*, *Today* and *The News Hour*, *Reader's Digest* and *Grit*, and yes, heaven help us, the *National Enquirer* and the *Star*, *Hard Copy* and *Inside Edition*. Then there are the 1,500 other daily newspapers in large cities and small towns, as well as several thousand weeklies; thousands of magazines, mass circulated and niche-marketed; radio and television stations, 50,000 watts on a clear channel to 500 watts, VHF or UHF, affiliated with networks or independent; and cable networks defying enumeration. These media voices vary in countless ways; they have different aspirations, serve different needs. The media are no more monolithic than higher education.

Part of the problem is that the typical academic and the average journalist do not understand well what the other does—even though they might think they do. As scholarship is judged, journalism looks too easy. What academics write professionally is usually read only by other academics, and often only by those who must read it. As a consequence, they have little sense of how difficult it is to produce a piece of work that someone might find intrinsically interesting. Indeed, academics have been known to smirk at one of their number, Paul Samuelson or Milton Friedman, perhaps, who writes too often or too successfully for the popular audience—at least until he wins the Nobel Prize. Perhaps the most devastating opprobrium that can be applied to a piece of scholarship is "This is not a bad work, but it's 'journalistic.'" This is the equivalent of condemning the work as glib, shallow, lacking in serious meaning.

Journalists fancy themselves as tough-minded and skeptical, with a touch of *The Front Page* in them, yet usually well-educated and sophisticated enough to use the proper fork. They perceive academics as people who are usually smart, but often fairly boring and long-winded. They lose patience with meandering campus discussions and delays in resolving issues. And journalists have little sense of the complexity and brutality of academic politics.

How academics and journalists do their work differs fundamentally. It is one of the conceits of journalism that a good reporter can learn enough about a subject in 25 minutes to write a story about it. This skill relates directly to the pace of journalism. Journalists are intellectual sprinters. They deal with assignments rapidly; they have a low threshold of boredom; they are eager to move from one task to another. This is a style that annoys many academics, flying in the face of their training and responsibility. Academics are more often the long-distance runners. An academic may spend months or years working on a problem, turning it over and over in the mind, examining every facet, searching for any nugget of information that will add to the body of knowledge. This effort may lead to an important finding, or it may lead nowhere at all, but it is what scholars do.

Given the tone of patronizing tolerance that journalists and academics frequently exhibit toward one another, it is ironic how easily each can be flattered by the other's attention. Journalists are pleased to be invited to speak on campuses and to participate in university symposia. Professors and administrators like to be quoted in newspapers, interviewed on television, or asked to write Op Ed essays. Both journalists and academics want to be invited to join corporate boards.

Leaders of both groups speak frequently about how important it is to understand one another. For journalists reading the case studies here, the tribulations of leaders in higher education should be informative. But this book is addressed more pointedly to those directly concerned with education—presidents and other administrators, trustees, public-affairs officers, and professors. As an experienced journalist, I feel a responsibility to caution them about their dealings with the media today—because coverage of education ranges from mediocre to woeful. Educators must be prepared to go beyond halfway in this relationship—not because they owe anything to the media, but because coverage of education isn't getting any better; in many respects it is getting worse.

Some of this weakness accompanies broader trends coursing through the mainstream media: a decrease in seriousness of coverage generally, abbreviated stories, trivialization, blurring of entertainment and news, and a supermarket-tabloid approach to stories about personal lives. Further, the coming of the information age affects journalists more than most, and it confuses them. They worry about how to respond to newfound competition and how to serve their readers and viewers in the technological age. We do not examine here, however, the media broadly but rather how they deal specifically with education.

In the last two or three decades, most of the media, larger news organizations and smaller, have vastly improved their coverage of business, medicine, science, and the arts. Yet in that same period, the quality of coverage of education, and its treatment as a *hot topic,* has diminished. The 1960s were notable for serious reform efforts in elementary and secondary education that were different from such efforts today in that people believed significant reform was possible. Journalists reported in depth on early childhood education and tried to explain the New Math. In higher education, journalists took seriously the Berkeley-born student protests against "depersonalized" institutions well before the movement came to be dominated by campaigns in favor of civil rights for blacks and against the Vietnam War. It was a consuming time.

In 1970, *Newsweek* recruited me from Dow Jones because I had developed a reputation for covering education seriously. In more recent years, when *Newsweek* needed someone to write about education, it often promoted a researcher or passed the occasional story to any writer available. A few years ago, the person who held the job of education writer at *Time* became a political writer. When she asked to whom she should give the files she had scrupulously kept over the years, she was told it didn't matter; *Time* had decided that it didn't need someone specifically assigned to follow education.

Anyone can see by looking at newsmagazines that they devote less space to education than they once did. Similarly, editors of one of the country's leading newspapers told their top education reporter that the paper would not run stories on higher education longer than 1,500 words, including the exposition required to give the casual reader some sense of what the story is about. How can a reporter do justice to a subject like diversity, or research integrity, or even a single tenure struggle in less than 1,500 words? But the problem is more insidious than a reduction in quantity . Rather than covering education in a temperate way, too many news organizations now often report its difficulties argumentatively, as if increasing tuition were an administrative conspiracy against parents, or as if professors who didn't teach three classes a semester were deliberately cheating students.

The importance of the news media at all levels should also be clear to senior academics at a time when the nation is conducting more of its business in public. No longer can corporations, politicians, or universities simply make private decisions in what they perceive to be their own best interests, as many of the powerful once did, without considering the public response. They owe it to themselves and to their constituents to try to understand media priorities.

To many academics, media attention is there when you don't want it and not there when you do. Many academics think their research, or that of friends, is deserving of a story in a newspaper or on television. It is overlooked, they assume, for one of three reasons: the university's news bureau is not doing its job, the news organization is not smart enough to recognize an important story, or the news organization is biased in favor of other institutions and researchers. All researchers need do is look at the journals of their own and a few other disciplines to see the volume of fresh information they are competing with for space in the media, to say nothing of news stories about wars and elections. But frequently they don't.

I remember vividly hearing a professor of musical composition denouncing the press for not having noticed his sonata, which had been performed once by a chamber group in his community. Similarly, a veteran news officer recalls with a smile that when he began his new duties at a major Midwestern university one of the deans told him, "It's really quite simple. We need to get a story in the *New York Times* every couple of weeks."

The *New York Times* comes up a lot. It is the most important newspaper in the United States not because it is the best, which it may be, but because it is the most influential among other important journalists. Watch the flagship news programs on the three major broadcast networks almost any evening. Obviously you will see breaking news stories similar to those reported in the *Times* that morning; but you are also likely to see a feature story or two that the *Times* has discovered. Take, for example, a scam pulled off by a university scientist on a pretentious academic journal. A story like this may have gone almost unnoticed for days or weeks, but when the *Times* becomes aware of it and plays it on the front page, it is quickly covered by other news organizations as if it were fresh.

Much like the *Times*, the *Wall Street Journal* and the *Washington Post* possess enormous influence, again, not just because they are excellent newspapers but because they are read carefully by leading editors and television news producers, who begin their days by combing through them. These publications are the local newspapers (although the *Journal* can be found anywhere) of the cities where the most powerful journalists live. No matter how important the *Chicago Tribune* might be in the Midwest, the *Los Angeles Times* on the West Coast, or the *Atlanta Journal-Constitution* in the Southeast, these papers cannot set the national agenda like those published in New York and Washington, D.C., simply because it is less convenient for journalistic decision makers to read them. Network news divisions and newsmagazines may be more independent about constructing their own story lists than they used to be, but the impact of the *New York Times*, *Wall Street Journal*, and *Washington Post* is disproportionately high on any issue, education included.

This helps explain, among other reasons, why private institutions tend to lead the national higher education agenda. Setting aside quality comparisons, Northeastern private colleges and universities most regularly enter the consciousness of journalistic decision makers because a disproportionate number of leading reporters and editors have attended them. And just as important, those who haven't attended those institutions, but now live in New York and Washington, have become acculturated to wanting their children to attend them. Make no mistake: To savvy admissions officers, children of prominent journalists are sometimes more valuable than children of investment bankers.

It would be enlightening to see the effect on coverage of higher education if newsmagazines and leading television news operations were relocated to Chicago. One wonders how much increased influence the Big Ten universities—which are to public higher education what the Ivy League is to private— would develop. And how much increased attention the array of excellent Midwestern liberal arts colleges would receive. A small example of how such conditions might play out is demonstrated by the number of Southern institutions featured on Atlanta-based CNN broadcasts. CNN producers find it convenient and inexpensive to dispatch a crew to Emory, Agnes Scott, or Florida State to do a feature or illustrate a large story, just as New York producers think of Connecticut or Massachusetts for their stories.

An easy illustration of the Eastern impact on media coverage of education is the matter of college costs. News stories commonly quote top-of-the-line prices—those charged by the Ivy League and the excellent smaller institutions in the region—as the apparent standard for a year in college, when only a tiny fraction of students nationwide attend institutions charging such fees. Their tuition prices are nearly twice as high as prices at the average private college, six times as high as those at the average public college, and immeasurably higher than the two-year colleges whose students mostly live at home inexpensively. In 1995, *Newsweek* ran a cover story headlined "The Thousand Dollar a Week" college year, trumpeting the $28,000 cost of an academic year at institutions holding classes only 28 weeks a year. It is legitimate to ask, as the magazine did, why the number of weeks in a semester has dwindled so markedly in recent decades. Still, the cover line was a gimmick; for many reasons, a college year means more to students than two semesters of classes. Even granting that the magazine issued a throwaway disclaimer that this wasn't the cost at most colleges, it would never have treated the article as a cover story had not the $28,000 figure applied to the famous Northeastern institutions that *Newsweek* editors feel closest to. One explanation of their influence is as simple as the words *human nature*. Journalists are people whose work is affected by their personal lives, just as is everyone else's.

It is also easy to overlook the fact that news coverage is governed by space and time. Deadlines, of course. But a newspaper or magazine commits in advance to a given number of pages per issue and a given number of columns for news stories. A television news broadcast reports the stories that will fit in a half hour, minus advertising time. Some days are newsier than others. On a day when attention-getting events such as important political decisions or natural disasters do not dominate the news, a positive feature about educational innovation may find its way to the front page or the top of the evening news; or, a seemingly modest scandal in a university may receive inordinate attention. Conversely, on a busy news day, what journalists call "good-news" features tend to be pushed aside, just as lesser scandals may be almost completely overlooked. A broader lesson of coverage is that journalism is an imprecise process, in which decisions are made for a variety of reasons in a variety of circumstances.

This cannot be a full treatment of the operation of journalism but rather a primer on understanding it. The Afterword that follows the chapters of case studies will offer a few suggestions on how colleges and universities can organize their public-affairs operations to meld in the most satisfying possible ways with the operations of journalism. A final note for now: One of the most important aphorisms of journalism, worthy of being remembered by anyone who deals with journalists professionally, is "When dog bites man, it is not news. When man bites dog, it is news." News, good or bad, is by hypothesis other than routine.

CHAPTER 1

How High the Cost
Indirect Costs at Stanford University

Not long after the humiliation of Stanford University by the Dingell congressional subcommittee, Frank Press, director of the National Academy of Sciences, assembled a small group of university presidents and leaders of the science establishment to assess the impact on American research of the struggle over indirect costs. The discussion quickly turned to Stanford bashing—the mistakes it had made, the stupidity, the terrible problems it had caused for other universities. After about 20 minutes, Harold Shapiro, the president of Princeton University, said quietly, "I really don't know what they did at Stanford, and I suspect that not many people know what they did, so I can't pass judgment on that. But I know one thing. Somehow or other, they have managed to create one of the world's intellectual treasures, and we'd better be very careful that we not act in a way that destroys that."

Shapiro's measured response contrasted with that of many other university administrators, who saw Stanford's public clash with the government in 1990-91 as a fouling of the research nest. "I certainly think it was generally felt by university presidents," conceded Donald Kennedy, who was then Stanford's president, "that the whole inquiry, the Dingell hearing, the 20/20 broadcast, were damaging to higher education as a whole, and damaging to the future of indirect-cost recovery, as indeed they were." Kennedy said he received encouragement from presidential colleagues, many of whom told him the same thing could have happened to their institutions, but, "It's easy when something has given you grief to be pretty annoyed at the source."

It was worse than Kennedy understood at the time, said his friend, Robert M. Rosenzweig, a former Stanford vice president who was then president of

the Association of American Universities, which represents the major research universities in Washington, D.C. "Other university people tended to
believe the [negative stories about Stanford]. There were lots of jokes, and lots
of nasty cracks. I don't think the other presidents were angry; it was people at
subordinate levels. [Not so much anger as] disdain, scorn—how could Stanford
have been so stupid, and it probably served them right [since] Stanford had a
reputation for being aggressive in indirect-cost recovery."

In kindergarten, the teacher would have said Stanford didn't play well with
others. It scratched for every research dollar from the government; it distanced itself from the Ivy League admissions consortium; it picked fights with
TIAA-CREF, the principal higher-education retirement funds. Perhaps
Stanford was spoiled. After a century of nearly unstinted growth and success,
this first great private university of the American West had become one of the
great universities of the world—its scientists among the masterminds of the
genetics and technological revolutions, a fount of political and economic
thought across the ideological spectrum, and at the same time one of the most
selective undergraduate colleges in the nation.

But academic excellence is only part of Stanford's panache. It has Golden
State weather, an ever-green, palm-trimmed, Mediterranean campus with a
quadrangle developed by Frederick Law Olmsted, set in the stylish community
of Palo Alto, tucked into foothills near the Pacific and convenient to San
Francisco. The year 1991 marked its centennial, and Stanford had it all—the
academic excellence; the financial security (it was successfully completing the
first billion-dollar campaign in eleemosynary history); the admiration, even
envy, of other institutions; and certainly an unmatched self-confidence—
some would say hubris—about its present and future. It also had one of the
best public images of any university in the nation, carefully nurtured over
nearly half a century.

Not that Stanford lacked for public-affairs crises; it had enough to fill its
own book. They ranged from the almost ludicrous—two executives of the
university's non-profit bookstore were discovered to be paying themselves six-
figure salaries and driving bookstore-provided luxury cars—to the stunningly
serious: in the midst of the indirect-cost fight, Dr. Frances Conley, a prominent professor of neurosurgery at the Stanford School of Medicine, resigned to
protest sexual harassment at the school, specifically the promotion to department chair of a doctor whose "attitudes and verbal behavior have been
offensive to me," as she put it mildly in an essay for *Stanford* magazine. She was
persuaded to withdraw the resignation after the other physician's promotion
was withdrawn and he agreed to medical treatment.

Kennedy relished presiding over an unceasingly bubbling academic caul-
dron. An energetic campus clash over the revision of a freshman "Western
Culture" requirement to a program called "Culture, Ideas, and Values," which
included more works by and about women, Africans, and Asians, touched off

a national debate over curriculum reform and "political correctness." "I thought the public debate, as it eventually unrolled, was very healthy," said Kennedy. "We were largely misunderstood, the secretary of education [William Bennett] got after us, but we were really talking about the right things: What ought to be the common intellectual property of educated men and women. Our faculty had a terrific process for resolving the issue, and I thought that the university was out there doing exactly what a university ought to be doing."

Indirect costs may not have been the only thing this much-blessed university had to worry about, but it was the most serious—serious in the scope of its impact on American research, and beyond, on all of American higher education. Here was one of the preeminent universities in the world accused of frittering away taxpayer dollars on yachts and commodes, and of covering its tracks with bookkeeping pettifoggery. What did that tell us about other institutions? And what if Stanford had indeed cheated the government out of $200 million or $300 million or whatever escalating figure its accusers came up with on a given day? How would its endowment and budget survive? Indeed, how would other universities cope with the millions of dollars potentially at stake?

Until it flashed across the national consciousness in the autumn of 1990, *indirect costs* was an almost unknown term to people unconnected with high-level research at American universities. Indirect costs can be defined (simplistically) as the overhead incurred by an institution to support research—costs ranging from electricity for lights and computers, and salaries for secretaries and custodians, to the operation of the library and the depreciation of buildings. Since these expenses cannot be laid precisely on specific research projects, a percentage of overhead is assigned to research. Thus, if the federal government makes a direct grant of $1 million for research to a university with a 60 percent indirect-cost recovery rate, it gives the university a total of $1,600,000, calculating $600,000 of that to cover indirect costs. (Indirect-cost rates vary considerably among universities, from about 40 percent to more than 70 percent; the rates depend mainly on the size of the institutions, the scope of their research, and the cost of services in their communities.)

Beyond the recovery rate itself, the government and universities must agree on the kinds of costs that actually support research. The library and computer labs are easy. But if the president holds a reception in his home for government officials, scientists, and corporate executives whose companies might apply the research conducted at the university, is a percentage of the expense for food and drink applicable to indirect-cost recovery? How about the flowers? Depreciation on the dining-room table and the Oriental rugs? The house itself?

Under ordinary circumstances, universities used a default rate for calculating indirect costs as promulgated in a federal Office of Management and

Budget paper, known as A-21. But because some universities contended that the default rate did not appropriately reimburse them, they were allowed under A-21 to sign supplementary agreements known as Memoranda of Understanding (MoU's). Over a decade, Stanford's accountants negotiated more than 100 MoU's with the Office of Naval Research (ONR), which was the federal agency designated to administer government research contracts with Stanford and a number of other universities. (No other university signed more than a dozen MoU's. But the ONR accountants who negotiated the MoU's at Stanford apparently recorded them differently than others did. In one case, for example, after negotiating two basic agreements for equipment inventory and buildings, the government accountants numbered the subparts so that it appeared there were 32 MoU's, not two. "This misunderstanding was to plague us," said one Stanford authority, creating "an image that [our] coverage by MoU's was unique [when] it was only more highly catalogued.")

To ensure that such agreements continued to be appropriate, the MoU's were supposed to be audited annually by another federal office, the Defense Contract Audit Agency (DCAA). But for reasons that have never been clear—overwork, incompetence, carelessness in the DCAA have been cited—the Stanford audits were pursued erratically and not completed over the entire decade beginning in 1981. This bureaucratic blunder was also to cause enormous anguish for the university.

Stanford officials liked to call their indirect-cost recovery style "very sharp pencils," as in, "Our accountants used very sharp pencils," a statement I heard spoken with pride by three different high-level university executives. Stanford's chief pencil-wielders at the time, William F. Massy, vice president for financial affairs; Frank Riddle, controller; and Janet Sweet, assistant controller and the indirect-costs specialist, helped run seminars for other universities' business officers on how to get the best indirect-cost recoveries. All of them have left their positions for one reason or another.

Some observers saw Stanford's tough stance as pure greed, a gambling style intended to finagle every possible penny out of the government, even if it risked comeuppance, financial and visible. "It depends on how you want to look at it," a Stanford executive said in defense. "You could interpret that as saying, 'See, we didn't think we were doing anything wrong; otherwise we wouldn't have been going around and talking about it.'" On the other hand, if this policy is fostered relentlessly from the top levels of administration, what is to keep lower-level accountants, those with less experience and skill, from trying to cross the bridge too far?

Because Stanford did so much research business with the federal government, the ONR actually assigned accountants to work from the university campus. Over the years, they got along fine with Stanford's accountants—too well, some government auditors later hinted. Then in late 1988, a new ONR representative, Paul Biddle, arrived, and almost immediately began raising questions about research policies and charges. To Stanford officials, he was a sloppy craftsman and a personally obnoxious troublemaker who began tampering with arrangements that had been agreed to by the government and had worked well for years. But they knew trouble when they saw it. They alerted Kennedy, who invited Biddle for coffee, telling him that if he had problems, he should bring them directly to the president's attention. Biddle never called back.

Paul Biddle saw himself as a white knight intent on saving the taxpayers from sweetheart deals put together by a grasping university and complacent bureaucrats. In an adoring profile that appeared in the January 1992 *Reader's Digest*—under the headline "He Caught the Campus Chiselers"—Biddle was pictured not only as a lonely struggler against Stanford and his ONR superiors, but as almost divine. He was so discouraged, the article said, that "One Sunday after church he approached his minister for advice. 'You've found coveting of taxpayers' money,' said his pastor. 'You have a duty to do something about it if you can.'" The article concluded with a quote from Biddle: "I think probably God is looking for a lot of little people to get America back onto the straight and narrow."

After a few false starts, this little person finally connected with Michigan Democrat John Dingell, whose staff knew how to market a "whistle blower." At the time, Dingell was considered, in the words of a *Wall Street Journal* editor, "the most feared inquisitor in Washington." His power base grew from his chairmanship of the House of Representatives Energy and Commerce Committee. Appointing himself chairman of its Subcommittee on Oversight and Investigations, he expanded the staff about twentyfold to well over 100. Dingell liked to claim that millions of dollars in taxpayer money had been saved by his investigations; not the biggest money saver but surely the most vivid icon was the $640 toilet seat purchased by the Pentagon. According to one analysis, he had "perfected the art of the congressional investigation. . . . characterized by politically sexy charges and the frequent use of juicy leaks to the news media. His hearings often leave a trail of unresolved charges and damaged reputations."

Dingell's staff was led by two men named Peter Stockton and Bruce Chafin, whose standards of professionalism and fair play, as recounted by several university authorities (not all of them connected to Stanford), can barely be described here in printable terms. Officials of one distinguished research university (again, not Stanford) were once summoned by the subcommittee and told to include a particular administrator in their party; since he was unavailable, the university brought a close colleague. Either Stockton or Chafin, the source cannot remember which, confronted these prominent university officials in a public lobby with the words, "Who the f— do you think you are!," informing them that he expected to see exactly the people he wanted to see exactly when he wanted to see them.*

"The Dingell crowd were bad people," said one higher education representative in Washington. "They were the underbelly of the House of Representatives, they were bullies, they were cynical. They weren't interested in substance. They didn't give a damn what Stanford had done or hadn't done. Once they got hold of the issue, and they saw that it had a lot of public resonance, they were just going to drive it for all it was worth." What did they get out of that? "A lot of publicity for the Dingell committee. I think they got a lot of personal satisfaction out of it. They were really some of the most unpleasant people in town."

In late August 1990, Dingell informed Stanford that it was to be the subject of an indirect-cost investigation. In October, a horde of investigators commissioned by the Dingell subcommittee and the ONR and DCAA decamped to Palo Alto where they demanded, and received, complete access to Stanford's books. The indirect-cost records contained hundreds of thousands of entries, nearly all made by staff accountants. So as government auditors began to pore over the books, they soon had more information than the university's top executives, who obviously could not keep up with all the details about the records. "There was always a dissatisfaction [among outsiders] that enough wasn't known, enough wasn't being done," said Larry Horton, Stanford's director of community and government relations. "People were asking questions to which we did not have the answers. No matter how much you tell people you don't have the answers, they don't like that. They'd say, 'What do you mean, it's your information, isn't it?' And they would think that you therefore were hiding it, as opposed to finding out what it is."

When the government investigators hit upon an item that they considered suspicious—or media catnip—they dripped it to reporters. So Stanford executives would frequently learn about their alleged malfeasances in the newspapers, and since they didn't know where to look in the sea of numbers for anything particularly fishy, they were frustrated in trying to respond. "The DCAA was doing audits, and every time they found something good they would pass it to the subcommittee staff, and the staff would leak it," said Kennedy. Stanford was especially bedeviled by the dominant regional newspaper. "We had a newspaper down the road, the San Jose Mercury News, and a reporter who was absolutely gobbling up everything that Dingell threw him. I've always been curious who benefits from leaks, and what kinds of commitments they have to make, but the Mercury News was eager for leaks and they were getting the results."

---

*For a report of similar Dingell subcommittee operations, see the article, "The Assault on David Baltimore," by Daniel J. Kevles, in The New Yorker, May 27, 1996.

The moment Stanford officials realized that the issue had reeled out of control was when they learned about the yacht. Their yacht. The yacht they didn't know about, but a twentysomething investigator for the Dingell sub-committee did.

When a local paper quoted an anonymous congressional source as saying, "We don't want to be paying for putting in tennis courts, or for a 65-foot yacht," the university went on a yacht hunt. "From the very first mention of the word 'yacht,'" said Horton, "we knew this was a very, very important issue, and could potentially create a serious public-relations problem if it was not handled properly. We didn't even know there was a yacht, we didn't think there was a yacht, and we certainly wanted to make sure there was no federal money in a yacht."

They started, logically enough, with the Hopkins Marine Station, an academic program that Stanford operated on the Monterey Peninsula, but instructors there had never heard of it. Later someone suggested that if the university had a yacht, it might have been a contribution, so the development office would know about it. Sure enough, a donor had sold a yacht to the university three years earlier for $100,000, well below its appraised value. It was stashed with Stanford's Department of Health, Physical Education, and Recreation until it could be sold, presumably for a huge profit, after the slumping yacht market revived. In the meantime, the lavish yacht *Victoria* was berthed in Oakland, 30 miles from Palo Alto, where it was used primarily by members of the Stanford Sailing Association. President Kennedy had never seen the yacht. To this day he has never seen the yacht.

On Horton's orders, the controller's office scoured records of the sailing club, athletic department books, all salary accounts, and anything else they could think of, until they had determined to their satisfaction that nothing connected with the yacht had been charged to indirect costs. "We knew that we had to be totally accurate about this. . . . Everyone who worked on this knew that if we were wrong on this, it would be very serious." Armed with the controller's report, Horton faxed to Leila Kahn, the young Dingell investigator whom Stanford had targeted as the source of the yacht leak, a letter that he himself characterizes as "brash":

> I enclose a copy of the newspaper article in which an anonymous congres-sional source stated that the government does not want to be paying "for a 65-foot yacht." During your visit to Stanford, you also inquired about a boat which Stanford owns and the effect of this boat on indirect costs . . . I believe the boat you refer to is the *Victoria*, a 72-foot vessel that is moored in the San Francisco Bay, in the Oakland estuary. . . . Stanford uses the donated boats to teach students to sail. . . . [They] are also used, free of charge, by a variety of community groups, such as the Ronald McDonald House and the Make-A-Wish Foundation. . . . *Neither the* Victoria, *nor any vessel obtained by Stanford through the boat donation program, has any*

effect on Stanford's indirect-cost rates for sponsored programs or staff benefit
rate, nor does it affect charges to the government in any other way [emphasis
added]. . . . If you have any further questions, please do not hesitate to call.

Not long afterward, a producer for the ABC News program *20/20*, who was
researching the indirect-cost story, called to thank Horton for his assistance.
In passing, Horton recalled, the producer suggested that Stanford do more
checking into its yacht, since the DCAA appeared to have found a connection
to it in the depreciation accounts. Horton called assistant controller Sweet,
who when she heard the word *depreciation* simply whispered, "Oh." The reason
the controllers had not checked the depreciation accounts was that the yacht
did not belong there, Horton said. "It's as though you're missing a sock, and
you look in the sock drawer, and then you look in the laundry bag, and then
you look under the bed, and you look every place where you think socks are,
and you didn't look in the tool shed in your garage because it shouldn't have
been in the tool shed."

Of course, when they rechecked, controllers found that depreciation on the
yacht had indeed been included among indirect costs. No one is certain how it
got in the depreciation pool, except by a blatant mistake, perhaps a coding
error among the three million or so items the office handled annually. And
how did the DCAA so quickly find the sock in the tool shed? Subcommittee
staffers have said publicly that one of their number, while cruising San
Francisco Bay on a tourist boat, had heard a tour guide point out a yacht
belonging to Stanford. Or, as some suspect, the source could have been a mole
in the Stanford system.

So there was nothing to do now but confess to the subcommittee, in what
Horton characterizes as a "very humble" letter: "I write now to tell you that—
although we believed that the information I provided you was accurate—we
recently learned that it was in error. . . . The *Victoria* and some other
equipment items donated to or purchased by the Department of Athletics
were inadvertently included in the equipment depreciation pool, part of which
was allocated to Organized Research. . . . The total amount that was incorrectly allocated [for fiscal years 1981-1988] was $184,286. . . . [We have]
repaid the full amount incorrectly allocated to the government. . . . We view
this matter as a serious error. . . . Needless to say, we regret that my letter of
October 25 contained incorrect information."

It might be regarded as curious that the DCAA knew of the mistaken entry
for the yacht, yet didn't tell Stanford. If Horton hadn't learned about it in a
casual telephone call from a television producer, the university might not have
found out until the subcommittee hearing, months later, which would have
given Dingell a "gotcha" for the ages. Logically, if informing Stanford at once
would have expedited the refund to the government, why didn't the DCAA
do so? No one knows for certain, but some people think that this illustrated the

relationship between the DCAA and the Dingell subcommittee, or, to put it another way, the DCAA's and other government agencies' fear of the Dingell subcommittee.

After nearly a year of sniping from Biddle and half a year of government investigations and media leaks, the Subcommittee on Oversight and Investigations of the House of Representatives Energy and Commerce Committee, chaired by Representative John Dingell, held a one-day hearing, March 13, 1991. It was a catastrophe for Stanford. Dingell opened by accusing Stanford of a "brazen catch-me-if-you-can attitude" and dropped more bombs that investigators had hidden from the university. One was an "Italian fruitwood commode"—in reality an antique chest of drawers—which the uninitiated thought was a toilet and at any rate sounded suspiciously like a Pentagon toilet seat. (Dingell, who almost surely knew better, appeared to encourage misunderstanding by juxtaposing the two in his opening statement: "Stanford has made Secretary Weinberger look rather frugal with his $600 toilet seat. Stanford recently purchased an early nineteenth-century Italian fruitwood commode.")

After other members of the subcommittee took turns lambasting the university, three sets of government witnesses appeared. First came testimony from Congress's own General Accounting Office, then the DCAA, and finally the ONR, the latter two, of course, having had oversight responsibility for years on Stanford's indirect costs. The DCAA, which had irresponsibly failed to complete required audits for a decade—during part of which Biddle was one of its Stanford auditors—blamed Stanford and the ONR. The ONR blamed incompetents among its own ranks.

After five hours of punishing fire, President Kennedy took his place at the witness table. He was conciliatory but refused to offer a *mea culpa*, because he had been advised that doing so would surrender legal ground needed in the negotiations ahead. Conceding mistakes, Kennedy contended that Stanford had done nothing illegal. But committee members kept throwing visible symbols, like sets of silver and cedar closets, at him, and his lawyerly contention that many of the university's actions had been "technically allowable" seemed a lame defense. Oregon Democrat (now Senator) Ron Wydens, a Stanford graduate, called it "a very sad day for one of the world's great universities," and Texas Democrat John Bryant mocked Kennedy for "stonewalling this committee like a common politician."

Looking back at the dilemma he faced that bitter day, Kennedy said, "If you're in the kind of momentary crisis that we were in, there's always a temptation to reduce momentary damage without thinking about whether that compromises a longer range interest. Now here I am, I'm going up there [to Capitol Hill], I'm going to get personal, public humiliation, it's going to be tempting for me to reduce that pain and not to think, as I should be thinking, about the long-range institutional investment. What in fact we did in that hearing was to make the best case we could for the method, for the innocence of Stanford employees of any kind of wrongdoing, and for the fact that we had played by the book." In the aftermath, Kennedy said, "We really got abuse in the newspapers, the 20/20 piece was a really bad piece. So it's embarrassing, the papers have some fun with you for awhile, the television has some fun with you for awhile, but it isn't very permanent."

The 20/20 pasting came a few days after the Dingell hearing. Introduced as a segment on government waste, "Your Tax Dollars at Work," the story blended Stanford fight songs and campus beauty shots with reporter Stone Phillips's cynical voiceover on the university's indirect-cost practices; respect-ful interviews with a gracious Biddle (who joked warmly when not expressing outrage at the university's behavior); and tough questioning of President Kennedy, a man usually quite comfortable in public who here looked stiff and suspicious responding to "questions about audit items that we had never seen." Phillips fed Biddle a line that some people thought him a "loose cannon," enabling him to respond, "We need more loose cannons in government," and enabling anchorwoman Barbara Walters, in the epilogue, to intone, "Here's to loose cannons."

The clearest illustration of how much ABC News, notably Phillips and producer Bill Willson, misunderstood about the case came when Walters asked if it was possible that the Stanford overcharges could be as high as the $200 million occasionally mentioned in news reports. Some people think "that may not be too far off," Phillips replied, citing "beach trips, movie rentals, and even a retreat for trustees at Lake Tahoe." These examples, worthy or not, amounted to peanuts; the $200 million figure could only have been possible if the MoU's, the special agreements that Stanford had negotiated with the government for indirect-cost accounting, were invalid. Although the univer-sity provided 20/20 considerable material about the MoU's, the 10-minute-plus segment never mentioned them—evidence that 20/20 did not grasp their significance or didn't care.

Not that ABC News was alone in missing the big point. The intense press coverage focused on the visible embarrassments at Stanford, such as the yacht and a new bed at the president's home (he had recently remarried), charges in the thousands of dollars not millions, for which the university reimbursed the government. When the media reported allegations from Biddle and later government auditors that Stanford could ultimately owe the government from $200 to $400 million, they usually left the impression that such overcharges resulted from an indirect-cost rate set a few percentage points too high or too many items incorrectly included. In fact, the colossal charges could not have been assessed except for some kind of fault or illegality in the MoU's. It was not as if the media didn't know about the MoU issue. Both the government agencies and the university discussed it openly, and news stories mentioned it as early as November 1990. But whether the MoU dispute appeared too esoteric to bother with, or not as "sexy" a story as the yacht or the president's bed, its gravity never became a subject of widespread public discussion.

The lack of understanding about the MoU's led to an important misunderstanding of Stanford's public position. The university could not, as many then suggested it should have, admit its errant ways, apologize, and promise to do better next time. "In the first place, there were charges out there that Stanford had conspired with Navy employees," said Kennedy. "Am I supposed to say, yes, we've engaged in criminal conduct, when we haven't." Besides, everyone agreed that throwing "some kind of concession" to a man like Dingell wouldn't make any difference anyway.

A month after the hearing, the ONR, which had become either emboldened by the Dingell subcommittee or terrified by it, unilaterally canceled its MoU's with Stanford retroactive to the previous autumn, which covered the then-current fiscal year. A terse ONR press release gave virtually no explanation. It said only that "The Navy's unilateral decision [came] after negotiations between the Navy and Stanford did not produce an agreement." That action truly frightened the university. At the time, a decade's worth of MoU agreements theoretically remained in play, since the DCAA had failed to complete its audits and close the books for the period since 1981; and Biddle and some DCAA auditors were claiming that all these MoU's were invalid. If so, Stanford's receipt of tens of millions of dollars more than it would have received under the A-21 default system was equally invalid.

"Our decision to speak up stoutly for the view that we were playing within the rules, and could defend on the individual charges, was the right one," said Kennedy. "I think subsequent events proved that. Had we just rolled over, we would have had a much harder time in the later legal action with the Armed Services Board of Contract Appeals, in what for us was the absolutely key issue, and that is, are the Memoranda of Understanding legally binding contracts? Of course they are, and if you gave on anything, you're going to slide down slowly. There was no way we could give on that point . . . with sixty to eighty million dollars [or more] at stake." Finally in the fall of 1994, after excruciating negotiations, Stanford made what Kennedy called "a token payment" and the government acknowledged the validity of the MoU's.

The token payment was about $1.2 million, but Stanford paid dearly to fight the charges. With its own accountants overwhelmed and shell shocked, the university hired the firm of Arthur Andersen & Co. in January 1991 to evaluate its accounting systems as a counterforce to the government auditors. At the same time, it moved to strengthen the credibility of its program by establishing a Special Advisory Panel on Standards for Accountability for Federal Research Costs, whose members included Bobby Ray Inman, the former deputy director of the Central Intelligence Agency, Father Timothy Healy, the former president of Georgetown University, and Joseph Connor, chairman of Price Waterhouse World Firm Ltd. To negotiate with the ONR and the DCAA, and to prepare for the Dingell subcommittee, it had already supplemented its house counsel with the high-powered Washington law firm of Arnold & Porter.

Stanford's influential in-house legal staff consisted of two dozen lawyers headed by John Schwartz, who was a confidant of Kennedy's. As the indirect-cost battle grew more precarious, the lawyers insisted that the university hang tough. "At some point the legal office decided," said a person who attended critical meetings, "that the exposure here was so great—we were talking about the survival of the institution—so that all other considerations had to take second place to the legal case. We couldn't afford to worry about the court of public opinion. We had to keep the legal case pristine." Ultimately, this administrator pointed out, the tough legal approach worked: "Our lawyers had a right to say, 'We won.'"

The potential damage to its image, however, led the university to seek outside public-relations counsel. Oddly, the Stanford community and the media seemed to accept expensive outside accountants and lawyers but found hiring a "PR man" unseemly. The public-relations man selected was Frank Mankiewicz, a Hill & Knowlton vice president who had been Robert Kennedy's press secretary and had served as president of National Public Radio. "He was enormously helpful," Donald Kennedy said. Besides advising Stanford officials as they prepared for the hearing and for their meetings with the press, he worked with the Arthur Andersen auditors and both the university's and the outside lawyers, offering counsel on how their actions would look to various constituencies. "I was perfectly aware that taking on that kind of help can open you up to criticism," Kennedy said. "I was much more worried about criticism from inside the institution than outside, faculty saying, what do we need that sort of thing for. But it was very worthwhile."

Asked about the fees paid to Mankiewicz, reportedly $400,000, Horton said with a smile, "You can run up bills in a big hurry." Stanford had too much at stake, of course, not to deal with the problem at whatever cost. What then was the cost for lawyers, accountants, and related services by the end of the crisis? About $37 million.

The price paid by Kennedy was his job. As pressure built through the academic year 1990-91, culminating with the Dingell hearing and the 20/20 program, Kennedy repeatedly said he would not give up his post. In the spring, after the hearing, he turned his attention to essential budget cuts, which had less to do with indirect-cost recovery than with the $170 million in damage the campus had suffered from the 1989 Loma Prieta earthquake. During the rigorous weekly budget meetings, Kennedy recalled, "I began to be conscious of the fact that it was very hard [for anyone] to concentrate on the long-range future, in view of all of the furor that there was about the chaotic situation in which we found ourselves. There was lots of speculation: 'Can the president survive this business?' 'Is he a lightning rod?' 'Is his continued presence going to mean that it's very hard to close this issue out, resolve it?'"

Kennedy's first instinct, and that of his wife Robin (she had been a Stanford lawyer), was to "ride it out, and a lot of people urged me to do that. But clarity is very important to an institution, clarity about the future. . . . I sort of soaked this up for [awhile], I talked to a few friends, and I just decided that it wasn't going to work, unless I put an end point to it, and made it clear that people could start looking ahead." So Kennedy announced in July 1991 that he would resign after the following academic year, 1991-1992, completing 12 years in office. One university executive called it "the pound of flesh extracted from us." Stanford undertook a year-long international search, which culminated in the appointment of Gerhard Casper, the provost of the University of Chicago; Casper became Stanford's president in September 1992.

As the university struggled through this fearsome crisis, one of the most glorious images in all of American higher education was inevitably bloodied. Stanford is a terrific place, but its particularly admiring treatment in the media was the finely wrought product of half a century of openness and confident public-affairs judgment. In most of the other cases evaluated for this book, institutions concluded after the fact that they were less open than they might usefully have been, and in particular that the principal news officers were not as well informed as they might have been; Stanford is perhaps the only one that determined it should have been less open in its relations with its publics. The extraordinary openness must be understood in the context of Stanford's personalities and traditions. Because Stanford has long served as a national paradigm of university public-affairs strategy, a serious examination of how it got there is in order.

The starting point must be Bob Beyers—a legend in the ranks of university news officers. There have been equally skilled public-information officers at other institutions, but an experienced journalist covering higher education nationally counted on Beyers, who ran the Stanford News Service for two decades until 1989, to produce thorough information on short notice; further, he produced candid information, even if it did not always redound to the benefit of Stanford. The office functioned like a newspaper "city room." A half dozen or so "beat reporters," covering various elements of the university, turned out lengthy articles that read more like news stories than press releases. Because the writers were insiders, their articles offered knowledgeable inter-pretation as well as basic facts.

Stanford News Service reporters, and frequently Beyers himself, covered everything, from student protests against the administration to racial clashes among freshmen to tumultuous faculty senate meetings. Beyers was known to report details of a student fracas to the Associated Press, and only then call the president of the university to make sure he knew as well. Perhaps the most telling example of connecting Stanford to the news—an example extreme enough that some people mistakenly consider it apocrypha—concerns Ted Bundy, who was executed in Florida in early 1989 after confessing to more than 30 murders. Under the headline, "Serial Killer Bundy Had Stanford Link," Stanford issued a press release that began as follows: "The ghost of Ted Bundy may haunt Stanford. . . . Stanford Registrar's Office records show that he was a nonmatriculated student here in the summer of 1967. . . . Whether Bundy might have been involved in one or more unsolved murders in the Stanford area probably will never be known for sure. But more than a decade later, [a Stanford psychiatrist] vividly remembers the chill he felt on learning that Bundy had been a frequent visitor in the Bay Area during 1973-74." (The legitimacy of issuing such a press release caused bitter arguments within the news service; true to form, however, the university's top administrators uttered not a word of criticism after its distribution.)

During a campus labor union organizing campaign, Beyers recalled, the Stanford News Service began a press release, "Stanford is the J.P. Stevens of higher education, according to [a union leader.]" The story continued with accusations from both the administration and the union. This astonishing press release, which surely would have been unacceptable at nearly any other university, was characterized by Beyers as an effective approach to a sensitive issue: "It gives [the university] a chance to get its reply out. And it gives you credibility."

Beyers's theory is that by releasing information before it surfaces in the press, a university gains control of the story: "You can announce that you realize you have a problem, and you're working on it. You get your [side of the] story in the press. The first story that breaks is that the president has done something [to solve the problem]." Beyers remembered "screaming, shouting, pounding on the table" when university lawyers wanted to squelch the news of a campus safety issue, which President Kennedy had already taken action to remedy. "We put [the story] out, and the [San Jose] *Mercury News* was mad as hell. We beat them on their own story. But the key thing was that the problem had been identified, Kennedy was out there, he had appointed a commission, we were in the driver's seat." Further, Beyers contended, the short-term damage from an apparently negative early story can alleviate long-term damage. "You may take a hard hit right up front, to the university or to an individual, but then it's out of the news, it's finished, and you showed you knew what was going on."

Obviously, no news director operates like this without the approval of his bosses, and Stanford's reputation for candor at the top was unmatched in

American higher education. The strategy began with Wallace Sterling, the university's towering post-war president, who had himself once worked for NBC News. A series of notable vice presidents for public affairs embraced openness: first Lyle Nelson, the architect of the information policy; then Frank Newman, later president of the University of Rhode Island and of the Education Commission of the States, then Rosenzweig, later president of the Association of American Universities.

"How Lyle sold it to Wally Sterling and Fred Terman [the provost at the time], I have no idea," said Rosenzweig. "Part of it was that there was not a lot going on here then that was very controversial. One could see easily the benefits of ingratiating yourself with the national press. The response was so favorable and flattering. It was only when things got tough, in the 1960s, that real challenges to that policy came. . . . At the time of student protest, [trustees] didn't like the idea of going to lunch at the Pacific Union Club [in · San Francisco], or wherever they had lunch, and having their friends come over and nudge them and say, 'What's going on down at Stanford? Can't you take care of those kids, make them behave?'

"There was a lot of pressure then, to make it look better than it was. I can speak with personal knowledge of that period, and it really was Dick Lyman [then provost, later president of the university] who held the line. Dick does believe that there is a right way and a wrong way, and the right way for an institution that's based on free and open communication is to conduct all of its activities, to the extent reasonable and possible, in that spirit. When I came to have something to do with it, I always believed, and still do believe, that you can't run two universities. You can't run a university that has one set of academic values and another set of management values. You take some knocks, but, well, the knocks are worth taking because the benefits outweigh the disadvantages."

The policy not only continued after Kennedy succeeded Lyman as president but increased in the proportion that Kennedy was instinctively more of a public person. About Beyers, his news service head, Kennedy said, "He was really a treasure. His great value was that he was seen by the internal Stanford community as having very independent status, of calling it as he saw it." But the president himself, a man comfortable with language and with facing the public, served as the university's principal and outspoken voice on many critical issues, perhaps too much so.

Kennedy's eagerness to step forward on almost any issue was addressed presciently by John Burness, then a vice president at Cornell University and now senior vice president for public affairs at Duke University, when he conducted an audit in 1989 of Stanford's public-affairs division:

> One additional aspect of Stanford's new-found prominence bears attention. To most of its publics, the president of a university is the personal

embodiment of the institution. As General Eisenhower learned when he became president of Columbia, the faculty are the university. But, to most students, staff, alumni, trustees, and the general public, the president is seen as the symbol of the institution. Apparently because President Kennedy is so good at it, and also because he seems to enjoy it, he appears to be the public spokesman for the institution on virtually every controversial issue. Given Stanford's new prominence, it would be a serious mistake to let that practice continue, unless the institution wishes to use up the president's credibility; the position needs to rise and remain above the fray. Crassly put, the president is too valuable a commodity to be used in this fashion, and it is incumbent upon Bob Freelen [then vice president for public affairs] and others at Stanford to play a more active and aggressive role as public spokesmen for the institution. This will, of course, necessitate a degree of media training for some of those assuming this responsibility, but it is a wise investment that Stanford should make.

Kennedy himself was not persuaded by this assessment in the Burness report. He recalled thinking as he read it that it was "interesting," but he couldn't think of specific issues when he "should have been quiet."

Burness had been invited to conduct his audit as a neutral authority acceptable both to Beyers and his boss Freelen, whose relationship had degenerated to communication by written memorandum. Freelen thought Beyers didn't manage well and would do things only his own way; Beyers thought Freelen was squeezing the university's cherished tradition of openness. The report angered Beyers, who resigned that autumn of 1989, coincidentally on the eve of the Loma Prieta earthquake, which caused literal upheaval on campus. Freelen, who later left in the wake of the indirect-cost clash, conducted a lengthy search for a successor that left the news service with "acting" leaders and a general absence of confidence at a time when it was much needed. "There was an unsettled relationship and a feeling of uncertainty and non-involvement from some people in the news service," one highly placed Stanford administrator remembered, "maybe even suspicion about how things were going."

Terry Shepard, a former reporter and editor at the *Los Angeles Times* who headed the University of Illinois information office, took over the Stanford News Service in April 1991, a few days after the Dingell hearing. The luckiest break he got was that his wife and small children remained in Illinois until the end of the school year, so that he could work from dawn to midnight trying to "get a handle on all this stuff. . . . The big problem was that the university could never catch up with what it needed to know. Our accounting systems were so complex. There were so many documents, and the charges were so broad, and the government had so many things, and auditors were running around every place. We were trying to tell everybody everything we could find out—we just couldn't find out everything."

Shepard, who has since been promoted to director of university communication, said, "I don't think there's any doubt that people are a little more cautious now, because the indirect-cost issue was such a threat to the very existence of the place, and it happened in ways that people still don't completely understand. Anytime you go through, if you will, a life-threatening experience, you're going to be more careful. So it's not that the place is less open as it's just more careful."

Upon his promotion, Shepard hired as his successor at the news service another veteran journalist, Doug Foster, who was the editor and publisher of *Mother Jones*. When Foster left to join the journalism faculty at the University of California, Berkeley, the position went to Alan Acosta, a two-time Pulitzer Prize winner at the *Los Angeles Times*. Shepard described the current news service operation as "doing what real news people do, which is to make news judgments on various grounds. First, is this news at all to people on the outside, not just flooding out everything. But we're also making judgments about the university's image, about timing, about context. Having been in the news business, we know how things can get twisted and distorted, and taken out of context. What we're trying to do is provide the context, trying to get accurate, truthful information out, but in a way that it is understood." Would he consider himself a "gatekeeper?" Yes, "that comes naturally to us, [knowing] that raw information is not always accurate."

But years after the indirect-cost crisis, Shepard's efforts to provide context—and the more cautious public-information philosophy espoused by new President Casper—still run into trouble when they appear to tamper with Stanford's reputation for candor. In 1995, for example, at the urging of several trustees, Shepard developed a corporate-style "Strategic Communications Plan." "I resisted it for quite some time," he said, because "I didn't think a corporate communications plan fit what a university does." He checked with other institutions—Duke's Burness labeled it a waste of time—and found no existing plan that "made sense to us." But when it was pointedly suggested to him that the university might hire an outside public-relations firm to do the job, Shepard decided he had better do it himself.

As finally published, the 30-page plan was stuffed with caveats:

"We emphasize that this is a *communications* plan, not a substitute for substance or a panacea for all our problems."

"Stanford is not a symphony orchestra, where each player devotedly follows a detailed score note by note. It is, at best, a jazz ensemble, with many soloists and individual improvisations."

"Finally, we must acknowledge that a university is very different from a corporation. Generally speaking, a successful corporation has a clear and disciplined command structure, tangible products, defined target markets, and a dominant goal of economic return. . . . We cannot 'market' or 'advertise' Stanford the way one would a commercial product or corporation."

The plan did, however, cite with approval various public-relations gim-
micks, like the "Seven C's of Communication" and the "Four F's" of university
goals. And the cover page offered six adjectives that could be used to describe
"the essential Stanford": "incomparable," "challenging," "vibrant," "bound-
less," "stunning," "pioneering/Western." Leaked to the press, the communications plan was quickly ridiculed: "Stanford Spin Job" [San Jose *Mercury News*];
"Immodest Stanford" [*Sacramento Bee*]; "New Speech Code" [*Stanford Daily*].
After the kind of raucous faculty meeting that Stanford was accustomed to, an
embarrassed President Casper announced that he was withdrawing the plan.
"This was the most ridiculous uproar about nothing that I had ever encountered," Casper told the *Mercury News*. "We really have more important things
to do. . . . I think in the end it failed."

Shepard was hardly pleased to be labeled as the author of a plan he had
never wanted to prepare. "I was not that unhappy to have it withdrawn," he
said, although "I was not thrilled about the context, the way it got withdrawn."
The offending six adjectives were nothing more than "category headings,"
Shepard insisted. "Of course they sound silly by themselves. The news stories
made it look as though I was proposing that everyone go around chanting this
mantra, and to use these words, and only these words, and always these words,
which was never the intent."

Almost at the same time, those skeptical about Stanford's new public-
relations posture received further ammunition. For years the university's
official communication to alumni had been the *Stanford Observer*, a tabloid
produced four to six times a year by the news service with digested stories from
the weekly faculty-staff newspaper. Foster, then head of the news service,
wanted to replace the *Observer* with something slicker, but Stanford already
had a magazine, the quarterly *Stanford* magazine, which was so good that it had
just earned the Robert Sibley Award as the nation's best university magazine
for the second time in five years. *Stanford* magazine, however, was published by
the Stanford Alumni Association, obviously affiliated with the university, but
privately incorporated, with a fierce sense of independence. Among the
successful enterprises it operates, on a $23 million budget (in 1996-97), are
the prestigious Stanford Professional Publishing Course offered every summer
and the redwoodsy Stanford Sierra Camp at Fallen Leaf Lake, which is
regularly sold out to families, university events, and retreats for non-profit
organizations.*

---

*The serene Fallen Leaf Lake is commonly misunderstood to be an arm of Lake Tahoe.
Mentioned during the indirect-cost investigation as the site for a Stanford trustees' retreat, its
location added to the university's embarrassment because it appeared to be related to the
gambling glitz of Nevada's Lake Tahoe. In fact, the isolated Sierra Camp is in California, a 45-
minute drive from the Nevada border.

Was it wise to have two magazines geared toward alumni? After considerable debate, a high-level task force reached what might be described as an inverse Solomonic compromise. The two publications would be prepared separately, on different paper, and the section representing the voice of the university, with no advertisements, would be inserted into the middle of the glossy, ad-rich alumni magazine. The upside was one terrific publication with less distribution waste. The downside was jarring readers with different voices, different design, different paper, a different commercial look.

A silly idea, Foster thought at first, but he eventually agreed. A silly idea, thought Bruce Anderson, a Stanford alumnus and *Sports Illustrated* veteran who had won the two Sibley Awards in five years as editor; he quit. To replace Anderson, the Alumni Association recruited Bob Cohn, another alumnus, from the *Newsweek* Washington bureau. The early issues produced some rocky moments, but intriguing magazines, and Cohn said he was optimistic. At the least, the Stanford administration found an avenue to alumni that it had not been granted or sought before.

The new attitude toward dissemination of information reflected the change at the top, from Kennedy, that most outgoing of university presidents and a longtime Stanford faculty member, to Casper, a newcomer to the institution. Casper was, first of all, a lawyer, trained to be cautious. More important, he had spent his career at Chicago, a small, highly intellectual institution with a conservative academic culture. "I think [Casper] has a sense that *private* means something," said Shepard, "and if you're a private university, you do have some right to conduct your own business that's different from a public university." Further, "Gerhard does everything a little more quietly."

One Stanford administrator who has observed both Casper and Kennedy said they simply have a different working style: "Don is a natural leader, and he will jump out in front and say, 'OK, that's a great idea, everybody follow me.' Gerhard, if he thinks something is a great idea, does a lot of quiet consultation, a lot of groundwork laying, gets things lined up, so that by the time the issue is public, there are fewer surprises."

When Casper took charge in the autumn of 1992, the status of the MoU's, involving tens of millions of dollars, remained in doubt. Negotiations and appeals continued for three and one-half years after the Dingell hearing, long after the news stories disappeared, and finally, in October 1994, Stanford and the ONR reached a settlement covering all the disputed years between 1981 and 1992. The university believed that it had established that its "procedures were not a unique, grasping, and irrational gaming of the system," as one executive wryly put it.

The official statement from President Casper sounded triumphant: "ONR acknowledges that it has no claim against Stanford for fraud or any wrongdoing or misrepresentation with respect to Stanford's indirect-cost submissions during these years. Over the course of these twelve years, Stanford conducted research under nearly 18,000 federally sponsored contracts and grants involving many millions of transactions and dollars. The settlement provides that Stanford will pay the government an additional $1.2 million . . . ONR has acknowledged that the documents governing Stanford's accounting practices [largely the MoU's] were valid and binding agreements." Casper's statement went on to note that as many as 30 federal auditors combed through Stanford's books before they concluded that the government had no claim for fraud, and that U.S. Department of Justice lawyers spent more than two years investigating allegations of fraud before they declined to join a lawsuit filed against Stanford by Paul Biddle.

The statement concluded: "Yet there is undeniable sadness in the hearts of those on the Stanford campus and elsewhere who admire and respect the University. There was much pain and distress as the public controversy developed. We regret the errors and inappropriate charges. But we also regret irresponsible accusations questioning the intentions and integrity of Stanford and University officials. Throughout this controversy, we asserted that Stanford had done no wrong. This settlement confirms that belief."

Although Stanford and the ONR had agreed that they would issue compatible statements, the press release distributed at the same time by the ONR read almost as if it referred to a different case: The ONR "announced today that it has achieved the two final major milestones in its program to reform its cost-setting procedures for university research grants and contracts. . . . [The ONR-Stanford] settlement includes an additional payment of $1.2 million to the government and dismissal of Stanford's appeals . . . . The appeals action brought by Stanford arose from government remedial actions taken after indirect costs at the University became a matter of public controversy."

The Navy's version went on to claim that it had implemented "a number of actions to strengthen its cost rate-setting procedures," including consolidation of negotiations at ONR headquarters rather than assigning its contract officers to work on specific campuses. It traced the history of the dispute with Stanford, including "a potential $185 million in questionable charges" had the MoU's been invalid. Then the Navy reluctantly acknowledged that it had lost the big battle—over the validity of the MoU's: The "charges had been made in accordance with the MoU's and thus had to be honored." Finally, it grudgingly conceded—at the bottom of page five of a six-page release—that the Navy "does not have a claim that Stanford engaged in fraud [or] misrepresentation . . . . This action finally closes the business dispute between Stanford and the Government and allows restoration of normal business relations."

It's hard to measure what the taxpayers gained from Biddle's whistle-blowing and Dingell's investigation of Stanford. In simplest terms, the university repaid something over $3 million (the final $1.2 million plus reimbursement for other errors, such as the yacht). Several other research institutions returned to the government a few million dollars more. Presumably further millions are being saved as universities treat their indirect-cost claims more cautiously and indirect-cost rates decrease. On the other side, already spent, are the salaries and expenses of the scores of investigators and auditors assigned to Stanford and other institutions, and the fruitless two-year Justice Department investigation of Biddle's claims.

Biddle appears to have gone to ground. After the lavish public praise from Representative Dingell at the hearing, the subcommittee staff dumped him. After the fawning interview on 20/20 and the Reader's Digest profile, the media began to take a more skeptical look. A profile of Biddle in a California newspaper reported that his "analysis of overbillings was so flawed it brought an outside expert to uproarious laughter." A Boston consultant, invited to critique Biddle's critique of indirect costs at the Stanford library, was quoted, "This guy seems so inept [his work] would be unacceptable in an undergraduate term paper." The story chronicled Biddle's original campaign to attract the Dingell subcommittee's attention, to organize Stanford faculty against their own university, and to unleash what he openly called a "media blitz" against Stanford. It claimed that if Biddle, who had earlier been a DCAA auditor, had done his job then, any doubts about Stanford's indirect cost billing would have been settled years before.

Biddle subsequently ran for Congress in the Palo Alto district and finished fourth among five candidates in the Republican primary. But during his 15 minutes of fame, he told one reporter, "I intend to be a rich man if at all possible," and he apparently planned to get rich at the expense of Stanford. A Civil War-era law allows a private citizen to sue, on behalf of the federal government, someone who has defrauded the government. If successful, the suit can induce treble damages and gives the original complainant one-third of the recovery. Biddle filed such an action, known as a *qui tam* suit, against Stanford, contending that the university had overcharged the government hundreds of millions of dollars. If his claim about the invalidity of the Memoranda of Understanding were upheld, treble damages could amount to nearly a billion dollars of which Biddle stood to receive hundreds of millions. Biddle persisted for years, through three sets of lawyers, even after the ONR conceded the legality of the MoU's. Although the university never thought he would win, it could hardly ignore the danger.

In late 1995, a federal appeals court threw out a different *qui tam* suit filed by a former government inspector, holding that a government employee whose job is to expose fraud cannot leave the government and collect on fraud he had uncovered in the course of his work. Not long afterward, Stanford's motion to dismiss Biddle's suit was granted. For reasons best known to himself,

Biddle continued to pursue an appeal, but the university thought this skirmish was effectively over.

Donald Kennedy now serves Stanford as director of the Global Environment Program in the Institute for International Studies. He still teaches undergraduate classes, still rides his bicycle around campus, and still cheers uproariously for Cardinal athletic teams.

Stanford is at least $37 million poorer, and it will be a long time recovering from the trauma. Horton, the university's veteran chief lobbyist, described it as "a sensitive bruise that has a great deal of pain. So every time you walk on that bruise, on that bruised foot, you feel it. But other people don't see it, they're not feeling the bruise. I think a lot of the way we look at things inside the university, the way we perceive them, is because of what we've gone through."

Prominent in Horton's tiny office on the Palo Alto campus are 21 volumes of documents and five volumes of press clippings (through 1994) on the crisis. The only high-level Stanford executive to retain his position after the fray and the change in the presidency, Horton contended that one cannot examine indirect costs as a public-affairs issue without considering its broader implications. "It was first and foremost enormously a substantive matter," he said, "with profound questions about the relationship between universities and government. It was a tremendous political problem, dealing with investigations and allegations of improprieties. All of those things have profound public-affairs implications, so I'm not at all suggesting that there weren't public-affairs dimensions. What I'm suggesting is, the public-affairs dimensions can't be understood in isolation from the substance."

Not surprisingly, Horton expresses disappointment at the media treatment. "I thought that in a case like this, in which there were accusations, people would look at both the source of the accusations, and about the credibility of those who were making the accusations, and at the other side of the story, which was almost missed completely. It was clear to me at the time that the battle of journalism had clearly been lost." But he is optimistic: "Sooner or later this thing will be put in perspective. The facts will be sufficiently digested, and the question of whether there was wrongdoing, or the suspicions that people have, I think will be settled, and the university will come out very well. The more serious matter for an institution is the battle of history. However painful it is in the short run, in an institution like Stanford, the long run is always most important."

In the longer run, the reality of the Stanford case turns out to be much different and more complicated than it was reported in 1990-91. It offers important lessons in both university behavior and the behavior of outsiders, such as the federal government and the media. None of these forces acquitted itself skillfully or nobly.

CHAPTER 2

Lightning in a Bottle
Cold Fusion at the University of Utah

Universities are places which are supposed to be cauldrons of ideas and debate, and they shouldn't be tranquil places. . . . There is something beyond politics, and there is something beyond public relations, and that has to do with the vigorous pursuit of ideas. By damned, if you can't do that in a university, where can you do it? And in the process of that, you're going to have human foibles all over the place.

Chase N. Peterson, M.D.
President of the University of Utah, 1983–1991

I think that we avoided a real rupture in the faculty here by a very narrow margin.

Hugo Rossi, former Dean of the College of Science
University of Utah

"SALT LAKE CITY — Two scientists have successfully created a sustained nuclear fusion reaction at room temperature in a chemistry laboratory at the University of Utah. The breakthrough means the world may someday rely on fusion for a clean, virtually inexhaustible source of energy." So began a press release from the University of Utah, issued March 23, 1989. The announcement stunned the scientific world, as well it should have. To create energy in a fashion so simplistic and so inexpensive could change not merely the course of energy production but the future of the world.

To this day, however, there is no agreement about whether the two chemists, B. Stanley Pons and Martin Ernest Fleischmann, had done what they claimed, or, indeed, whether what they claimed is possible. One expert called it "a scientific controversy not seen for a hundred years." A preponderant number of scientists who have studied the issue insist that cold fusion in a tube looks more like a perpetual-motion machine than a nuclear reactor. Yet the two chemists, and a number of other legitimate scientists, continue to tread the same path and continue to report intriguing results.

Dr. Chase N. Peterson, whose unwavering support of Pons and Fleischmann cost him his job as president of the University of Utah, refuses to give up. "There is huge denial on the part of the orthodox physics community that anything's happened. They say everything is nonsense," he said to me in his small office at the University Medical Center where he remains on the Utah faculty. "But would you be influenced in writing your book if I could tell you with absolute certainty that 5 years from now Con Edison will have a cold fusion generator? I just present for your consideration the possibility that it might be a somewhat different chapter if 5 years from now, or 10 or 20, we'd have a Con Edison generator."

We don't know whether this scenario can develop, but we do know that the fallout from the cold-fusion announcement shook the University of Utah like an earthquake in the Wasatch Range. It drove out the president, embittered longtime friends and colleagues, and embarrassed the university and the people of the state of Utah. It also provided hard lessons in challenging the science establishment, going public with a major scientific announcement, and dealing with lawyers.

Cold fusion exploded publicly that day in March 1989 when University of Utah officials announced at a press conference that Pons, the chairman of its chemistry department, and Fleischmann, an electrochemist at England's Southampton University, had created fusion in a table-top experiment at room temperature. The response was instantaneous, and not merely among scientists; everyone could understand the awesome potential of the achievement. The announcement made front pages everywhere, and both *Time* and *Newsweek* did cover stories. In *Newsweek*'s "The Race for Fusion," the report that two chemists "had created nuclear fusion in a bottle, using little more than water, wire, and electricity . . . was as if someone had said he'd flown to Mars in a prop plane."

The reaction from physicists, who considered the study of fusion their special province, was nuclear in its intensity. For nearly four decades, physicists around the world had sought ways to harness fusion for energy, developing complex equipment and conducting elaborate experiments at a cost of billions of dollars. They theorized that controlled fusion could be usefully achieved only under extreme conditions, such as those created by heating charged gases of hydrogen nuclei to temperatures of millions of degrees; yet no one had mastered the equipment necessary to achieve optimum conditions.* Perhaps in a few years, perhaps in a few decades, someone would. Now two unheralded scientists—not even physicists but electrochemists—were saying that they had accomplished the feat, in an inexpensive university laboratory and at room temperature. It was unthinkable.

At a meeting of the American Physical Society a month after the Pons-Fleischmann announcement, paper after paper denounced their claims, and "a roar of applause" from 1,500 physicists greeted the statement from physicist Steven E. Koonin of the University of California, Santa Barbara, that the experiment "suffered from the incompetence and delusion of Pons and Fleischmann." Koonin went further in a *New York Times* interview: "It's all very well to theorize about how cold fusion in a palladium cathode might take place. One could also theorize about how pigs would behave if they had wings. But pigs don't have wings."

By contrast, chemists reveled in this apparent triumph by one of their own in a field usually considered to be outside the area of their expertise. Pons "received sustained applause from 7,000 chemists" at the national meeting of the American Chemical Society (ACS) three weeks after the announcement, and Clayton F. Callis, president of the ACS, evoked "long applause" with an

---

*The following are popular definitions of fusion and of the cold-fusion experiment, which appeared in *Technology Review,* the magazine of the Massachusetts Institute of Technology, May/June 1994: "Fusion requires the joining together of two atomic nuclei, both of which have a positive electric charge and so repel each other strongly. Scientists had thought that only by making the nuclei extremely energetic could they overcome this electrostatic repulsion, sometimes called the 'coulombic barrier' (a coulomb is a unit of electrical charge). 'Hot fusion' does this by ripping the electrons off atoms of the two heavy forms of hydrogen—deuterium and tritium—at very high temperatures, thereby creating a cloud of ions, or plasma. Huge magnets generate fields that hold the plasma together long enough for some of the nuclei to crash into each other and fuse. This fusion reaction creates tritium and helium nuclei, as well as a shower of neutrons and gamma radiation." The cold fusion experiment: "Pons and Fleischmann's experiment—the basic model for much of what has been done since—is based on electrolysis. An electrode pair consisting of a strip of palladium surrounded by a coil of platinum wire is immersed in a container of 'heavy water'—that is, water in which deuterium takes the place of ordinary hydrogen. (Deuterium is a commonly occurring form of hydrogen that has one neutron in its nucleus in addition to the one proton that all forms of hydrogen have. Deuterium atoms undergo fusion reactions; ordinary hydrogen atoms do not.) A salt, typically lithium deuterhydroxide, is dissolved in the heavy water to make it more conductive. When a voltage is applied to the electrodes, an electrical current flows through the liquid and causes the heavy water to decompose into its constituent atoms, deuterium migrates to and dissolves in the palladium electrode and oxygen is released as a gas at the platinum electrode. As deuterium builds up in the palladium, it supposedly undergoes the fusion reaction. The palladium's atomic lattice captures the energy released by the reaction and the metal heats up."

"expression of satisfaction that chemists rather than scientists from some other discipline were getting credit for what might be a monumental discovery."

Although Pons and Fleischmann had introduced the discussion, the physicists' cutting counterattacks soon dominated public attention. Uncertain about the validity of this extraordinary claim, and given no warning, science reporters at major news organizations spun their rolodexes for guidance about nuclear fusion and came up with physicists to comment. Also surprised, and usually angry, most physicists immediately pronounced the science flawed and the method of announcing the finding—at a press conference rather than in a peer-reviewed journal article—unconscionable.

The familial clash between chemists and physicists at the University of Utah grew particularly nasty. Utah's Department of Chemistry ranks among the nation's elite, and Pons was then serving as its chairman. Nevertheless, none of his departmental colleagues was working on cold fusion, and few knew enough about the experiments to explain or defend them. As it happened, no one in the university's physics department was even working on nuclear fusion, and its faculty was blind-sided by the announcement. Utah physicists who were called by reporters from Salt Lake City and elsewhere were embarrassingly ignorant about this momentous experiment conducted in a neighboring building.

Thus, Utah's chemists were sympathetic but neutral, and its physicists, especially after they heard from colleagues around the country, were condemning. "The anger between the physicists and chemists caught me totally off guard," said Pamela W. Fogle, director of university communications, who, as a former science writer, had worked often with scientists in both departments. "I never would have anticipated or expected it. . . . [I would] never have dreamed that there would be this kind of discord and anger. And a lot of it seemed to me to be irrational anger, just people losing it completely. I mean, you could not open a conversation and get a rational discussion."

However valid their science, Pons and Fleischmann turned out to be public-relations disasters. Fleischmann, whose family fled Czechoslovakia for England in the 1930s, became one of his adopted country's leading electrochemists. He also mentored Pons, who earned his doctorate at the University of Southampton. Fleischmann worked mainly in England, traveling occasionally to Salt Lake City, where he collaborated only with Pons. His innocence about media relations caused one of the seemingly endless complications with the cold-fusion announcement.

Although he knew that a press conference had been scheduled for March 23 in Salt Lake City, Fleischmann spoke freely to a reporter for the *Financial Times* in London the week before. The reporter, who was heading off for an

Easter weekend holiday, left his story with the paper, and it appeared on the wires the day before the Utah press conference. This enabled at least one major U.S. newspaper and one Salt Lake City television station to produce stories in advance, increasing the aura of science by hype. Fleischmann later said he had not understood the "embargo" of an announcement and had not realized he was doing anything wrong; there is no reason to disbelieve him.

Fleischmann took only a small public role in the furor after his original announcement, leaving Pons, who was just as inexperienced in such matters, as the centerpiece of the American controversy; his increasing discomfort—some have said paranoia—about all the attention exacerbated the university's problems. A North Carolinian, Pons attended Wake Forest University before earning his doctorate in England. Although he had come to Utah only six years earlier, he was well-regarded enough professionally and amenable enough personally to have been elected by his colleagues as chairman of the university's internationally respected chemistry department. University Communications Director Fogle says she had maintained a cordial relationship with him.

Pons's attitude and demeanor began to change as challenges grew heated. "When I first talked with Pons and Fleischmann," Fogle recalled, "they were candid and open with information, what I had come to expect as a science writer." But soon afterward, apparently upon the advice of lawyers, they stopped responding to questions or describing their work. "That was very frustrating to me as a communicator," Fogle said. A university scientist who knew him before he was famous said, "Stan was very gracious, very articulate, he had a warm sense of humor. He was concerned about students, he was an excellent teacher, students really enjoyed his classes. He was highly regarded in the chemistry department." Then within a month of the announcement came a startling change. "I think that the controversy hurt him deeply. He did not know how to deal with it, and it was at that point he started relying on his friend Triggs. He relied more and more on Gary as it got tougher and tougher."

Gary Triggs was a childhood friend, who was a lawyer in North Carolina. University authorities attribute much of their problem immediately after the announcement to the fact that Pons now listened almost exclusively to Triggs, who apparently had no special expertise in either science or patent law. At one agonizing point, Triggs threatened "legal action" against Michael H. Salamon, a Utah physicist, who reported in the British journal *Nature* that he and his colleagues had rechecked the electrochemical cells on which the Pons-Fleischmann claims had been based and found no evidence of nuclear fusion. Salamon demanded that the university pledge to defend him as a member of its tenured faculty and indemnify him if necessary. At the same time, the university believed it was committed to defending Pons, also a tenured professor. Thus, it faced the ludicrous prospect of supporting both sides in an academic freedom lawsuit and indemnifying the loser. Ultimately, the university ended its relationship with Triggs, he apologized in writing to Salamon, and the suit did not proceed.

It is commonplace to blame lawyers in crises like these, just as it is to blame journalists, but here the excess caution of lawyers and the naivete of Utah administrators in dealing with them particularly cluttered the issues. Patent lawyers from California and Texas were called into the planning process months before the public announcement—that is, months before a report of the work was submitted to a journal and months before anyone except a handful of people knew about it. The lawyers focused not on the protocols of science or the intellectual reputation of the university but rather on enhancing the financial opportunities of the two scientists, the institution, and the state.

Utah's approach reflected the growing belief that a university deserves to benefit should its faculty's research prove lucrative. Peterson wanted to position Utah to gain financially from cold fusion, as Stanford University had from recombinant DNA, the University of Wisconsin from rat poison, and Indiana University from fluoridated toothpaste. He was particularly concerned with patents, since a few years earlier the federal government had given institutions the right to patent the results of federally sponsored research. To critics, Utah's thinking was dominated by greed rather than a sense of discovery.

At the same time, Utah further angered the scientific world by reneging on an agreement with Steven E. Jones, a physicist at neighboring Brigham Young University (BYU) in Provo. Having discovered that they were doing related work, Pons and Fleischmann agreed with Jones to make simultaneous announcements in separate papers for the journal *Nature*. According to Utah officials, Pons and Fleischmann soon developed second thoughts about the agreement. They decided that their work demonstrated energy production, while Jones's did not. But an additional factor made them, as one colleague said, "irate." Earlier they had sought a Department of Energy grant, and Jones, acting as a referee, is said to have asked repeatedly for additional information. Pons and Fleischmann came to believe that some of Jones's work was based on information derived from theirs, and therefore he did not deserve equal credit. So without so much as informing Jones or BYU, they arranged to publish in the *Journal of Electrochemistry* instead and proceeded to announce their findings at the press conference.

Peterson said that lawyers had advised him, Pons and Fleischmann, and James Brophy (the vice president for research) that the university risked losing international patents if news of the discovery became public before Utah had established its rights. In retrospect, other lawyers believe they were being hyper-cautious. But Utah officials found it hard to challenge their counsel, who said in effect: "We understand the stakes; we wouldn't be here if you hadn't thought to bring us in; we know more about how to handle this than you academics do."

Thinking first of the legalities and financial prospects, however, made an enormous difference in how the news was announced, and ultimately received. To protect their secret, for example, Peterson and Brophy did not alert Utah's own physicists, who might have injected caution into the process early and might not have been so aggressively opposed afterward. Worse, the fear of losing exclusivity pushed Pons and Fleischmann to rush their paper into the *Journal of Electrochemistry* before it had been thoroughly vetted by other scientists and before they had refined their own work; Pons pointedly said later that the announcement was premature. But facing science-by-press-release criticism, Utah authorities noted that the findings had in fact been submitted to the journal in advance of the public announcement (it appeared about a month later). They also dismissed as haughty the criticism of some physicists that the journal in question was "obscure." The *Journal of Electrochemistry* is small, yes, but this is because the field of electrochemistry is small.

Nonetheless, the process by which this article was published could hardly be considered routine. Under usual circumstances, a scientist sends an article describing a piece of work to an appropriate journal. The editor submits it to a qualified peer, perhaps two or three, who review the work, check some of the results, and perhaps question the author, who may then revise the article. Other interested scientists might receive pre-prints and offer corrections. (In this day of e-mail, information spreads far faster and more widely than it once did.) Here, Pons and Fleischmann—and probably their lawyers—rushed to publication because they feared that information was leaking out. They apparently requested the *Journal of Electrochemistry* to turn the article around within a few days. This meant little time for a peer to review the paper carefully and no time for a large number of scientists to even learn about it before the press conference. But such was the reputation of Pons and Fleischmann that the journal was willing to accept the article on their terms.

The lawyers, not the news officers of the university, even controlled the critical press release that accompanied the public announcement. Fogle says "three batches" of lawyers vetted it—"I'd never had lawyers review a news release"—eliminating important information that might have alleviated some of the initial skepticism among reporters and scientists. The original draft, for example, included specific details about the experiment, how it was set up and how long it took to generate the results. The fact that it often took months for the experiment to produce results was excised; thus, other scientists were not warned that they could not have overnight success in replication.

The draft also offered details on the paper, its title, the journal in which it was to be published, and when. The lawyers seemed totally dense about the significance of this information. They eliminated all of it, then, as a compromise, restored mention of the paper's submission to a journal in a single sentence on the second page. "The lawyers were beyond my control," Fogle said with resignation. "But these were concessions I would fight over, significantly fight over, if I had to do it again. I wish I had known what boundary I could push to get what I knew was needed."

Here are highlights from the University of Utah press statement, "embargoed for release" on Thursday, March 23, 1989, 1 p.m. MST:

> SALT LAKE CITY — Two scientists have successfully created a sustained nuclear fusion reaction at room temperature in a chemistry laboratory at the University of Utah. The breakthrough means the world may someday rely on fusion for a clean, virtually inexhaustible source of energy. . . .
>
> "What we have done is to open the door of a new research area," says Fleischmann. "Our indications are that the discovery will be relatively easy to make into a useable technology for generating heat and power, but continued work is needed, first, to further understand the science and second, to determine its value to energy economics."
>
> [After two more paragraphs discussing nuclear fusion, this is the entire second paragraph of page 2:] *Their findings will appear in the scientific literature in May* [emphasis added]. . . . [On page 3 of the release, the researchers address the background of their work:] Pons calls the experiment extremely simple. "Observations of the phenomenon required patient and detailed examination of very small effects. Once characterized and understood, it was a simple matter to scale the effects up to the levels we have attained."
>
> The researchers' expertise in electrochemistry, physics, and chemistry led them to make the discovery. "Without our particular backgrounds, you wouldn't think of the combination of circumstances required to get this to work," says Pons.
>
> Some may call the discovery serendipity, but Fleischmann says it was more accident built on foreknowledge. "We realize we are singularly fortunate in having the combination of knowledge that allowed us to accomplish a fusion reaction in this new way.". . .
>
> The research strategy was concocted in the Pons' family kitchen. The nature of the experiment was so simple, says Pons, that at first it was done for the fun of it and to satisfy scientific curiosity. "It had a one in a billion chance of working although it made perfectly good scientific sense."
>
> The two performed the experiment and had immediate indication that it worked. They decided to self-fund the early research rather than try to raise funds outside the university because, says Pons, "We thought we wouldn't be able to raise any money since the experiment was so farfetched."

Add insouciance to lack of detail.

At once the cold-fusion announcement was labeled "science by press release," which was particularly unfortunate for Utah since its Office of University Communications is one of the most admired in the nation. In particular, the office, headed for many years by Raymond Haeckel and since 1990 by Fogle, has earned the respect of science writers for its handling of a number of medical and genetic advances at Utah, including the artificial heart and the discovery of genes for neurofibromatosis, colon cancer, and common hypertension. But the public affairs office could not get a grip on the cold-fusion episode.

Fogle, who was then director of the news service under Haeckel, first learned about the project two months before the eventual release from Vice President Brophy, who said that a major story was coming but that he could not tell her whose work or what department. "I went back to him the next day," Fogle recalled, "and said, 'You know, Jim, I can't do anything to prepare for this story until I have a little bit of information. I've got a science writer who is going to need to research the area.' So he told me that there was work going on in the chemistry department on room temperature fusion. I knew about hot fusion, but I did not know about any other kind. So I sent Jim Bapis, the science writer, to the library and said, 'Learn everything you can about fusion, hot and otherwise.'"

"As a former science writer," Fogle said, "I'm familiar with all the hoops that you jump through before making a major scientific announcement, all of which lend credibility to the work that you're doing." Still, although outside lawyers had been consulting for months, the news service received no further information until a week before the announcement was scheduled. After a press release was hurriedly prepared, and edited by the outside lawyers, the news service was ordered not to distribute it in advance, even under embargo, either to newspapers and television stations in Salt Lake City or to key science reporters around the nation.

Everyone in the administration assumed that an embargo would be broken. But Fogle argued that if reporters at least had the release in hand, they would better understand what they were dealing with, especially when they began to call their stable of experts for comment. (As it happened, the experts on fusion might not have been able to help much, since they were physicists and this report came from a chemistry department.) Further, if they had no meaningful information about the announcement, national science reporters, most of whom are in New York and Los Angeles, would have little impetus to cover the press conference.

The administrators compromised. They created a single paragraph of information that Fogle was to use—and not expand upon—when calling key science writers around the country whom she dealt with regularly. She was also not allowed to invite the reporters to arrive a day early and study the information. Fogle remembers first calling Jerry Bishop of the *Wall Street Journal,* the nation's most highly regarded science reporter. "[W]hen he started asking questions, I realized I needed to answer those questions, so I did to the best of my ability."* Still, without the release, most reporters were reluctant to come, although some newspapers and television networks sent stringers. "I think the curiosity got them more than anything else," Fogle said. "But I felt as if I had not served the role I should have served in providing them with the information they needed to make the judgment. It makes for a little notch in [our] believability."

The university news service did not worry about the Salt Lake City media, with which it had excellent relations. Local television reporters were cooperating in arrangements to open Pons's laboratory on the morning of the news conference, for both television and still pictures, because everyone expected chaos after the announcement.

Then Fleischmann's ill-timed interview in England took effect. Fogle was at her desk at about 5:30 p.m. on the eve of the press conference when she received a call from Ed Yeats, the science reporter for KSL-TV in Salt Lake City, a friend with whom she had worked for a decade. Yeats said that he had called a researcher at the Los Alamos National Laboratory in New Mexico, who told him that the London story was on the wires. Yeats said he considered the embargo broken and was running an advance on that evening's news. A few minutes later, Fogle turned on the television set in her office and saw a computer-generated image prepared by Yeats with the help of the Los Alamos researcher. "My lord, that's what the experiment looks like," she remembered saying to herself.

The next day the press conference itself went smoothly, although reporters mainly ignored the introductory warning from President Peterson that the experiment might be fusion or it might only be interesting science. But no one was prepared for the reaction to the news. The university press office handled more than 1,500 calls in the following four weeks, from reporters, scientists, attorneys, brokers, literary agents, book authors, corporate executives, and philanthropists. At various times 10 staffers were responding to media inquiries, directing callers to researchers, and trying to quell false rumors. But tension increased between the lawyers—both the university's and Pons's, who

---

*So intense was the anger among some physicists that they attempted to have the American Physical Society national journalism award given to Bishop rescinded because he had won it for coverage of cold fusion. In a 1991 article for a National Association of Science Writers publication, Bishop assessed the episode: "If [the cold-fusion story] was true, it would be one of the big scientific stories of the century. If it wasn't true, there was going to be a lot of controversy. Either way, our readers would like to know what happened, and we could set it in context. . . . The concept that it's irresponsible to report things before they've been peer-reviewed simply doesn't apply in cases like this or in a lot of science reporting."

demanded secrecy—and the public-relations staff, who thought it important to provide clear external communication. And it didn't help that Pons and Fleischmann, who had been cordial and candid at the first press conference, had now stopped talking.

In the weeks following the announcement, the two chief boosters of Pons and Fleischmann's research, Peterson and Brophy, pushed for government and private financial support. In April, testifying before the House Committee on Science, Space, and Technology, Peterson exhibited a touch of the defensiveness that colored many of the university's actions: "What led to the Utah experiments? A capacity to see an old problem from new perspectives was required. Chemists, electrochemists, looked at a problem traditionally reserved for physicists. . . . I would like to think that it may not be by chance that it happened in Utah, a university which has encouraged unorthodox thinking while being viewed by the world as a conservative, even socially orthodox, place. There in fact may be something valuable in isolation from more traditional centers." His critics claimed that Peterson was campaigning for earmarked funds. He insists that all he sought was federal support for cold-fusion research, with which Utah would take its chances. In any case, no federal funding resulted. But an enthusiastic Utah state legislature appropriated $5 million almost at once, primarily to create the National Cold Fusion Institute, which was established in the summer of 1989 in the university's Research Park.

Six weeks after the announcement, the new celebrities, Pons and Fleischmann, were quickly added to the agenda for a semiannual meeting of the Electrochemical Society of America. One of the smaller scientific organizations, and unsophisticated about public attention, the society reacted badly to the novel circumstances. Organizers of the meeting angered reporters at the outset by demanding that they pay the full conference registration fee to hear the cold-fusion presentation—contradictory to the norm at scientific meetings, which reporters are usually encouraged to attend gratis. Only a handful paid, but Pons and Fleischmann agreed to participate in a press conference afterward.

Soon the schedule was falling apart, and the two chemists, who were supposed to speak in the late afternoon, did not get on until late evening, by which time everyone was tired and annoyed. And the Pons-Fleischmann presentation—much anticipated since this was their first opportunity to address their own scientific society—was a dud. Hugo Rossi, dean of the College of Science at Utah, who attended the meeting, was shocked. It was "so weak," Rossi said. "We had discussed what they were going to do, and I was convinced that they were going to come on very strong, with very important results. Instead they showed what was basically a silly video of bubbles in a tube."

If the presentation was weak, the press conference was a fiasco. The Salt Lake City newspapers and television stations were all represented, along with a sizable Los Angeles press contingent and some national science writers; as many as 150 reporters and a dozen television cameras jammed into a room much too small and much too hot. After a few timid questions, a physicist from the California Institute of Technology—a nonjournalist who had crashed the press conference—commandeered a microphone and began shouting loaded questions at Pons and Fleischmann. Soon everyone was grabbing microphones and interrupting each other; a number of people, some of them physicists cholerically denouncing the work, stood on chairs to shout. Pons and Fleischmann sat stony faced in the television lights, perhaps stunned, certainly angry. After a few minutes they announced that they would participate no longer, stood up, and walked out.

This was only one of numerous insults public and private. Physicists at Utah, pressured by their friends at other institutions, were demanding that the university disavow the research. In one bizarre case, a man who claimed to come from the Massachusetts Institute of Technology camped outside the door of Pons and Fleischmann's laboratory, trying to force his way inside when the door was opened. Telephone calls and faxes arrived from around the world, calling for more information or calling the experiment a fraud.

Pons and Fleischmann had a right to consider themselves harassed. And they were not prepared psychologically for stardom. Fleischmann appeared to have little understanding of American behavior; the relatively little time he spent in Salt Lake City was out of sight in the laboratory. That left Pons to oversee the experiments and respond to questioners both inside and outside the university. And this unassuming chemist, once regarded as friendly to colleagues and solicitous of students, changed. Fogle said that when Pons suddenly refused to speak with her, she could not provide answers to reporters that might have slowed the critical onslaught.

Dean Rossi was also puzzled. A mathematician himself, he thought he could moderate the clash among the university's chemists and physicists, so he had volunteered to serve as director of the National Cold Fusion Institute when it was established in 1989. But Pons and Fleischmann were "incredibly secretive," Rossi said. "Almost immediately, several laboratories [at Utah] in chemical engineering and in physics and in metallurgy started up experiments and tried to get basic information, filling in some of the details that were missing in the [original] article. Pons and Fleischmann felt this was harassment. [We thought] they should have been really anxious to have their colleagues at this institution rather than at other places confirm their results."

Rossi's doubts intensified after the Los Angeles meeting. "I began to think this wasn't just a kind of paranoia but was really their lack of confidence in their own work. I began to share the skepticism of some other scientists." Rossi said he then carefully reread their original paper and concluded that "it is a bad paper. It's confusing. It's contradictory. The data is massaged data; they don't present the raw data that they had."

Rossi says he had begun his role at the institute with an open mind and was supportive of the two chemists: "I felt that as a mathematician, my neutrality and objectivity were apparent. I saw my role as helping protect Pons and Fleischmann from the attacks from the outside and also helping them to work with other scientists, here and elsewhere, to get things moving." He recalled it as "a hard job that became impossible."

The tipping point for Rossi came a few months after the National Cold Fusion Institute opened. "Pons and Fleischmann wanted their laboratory to remain in the chemistry building. So I convinced them that I wanted a duplicate laboratory—run by somebody they chose, whom they really felt confidence in—running up at the institute in the Research Park. We hired a person who had been a post-doc with Pons, who had worked on electrochemical experiments that Pons felt very good about. I felt pretty good about him. I tried to make it really clear to him that he was working for me, but what he was to do was to replicate the Pons-Fleischmann experiments. Well, I discovered after awhile that he had instructions from Pons to do nothing [but] set up fake experiments. I discovered this with the help of the assistants who were working for him. [One of them] told me, 'You know, those tubes are running, and there are wires running from them, but they're not hooked up to the computer. Data are not being gathered.'

"[Pons and Fleischmann] were making the rounds of meetings. They were preparing for, and going to, a long meeting in Japan. Sometimes I think they just did not want anything happening at the Cold Fusion Institute. This was something that they had to permit to take place because of political pressures within the state, but they did not feel that it should operate. They wanted to have complete control over what was going on, so they told this fellow to just hold off [and] don't do anything until they came back. So I fired him. And Chevis Walling offered to gather the data for those experiments. Chevis Walling is an organic chemist, a member of the National Academy. He was on the [Utah] faculty, he has an outstanding reputation as a scientist, [and] he was a very close friend and supporter of Pons; so he was in the inner circle. Well, when Pons and Fleischmann returned from Japan, they were irate that I had fired [their man] and put Walling in charge of this. And they came in and just dismantled the cells and took them out."

Ironically, Walling thought the data were, on balance, positive. "If you do things one way," Rossi said, "which is pretty much the standard way of doing statistics, thinking of it as a Gaussian distribution, then you showed no heat. But if you thought of it as a Poussian distribution, which it really is, then you began to be able to make calculations which showed heat. It's a subtle point, though, and hardly was going to make a dramatic show. So we never told anybody except Pons and Fleischmann that Chevis felt that it was very slightly positive." They may have been annoyed partly because the support was lukewarm, Rossi surmised, "but I think what made them angry was that they wanted complete control over everything."

As months went by, scientists continued to battle. Confirmation of various elements and to varying degrees of the Pons-Fleischmann results came from such institutions as Stanford University, Texas A&M University, the University of Minnesota, and the University of California laboratory at Los Alamos, although some researchers who reported confirmations later backed off. In October, after a conference sponsored by the National Science Foundation and the Electric Power Research Institute, a group of scientists that included Nobel laureate Edward Teller, a leader in the development of the hydrogen bomb, recommended further study of the cold-fusion phenomenon, concluding that the Utah scientists' unusual findings "cannot be explained as a result of artifacts, equipment, or human errors." A month later, however, a panel commissioned by the Department of Energy found "the present evidence for the discovery of a new nuclear process termed cold fusion is not persuasive." Its report said it was "sympathetic" to "carefully focused and cooperative experiments" but saw no reason to give special preferences to cold-fusion proposals.

The next spring, at what was billed as the First Annual Conference on Cold Fusion at the Utah campus, scientists reported that 25 laboratories around the world had achieved some sort of positive result. "It is no longer possible to dismiss the reality of cold fusion," said Julian Schwinger, the Nobel laureate physicist at the University of California, Los Angeles. Critics complained that they had not been invited to the conference and pointed to some 250 experiments that had shown negative results. And coincidentally or not, the *Nature* article by the Utah physicist Salamon—critical of Pons and Fleischmann—appeared the very week of the conference. (*Nature* consistently refused to publish any articles in support of cold fusion.)

About this time, Pons and Fleischmann's two most powerful friends at the university began to lose their effectiveness. President Peterson's aggressive campaign on behalf of cold-fusion research was costing him credibility within the faculty. More significant, Vice President Brophy was growing progressively ill with cancer. Although he gamely continued to go to his office, mainly to deal with cold-fusion issues, he died the next year. Brophy was the person who had taken Peterson for a walk one day and told him that something important was happening in Pons's chemistry laboratory. (How and when Brophy himself learned about the experiments is not clear. He is said to have reviewed the original paper, but critics note that since he was not an expert in fusion research he may not have thoroughly understood the process.) Brophy had persuaded Peterson of the importance of the work and later attempted to persuade dubious faculty colleagues. He was ultimately the only person in authority at the university in whom Pons would confide. During the tense early days when Pons would no longer speak with Fogle, she and Brophy had a standing appointment to talk each morning at 6:30, so that she could prepare for the day's inevitable questioning. Brophy's death probably ended any hope that Pons and Fleischmann, the lawyers, the faculty, and the administration could ever work together on this project.

Brophy went to his grave a believer in cold fusion. Shortly before his death, he responded to questions posed by a visiting researcher, sometimes speaking too faintly to be heard. The transcript indicates that he thought himself almost blameless and the university more misunderstood than mistaken. One problem was the media: "Much of the press was more interested in the story of the story than in the story itself; that is, they were interested in the bizarre surroundings as cold fusion history developed rather than in the story of cold fusion. . . . The discussion in the press of the arguments, so to speak, between the physicists and the chemists was also blown out of proportion. There is a tense situation between physicists and chemists . . . a union-card aspect . . . [but it was] blown out of proportion."

Brophy deplored the time wasted responding to repeated questioning of the research. For this he particularly blamed the physicists. "The internal relations were mostly from the physics community, but somewhat from the external community indirectly. It was certainly true that officials from the American Institute of Physics were in contact with . . . members of our physics faculty, saying you guys better stop that nonsense going on out there or bad things will happen. So there was considerable peer pressure on our physicists, and to some extent on the chemists. . . . It was clear that people were acting emotionally rather than in a thinking way. The black hats, such as they were, came from the hot fusion community. . . . [T]here was certainly an organized campaign to discredit cold fusion based on the possibility of losing funding. . . .

"What we did properly in managing the issue once it became public was to act like a university that was supporting its faculty. But more could have been done to make our position clear. We weren't supporting cold fusion, we were supporting academic freedom. There were those of us who believed, now even more so, that the science of cold fusion is correct; while all the details are clearly unknown, and it will take longer than we had originally expected."

Brophy also saw the president as part of the problem: ". . . the personality of President Peterson, who in his openness and desire to be part of many things, openly embraced the cold fusion idea and made his presidency, and therefore the university, at the forefront. . . . There was no point at which we sat down and said, should we support this or not. It was the president's desire to go forward."

Peterson, a native Utahn, came to the presidency on an unusual track. After earning baccalaureate and medical degrees from Harvard University, he practiced in Salt Lake City and taught at the University of Utah Medical School. Then he was invited to become director of admissions at Harvard and five years later was appointed Harvard's vice president for alumni affairs and development. He returned to Utah as vice president for health sciences at the university, succeeding David P. Gardner as president in 1983. While vice president, he was "the man in the white coat," as one source remembered, who made regular television appearances when Barney Clark received his artificial heart. Some think he grew to like the limelight too much. "In things like the heart business, or cold fusion," said one longtime faculty member, "he so badly wanted to make a big national impression that I think it clouded his vision and he lost all sense of caution."

It's hard to find people who don't like Chase Peterson personally. After he resigned under fire, he was given an autographed copy of every one of the hundreds of books written by faculty members during his presidency, and he and his wife both received honorary degrees. "I like him a lot, I admire him a lot," one colleague observed, "but many on the faculty felt that Chase pretty much ran the university like a family business. They felt co-opted by the central administration. This was not the faculty's institution, it was Chase's own business."

For one reason or another, unrest builds up around almost every president as the years go by, and cold fusion gave Peterson's opponents, primarily the scientists, a big weapon against him. "I think that we avoided a real rupture in the faculty here by a very narrow margin," said Rossi, who worked closely with Peterson for many years before breaking with him over cold fusion. Rossi credits Joseph Taylor, another mathematician who was then academic vice president, and Craig Taylor, chairman of the physics department, with calming the mood. "The physics faculty and about half the chemistry faculty wanted to call for Peterson's resignation," Rossi said. "But we had a meeting and settled for a demand that cold fusion science be put back in the hands of the scientists, because by this time it was being run autocratically by Brophy and Peterson."

The action that ended Peterson's effectiveness was the transfer of $500,000 from the University of Utah Research Foundation to the National Cold Fusion Institute, in an effort to maintain cold-fusion research at a time when federal and private funds were unavailable. But the president first announced it as an anonymous gift: "a dumb thing that I shouldn't have done, a human weakness on my part," he says now. "I had transferred a half million dollars 10 times for different projects, and no one ever bothered to ask where it came from. It was entirely legal, but it was dumb. It made it look deceptive. I didn't have sufficient trust in the maturity of the community to take this, and I should have." Angry scientists said Peterson wanted to make it appear that cold-fusion research was attracting outside support. When the "anonymous gift" was identified, the faculty approved a resolution of "no confidence" in the president. He announced in June that he would retire after the following academic year.

The decision cooled the campus, but as a lame duck Peterson could do little for the cold-fusion project. In the fall of 1990, Pons unexpectedly put his house in Salt Lake City up for sale and took leave from the university; he never returned to the faculty. Since then, he and Fleischmann have continued to work together in Europe on cold fusion, but only Peterson has kept in touch with them. The month Peterson retired as president, June 1991, the state's multimillion-dollar appropriation for the National Cold Fusion Institute ran out; subsequently, the institute returned its equipment to the university's chemistry and physics departments and shut down.

Utah chose as Peterson's successor Arthur K. Smith, a political scientist who understood what it meant to walk into controversy, having served as provost under James D. Holderman at the University of South Carolina and acting president after Holderman's resignation (see Chapter 5). (Smith left Utah in early 1997 to become chancellor of the University of Houston system and president of the University of Houston.) Smith said he asked South Carolina chemists and physicists for their assessment of the Utah situation before he arrived as a candidate. They saw the cold-fusion experience as a lesson in "upholding the importance of the peer-review process in bringing scientific discoveries to light. . . . [Y]ou've got to be cautious about making announcements or claims in advance of replications by reputable scientists."

Smith said that both he and Richard Koehn, the vice president for research whom he chose to replace Brophy, had to pass "a smell test" on cold fusion. "The task I had," Smith said, "was to first deal with a situation in which people had been divided into believers and nonbelievers. . . . There was a substantial group of faculty that would have liked nothing better than had I, as the new president of the University of Utah, called a press conference from the steps of the Park Building [administration] and denounced Drs. Pons and Fleischmann and cold fusion as something akin to alchemy." Koehn, who had been a dean at the State University of New York at Stony Brook, says moderately that he had only been at Utah a few days before he was visited by various scientists to "essentially press their views of the issue."

The short-term, Smith-Koehn solution was to appoint a small group of university scientists to an ad hoc advisory council and to take no administra-tive action on cold-fusion issues without the council's knowledge. For instance, when lawyers asked for additional research as they continued to explore the possibility of obtaining patents, Smith and Koehn, who both appeared skeptical about the prospects, immediately informed the council that the work would be limited to strengthening the case for replicability and would go no further.

This related to Smith's longer-term anxiety: If something commercially valuable did result from cold fusion, the university's financial interests should be protected. To help accomplish this, in 1994 he and Koehn shifted the cost and effort of pursuing patents to a private company, while retaining the rights to license the patents and collect royalties much as it would for any other technology. The university received an advance payment "in the low six figures," which it could apply against the estimated $700,000 paid to patent lawyers since 1989. The university would share any royalties with Pons and Fleischmann.

Smith also pronounced himself "astonished" to find that this "$900-million-a-year conglomerate, with a big health sciences operation," did not have house counsel. Historically, the university had been represented by lawyers in the state attorney general's office, who had other responsibilities, other loyalties, and no special expertise concerning higher education. Now the university has "a five-person office, and I need them," Smith said. Hardly a day goes by without his meeting once or twice with the general counsel.

Creation of an in-house legal team is a positive, if tangential, consequence of the cold-fusion episode. Other long-range effects on the university are harder to measure. Authorities insist, with statistical backing, that the University of Utah suffered little measurable damage, either in funds or personnel, to its academic programs. For instance, National Science Foundation grants alone more than doubled from $8.2 million in 1988, the year before the cold-fusion announcement, to $17.8 million in 1994; private contributions grew from $34.7 million to $63.7 million; and the Utah legislature increased its appropriation to the university 34 percent over those six years. Enrollment in the graduate programs of the College of Science increased more than 15 percent, and there is no evidence of a faculty brain drain.

On the other hand, faculty members and administrators have had to listen to corny jibes about cold fusion. Koehn said that the first person in New York he told about moving to Utah chuckled and said, "Oh, you're going to work on cold fusion, I suppose." He conceded that some people around the country still laugh, but insists the furor is overrated. "I'm a geneticist [and] this institution is extremely excellent in genetics. The University of Utah is by any objective measure a very significant research institution, so I think the people in my community, geneticists whom I work with, saw that picture in a much more balanced view." This may be likely, but many Utah faculty think they will have to absorb the teasing for a long time. And more seriously, they believe that respect for the science they do wavered among their peers nationally and internationally for a number of years after the cold-fusion episode.

The university can justifiably claim rank in the second tier of research universities—no backhand compliment intended: not a Berkeley, Caltech, or MIT in many disciplines, but an institution where researchers have achieved notable breakthroughs in treatment of the heart, eye, ear, arm, kidney, and blood vessels. It is tantalizing to wonder about the reaction had the cold-fusion announcement come from one of the academic powers on either coast. The response might well have been more subdued, more respectful. At the same time, if it had come from chemists, no matter where, the physicists would almost certainly have been just as furious.

Some citizens of the state believe that their university is a bit too good. Utahns take great pride in education—the state is second nationally in the percentage of high-school graduates who advance to higher education, and it has the nation's highest literacy rate. They appreciate the technology developed within the state and understand that economic development follows education. They take pride in the university's achievements and what it has done for the state. Yet they worry about the academicians reared and trained in other states and countries who provide the core of the university faculty, more fearful than they like to admit that these intelligent and cosmopolitan newcomers could modify, through education, traditions they hold dear.

Utahns are sensitive about their conservative image as a place dominated by the Church of Jesus Christ of Latter-day Saints (commonly known as the Mormons elsewhere and as LDS in Utah). They can joke about it—in the spring of 1995, just before Salt Lake City was awarded the 2002 Winter Olympic Games, which it had been pursuing for two decades, a local newspaper headline read, "Is Salt Lake City Too Boring for the Olympics?"—or they can get defensive—the political editor of the *Deseret News* in Salt Lake City once compared the assaults on Pons and Fleischmann to the mediaeval Catholic Church's response to Copernicus and Galileo.

Utahns remember treatment like the churlish story written by Robert Bazell, an NBC News science reporter, in the *New Republic* a month after the cold-fusion announcement. Referring to Pons and Fleischmann, Bazell wrote, "University of Utah officials, imbued with that state's unique blend of chauvinism and xenophobia, were not only happy to play along but encouraged them." He embarrassed Peterson by juxtaposing the president's casual comments about the charm of states like Oregon and Maine with "murders [and] thefts of forged documents" in the Mormon church. He sneered at prideful stories in the local papers and state legislative support of cold-fusion research. The story was headlined, "Hype-Energy Physics" (note: not chemistry).

Peterson contends even now that Utah came under attack because it had violated too many "holy grails." For example, physicists, "who consider themselves keepers of the truth," were angered because chemists had invaded their preserve and perhaps endangered their careers. Like "the military-industrial complex" decried by President Eisenhower, Peterson sees "an industrial-research complex. There is big money in hot fusion, and if we turn out to be right, hot fusion, I guess, goes away." He estimated that researchers, primarily physicists, have collected $400 million annually since World War II to work on fusion. "That represents entire careers, and orthodontia, and college educations for whole families of people that have lived off this dole," Peterson said with some bitterness. "We hadn't realized how threatening that would be." Utah was also simply too candid, he said, in admitting its concern for patents and positioning itself to gain financially should cold fusion prove practical, even though other universities have profited from faculty research successes.

As Peterson is quick to point out, the physicists' scorn has not ended the search for cold fusion; on the contrary, researchers periodically report advances. The May/June 1994 cover story in *Technology Review*, the official MIT magazine, was titled, "Warming Up to Cold Fusion." Summarizing the assaults on cold fusion over the five years since the Utah announcement, the many failures of replication, and a number of intriguing successes, the article said:

> If the validity of the effect rested only on results reported during the first year after the initial claims by Pons and Fleischmann, this strange diversion from routine science would have joined 'n-rays,' polywater, and other excesses of the imagination. But enough reputable researchers have now published findings, produced from a broad enough range of experimental approaches, that it has become difficult to doubt that something is going on outside the explanations offered by conventional physics. What is happening might be fusion; it might not be fusion. But to dismiss the claims as the result of experimental error or fraud is no longer appropriate. . . .

> Early investigations of all new phenomena tend to be incomplete, prone to error, and difficult to reproduce. Further scientific investigations require money; the more complex the phenomenon, the more money is required. But dollars tend to flow toward research with a clear chance of success. Thus, many potentially important ideas never receive enough funding to enable scientists to understand them. To a large extent, this is the case with cold fusion. Skeptics maintain that the effect is not real and that funds should therefore not be wasted on studying it. Rather than invest a little money on the possibility that they might be wrong, skeptics actively try to turn off support. . . .

> The advance of scientific knowledge rests on the idea that before work is judged valid it must be evaluated by, and reproduced by, other scientists. While these procedures have kept science from making too many mistakes, they can also stifle new ideas. It is now virtually impossible to publish positive cold fusion results in certain journals because the editors or their chosen peer reviewers are convinced that the effect is bogus. This

creates a *catch-22*: the journals will not accept papers until more papers published in such journals show evidence for the effect.

A July 1994 page-one article by Jerry Bishop in the *Wall Street Journal* observed a similar phenomenon: "Five years later, cold fusion remains a pariah in the scientific establishment. The U.S. Patent and Trademark Office routinely rejects any patent application that claims to involve cold fusion, putting it on a par with perpetual motion. The Department of Energy hasn't funded a cold-fusion experiment since late 1989 and isn't likely to change that policy. *Nature,* the prestigious scientific journal published weekly in England, flatly refuses to publish any paper about cold fusion. And other journals ignore the field. . . . Nevertheless, cold fusion simply won't die a natural death."

Bishop went on to describe cold-fusion research—some seemingly quixotic, some well-financed by rational commercial interests—occurring in Italy, India, Russia, China, Japan, and the United States, where, for example, the Electric Power Research Institute was funding experiments by SRI International in Menlo Park, California. "A sizable following is building around cold fusion," Bishop wrote. Pons and Fleischmann continue to work together, now in the south of France, apparently comfortably funded by Japanese corporations. They also continue to claim significant advances, but, true to form, keep details private.

Certainly this episode did not lack for journalism. Besides thousands of news stories, at least eight books were being shopped around at one time or another, several of them by physicists anxious to discredit both the research and Utah's handling of it; only a couple found publishers. In addition, a Cornell University communications professor and an Indiana University sociologist landed a National Science Foundation grant to establish a "cold fusion archive" as part of research into the sociology of science. Indiana professor Thomas Gieryn described the scientific community as "highly moral," one that takes its rules and taboos seriously. At the same time, it is a community that "thrives on the competition" for jobs, the rights of discovery, and academic turf. Utah understands.

The pressures on the university's news service did not ease for years. Fogle tried to maintain a steady flow of information from the National Cold Fusion Institute as long as it remained open—concentrating within the borders of the state because taxpayer dollars kept the institute going. She worked closely with the dozen or so national reporters who continued to follow cold fusion after the initial flurry. But the experience left her cautious. "We backed off a little. . . . [W]e were very selective in those stories [on any subject] that we sent nationally, so that we knew that they were legitimate news stories."

It took Utah's research apparatus several years to return to the level of national recognition it had held in 1989. But Fogle thinks that the university's effort to be cooperative with journalists prevented long-term damage to its reputation: "We continue to have good research, we continue to put out good stories, and [the media] continue to use them. We have long had a good relationship with both national and local media, and we continue to have a good relationship with national and local media"—with one exception. "My perception is that the only relationship that is strained would be that with the *New York Times*. I think that Bill Broad [a *Times* science reporter] probably will always think of the University of Utah as some particularly backwater kind of place. We continue to get stories in there that are worthy of being published, [but] to this day it might be tough to get in [the *Times*] Science section if it's not a genetics story."

The whole university seems to be cautious on the subject of cold fusion. Its only official concern is to protect its patent rights. The top administrators are dubious about cold fusion; no university researchers are known to be working in the area. Pons and Fleischmann are gone; so is the National Cold Fusion Institute. The sense one gets at Utah is that people wish things hadn't happened as they did, and most of them doubt the electrochemists' claims, but they know they are an honorable university that produces high-quality scientific research. And as one executive says with a smile, "We don't know yet how this will turn out."

In a detached editorial a month after the 1989 announcement, the *Economist* welcomed the controversy in language that appears valid years later: "Even if Dr. Pons and Dr. Fleischmann are wrong, they will have done no harm. To complain that the furor over fusion wastes time and money is pusillanimous. It is providing excitement and inspiration in abundance. Theorists have awoken from dogmatic slumbers. . . . Whether this cold-fusion excitement heralds an age of trouble-free energy, or is merely a skirmish in the streets, it is exactly what science should be about."

CHAPTER 3

Bulldog Determination

The Jan Kemp Case at the
University of Georgia

S cholars have studied it, politicians and entrepreneurs have thrived on it, cynics have dismissed it—the phenomenon of 90,000 people in an open-air arena on a Saturday afternoon, most of them behaving as if the honor of their state will rise or fall this day according to the physical performance of a few dozen 20-year-olds. One can witness this phenomenon a half dozen times each autumn in places known as Death Valley in Clemson, South Carolina, or the Swamp in Gainesville, Florida, or under a blanket of red in Lincoln, Nebraska, or Norman, Oklahoma. Of the people who hold tickets to these events, a few thousand are academic colleagues of the young men on the field, but many are older, sometimes much older, likely to be extremely prosperous, and known to drive hundreds of miles in all kinds of weather to party with friends, eat and drink voraciously, and revel in this spectacle of community glory. They are called fans, and the event is called intercollegiate football.

We could argue endlessly about where this enthusiasm is most replete. But one of the leading contenders is Athens, Georgia, home of the University of Georgia (UGA) and the Georgia Bulldogs. The arena, Sanford Stadium, has been expanded seven times since its construction in 1929; it now holds about 86,000, counting the luxury suites, which banks and industrial giants rent for upwards of $50,000 per season. Seventy years ago, rows of privet hedges were planted just in front of the grandstand on both sides of the field, so that imaginative sportscasters breathlessly refer to each game there as being played "between the hedges." When the hedges were to be removed to widen the playing field for the 1996 Olympic soccer championship, Sanford denizens reacted as to a sacrilege until they were assured that new privet hedges, which grow like weeds, were already being nurtured and would be planted in time for football season.

The greatest moment in Georgia athletic history occurred in early 1981, when an unbeaten football team coached by the revered Vince Dooley and starring freshman Hershel Walker won the national championship by defeating legendary Notre Dame at the Sugar Bowl in New Orleans. Riding this crest of glory, few 'Dawg fans noticed a year later when a disgruntled English teacher named Jan Kemp filed a law suit against the university. She alleged that her contract had not been renewed because she had spoken out against unethical procedures in the Developmental Studies program, a remedial effort for students who had qualified for admission but needed extra help in reading, writing, and mathematics—in particular, preferential treatment for athletes and for children of highly placed families.

Jan Kemp's lawsuit finally went to trial in Atlanta in January 1986. After three weeks of testimony, a federal jury awarded her $2.57 million in damages. Ultimately, she settled with the university for $1.1 million. The putative issue was Kemp's right of free speech, and whether the university had violated it by punishing her for exercising it. The named defendants were the university's vice president for academic affairs, Virginia Trotter, and the director of the Developmental Studies program, Leroy Ervin. Both lost their jobs after the trial.

But on trial in the court of public opinion were the academic integrity of the university, especially as it related to intercollegiate athletics; and the administration of UGA's president, Fred Davison. The trial embarrassed the university within the state and around the nation. The Georgia Board of Regents, the governing body for all institutions of higher education in the state, jumped on the university with a brutal post-trial audit of the Developmental Studies program that turned up scores of instances of questionable practices as well as angry accusations among administrators. Davison, who had been a powerful president of the university for 19 years, resigned.

To this day, Davison and his supporters remain incredulous about the outcome. They blame the judge, defense counsel, plaintiff's counsel, and they blame political maneuvering in the state. But on at least one issue, they realize that they are at least partly to blame: UGA indisputably lost the critical struggle, outside the courtroom, over public opinion. And from this defeat have come enormous changes in the way the University of Georgia deals with its public.

To anyone associated with a university that plays "big-time" football or basketball—"revenue-producing" sports as they are known euphemistically in the National Collegiate Athletic Association—Georgia's tale possesses a "there but for the grace of God go we" quality. This is not to say necessarily that every institution could be found to engage in unethical practices of one kind or another, but, depending on one's standard of ethics, it is possible. At worst, corruption is blatant. Supporters of athletic teams—often called "boosters"— have been known to give cars, credit cards, and cash to athletes, who are theoretically amateurs allowed to receive nothing more than a tuition scholarship plus room and board. At what might be called the milder side of the spectrum, athletes receive complimentary tickets to the games they play, which they (or others for them) can sell at hundreds of dollars apiece. And the players can be guided into courses or academic tracks that will help them maintain their eligibility but give them little hope of graduation. On the other hand, perhaps athletes deserve more than a few thousand dollars in scholarship assistance when they produce tens of millions of dollars in revenue for their institutions, and networks cut billion-dollar deals to televise their games.

While those issues go afield from the current work, the Kemp case stands at the interface between athletics and academics. A Georgia native and graduate of the university, Jan Kemp held a position as assistant professor of English and coordinator of the English section of Developmental Studies in 1982. Based on trial testimony, she was either a challenging yet thoughtful teacher who cared intensely for her struggling students or an erratic shrew who played favorites in the classroom and did little scholarly research outside it.

Around this time, Kemp began complaining to colleagues and superiors about breaches in academic integrity, which concerned both how students entered and left Developmental Studies. At one side, Kemp, and perhaps a number of her colleagues, felt that some students—athletes and children of well-connected parents—were receiving preferential admission to the remedial program. At the other side, she thought that some students—almost always athletes—were being "exited" from the program into the academic mainstream even though they remained unqualified.

In any case, Kemp was demoted from her position as coordinator for English and later informed that her teaching contract would not be renewed. It is one of the dirty little secrets of the university world that for legal reasons an institution often cannot tell members of its junior faculty why their contracts become "non-renewed." University administrators were later to explain that Kemp had failed to demonstrate enough research progress that would lead to tenure.

Kemp saw the action as punishment for her having gored some sacred university cows. She filed an official grievance, which worked its way through the institutional process, and lost. Next, she hired Athens attorney Pat Nelson, who filed suit in state court, and brought into the case another Athens lawyer, Hue Henry, a dogged and imaginative litigator with plentiful experience both in civil rights cases and actions against the University of Georgia. They voluntarily dismissed the state suit and refiled in federal court, charging a violation of a nineteenth-century statute protecting free speech.

Henry sued the two academic officials directly responsible for the Developmental Studies program, Director Ervin and Vice President Trotter, plus the board of regents of the state university system, which was the university governing body. Naming the regents, presumably for their deeper pockets, added a significant legal development. It took the suit away from Athens, where the University of Georgia is a whale in a pond, to a federal district court in Atlanta, the cosmopolitan state capital and the regents' headquarters. The board of regents won dismissal as a defendant, on the grounds that the case concerned only the University of Georgia, not the 32 other colleges and universities in the state system, but the suit remained in Atlanta. The judge who drew the case, Horace T. Ward, was a black man who had attended Northwestern University's prestigious law school after being denied admission to the then-segregated University of Georgia. And four of the six jurors were also black in a case that would turn heavily on the treatment of black athletes.

After the usual systemic delays, legal maneuvering, and pretrial discovery, the case, entitled *Dr. Jan Kemp v. Leroy Ervin, individually and in his official capacity as Assistant Vice President for Academic Affairs and Director, Developmental Studies, and Virginia Trotter, individually and in her official capacity as Vice President for Academic Affairs*, went to trial January 5, 1986, in the United States District Court for the Northern District of Georgia, Atlanta Division, Civil Action File No. C83-330A. The trial lasted five weeks, and 53 witnesses were heard. The jury deliberated for 10 hours over three days. It awarded Kemp $79,680.95 in lost wages; $1 for loss of professional reputation; $200,000 in compensatory damages for mental distress; and $2,300,000 in punitive damages against Trotter and Ervin.

From start to finish, the defense insisted that the one and only issue in the case was whether the university had deprived Jan Kemp of her free speech rights. It conjured a strategy intended to prove that the university had not renewed her contract because of her incompetence, not because she spoke out against university practices. But Henry, Kemp's lawyer, stretched the playing field. He wanted the jury to hear all about the remedial program and the athletic program, and Judge Ward ruled that most of that evidence was relevant to Kemp's complaint.

Perhaps the judge's surprising ruling on the eve of trial stunned O. Hale Almand, a prominent Macon litigator who had been hired as defense counsel by the attorney general of Georgia and top-level university authorities. In his opening statement, he uttered what must rank as one of the most catastrophic sentences in the history of American jurisprudence. In reference to athletes enrolled in the Developmental Studies program, Almand declared: "*We may not make a university student out of him but if we can teach him to read and write, maybe he can work at the post office rather than as a garbage man when he gets through with his athletic career* [emphasis added]." To be generous, one must assume that Almand intended to make the point that three or four years of exposure to higher education, even without graduation, would help anyone. Hue Henry said he couldn't believe what he had heard. Neither could neutral parties. How the predominantly black jury heard Almand, one can only guess.

If the courtroom battle was a victory for the plaintiff, the public-relations battle was a rout. The attention-getting skill of Henry and the attention-getting demeanor of Kemp, which had kept the case in the public eye for months, ensured that it would be front-page news for the entire trial. They gave informal press conferences at recesses, lunch breaks, and the close of the court day. They returned reporters' telephone calls. They were open and friendly. They drummed on the theme that Kemp was more than a loyal, hard-working teacher struggling against the power structure of the university and the state government; she was trying to protect the university from itself.

The administrators didn't know what hit them. President Davison and his advisors seemed never to grasp the public import of the case. And he maintained his standoffish attitude toward the press that antedated the Developmental Studies issue: "Maybe I didn't spend enough time on public relations [in general]," Davison said. "We felt we'd let the record speak for itself about the institution. It may be today that you have to have a more structured presence [and a better] way to present yourself than we did. It just wasn't my way of operating, particularly."

But friends and associates of the president would go further. Scott Cutlip, then dean of the university's well-regarded journalism school and author of a leading textbook on public relations, was one of Davison's closest confidants. "Fred had an intense dislike for the media," Cutlip said, "and he was surrounded by people supporting that dislike." Cutlip even includes the president's wife and secretary, and, in particular, one of his own golfing buddies, Ralph Beaird, then dean of the law school, among those who harbored a "hatred of the media." How does Beaird himself remember it? "The fact is, the case created a media frenzy. Everybody with the media from New York and all over came down, and this was a Southern football team, a member of the SEC [Southeastern Conference], a football factory. We hire thugs and felons to play football, et cetera. That's the attitude they have; there's no civilization west of the Hudson River or south of the Hudson River. That's the attitude you have with the press."

Davison's view was not that intense, but one Georgia journalist characterized his approach as skeptical. "He didn't ever trust or like the media," this journalist said. "Fred stayed in his office, locked the door, issued these press releases, and wouldn't talk to anybody. It's not as if he closed the door [for the Kemp trial]. He had never opened it. I have this image in my mind, of them slipping press releases under the door." Another reporter remembered Davison's projecting "an absolute stone wall. 'They're out to get me' was his attitude toward reporters."

Tom Landrum, who was then UGA director of public relations (later to become special assistant to the university president), said that before the trial opened he asked Davison's closest advisors for instruction on what position his office should take. Advised to talk to Hale Almand, Landrum drove to Macon for a briefing and marching orders, which were: "I don't want this case tried in the newspapers. It's not going to be wise for the university to come out with any information, or with any campaign." Landrum reported back to the president's advisors, "and that was our posture. We did not attempt to override the attorney general's office, and we were pretty darn good about following what the attorney general directed us to do. It was a legal matter and they wanted it to be kept a legal matter." Still, early in the trial, when he saw the university take a daily pounding, Landrum asked again. This time he was told to wait until the defense case was presented; then everything would be all right. "Hindsight being 20/20, it would have been better to have done some things differently," Landrum said.

Tom Jackson, currently director of the university public information office but then an Athens-based reporter for an Atlanta television station, brings a similar perspective. In six years of covering the university while Davison was president, "I only interviewed him directly on camera in his office twice. He didn't want to comment on things. He didn't want to be one-on-one with reporters. At public events, where he had prepared remarks, they loved to have you present, but to just do an interview, and say, 'Can you respond to x, y, or z issue?' he was mostly unavailable."

Davison perhaps underestimated the importance of media ties because he had maintained such successful relationships with most of his other external constituencies. He was popular with the university's official alumni body, whose officers tried to persuade him to withdraw his resignation after the trial. He was well-regarded in university outposts, such as extension services, around the state. For years Davison had taken pride in making those centers feel a part of the institution, piloting his own Beechcraft Bonanza on day trips and hopping into a pick-up to visit farmers. "You could tell those [service officers] they were just as much faculty as those of us in Athens," Davison said. "When they believed it was when they saw me in Attipulkas."

On campus, opinion was more divided. Certain years the president avoided appearances at halftime in Sanford Stadium because he might be booed by the crowd. Support within the faculty was mixed, but that hardly seemed to matter. The professoriate was so complacent that few showed up for meetings of the campuswide university council, and the arts and sciences faculty senate didn't meet at all for one 13-year period. Davison and a small coterie of advisors ran the university with little external input or opposition. Among these advisors were Dean Beaird, Dean Cutlip, public-relations chief Barry Wood, and the late Jim Kinney, then executive assistant to the president.

(Beaird and Cutlip were widely considered instrumental in the appointment of Virginia Trotter to the academic vice presidency in 1977. In a similar job at the University of Nebraska, she had gained a reputation as a strong supporter of professional schools, and as a newcomer to the University of Georgia, she was thought to be unthreatening, even to those who were her hierarchical inferiors.)

Davison's critical base of support came from the legislature, a constituency he had cultivated for the nearly two decades of his presidency, and especially from Speaker Tom Murphy, an almost novelistic paradigm of the old-line Southern political leader, courtly, countrified, tough as an anvil. Although UGA was only one of more than 30 public institutions of higher education in Georgia, Davison persuaded the legislature of its overwhelming importance to the state as a research institution. He won funds to double graduate enrollment and nearly double library expenditures, research expenditures grew six-fold during his presidency, and Georgia became a national leader in the growing field of biotechnology. On the eve of the Kemp trial, Davison and the university were riding particularly high. The University of Georgia—established in 1785, it is the nation's oldest state-chartered university—had just marked its bicentennial with 18 months of academic symposiums and celebratory parties.

Davison's determined insistence on the university's premier role in the higher-education structure inevitably cost him points among fellow presidents in Georgia, and, as years went by, with the board of regents. He once reportedly said at a gathering of Georgia presidents that he had no peers in the room; his peers were the presidents of institutions like Cornell University and the University of Wisconsin. He also annoyed some of the regents, who in theory represented statewide interests but were protective of the smaller institutions in their neighborhoods.

Davison believes that 19 years in a visible presidency would cost anyone support. "I think I was still doing a good job," he said, "but every time you make a decision, you make a person angry—different people all the time. Probably the most remarkable thing is that I didn't make more folks madder than I did, because it was a time of turmoil. The first thing I did was limit the size [of the university]. I took the position that we were going to let our ability to generate quality dictate our size, not the other way around, and this was during the great growth phase. Everybody was for that philosophically, until it was their child, their constituent's child, but we stood firm and, I think, won their respect."

The breaking point, though, in the estimation of Davison and his associates, was the crumbling of his relationship with two governors of Georgia, George Busbee and Joe Frank Harris, and particularly with one of their chief political operatives, Thomas L. Perdue. Perdue rose to the rank of executive assistant during Busbee's second term as governor, then retained a similar position under Harris. A Democrat then, he now sells his services as a campaign consultant to both Republicans and Democrats.

Davison first clashed seriously with Perdue on then Governor Busbee's plan to take over the independent public television station operated by the university and drop it into a statewide network controlled from Atlanta. Davison argued that the state as a political unit ought not to control an influential television station, but Busbee wanted it as part of a broad telecommunications plan. According to one story, which a number of people voluntarily repeat, Davison tossed Perdue out of the president's home in Athens after an argument about the station. Their disputes grew nastier as Perdue increased his power over gubernatorial appointments, including those to the board of regents.

Davison and his friends believe today that the Jan Kemp lawsuit was allowed to play out as it did because it provided an "excuse" for Perdue and others in Atlanta to rid themselves of the president. As they see it, the regents, influenced by Perdue, were not uncomfortable with Hue Henry's strategy to extend the scope of the trial and in effect put the university, its president, and its athletic program on trial. After the trial, then Governor Harris denied accusations of political meddling, telling an Atlanta newspaper they were "an exaggeration; . . . it's totally in error." He said, "I don't think [Davison's] resignation was called for or was necessary." Some neutral observers think that Perdue and the regents were not determined to oust Davison but would have been content to embarrass him, just put him in his place. "I think Fred Davison would be president of the University of Georgia today if he hadn't resigned," said one. "He would have been slapped hard but he could have held on."

Illustrative of the clash is the selection of a lawyer to defend Trotter and Ervin, and in effect the university. The case was considered too big to be handled by anyone in the office of the politically ambitious state Attorney General Michael Bowers (then a Democrat, now a Republican). So Bowers (who resigned as attorney general in 1997 to campaign for governor) hired Hale Almand, who had gained a reputation as a tough federal prosecutor and had recently won an important corruption case on behalf of the state. The Davison camp contends that Almand possessed too little expertise in either civil rights or labor law to be given this assignment. Others consider this to be "Monday morning quarterbacking"; not only was Almand thought by university leaders to be a good choice at the time, but Davison and Beaird were instrumental in his hiring. After the trial, Attorney General Bowers told an Athens newspaper that "In 1982, when the Kemp case went to the courts, President Davison asked specially that Hale Almand be hired." Faded memories and differing perspectives make it virtually impossible to learn those particular details.

At any rate, Almand is considered by all hands to have performed unsuc-
cessfully. His "postman-garbageman" opening statement has become legendary in Georgia legal circles. "It was stunning, it made me nervous," his
opposing counsel, Henry, remembered, noting that Almand made his statement in front of a black judge and four black jurors. "I was wondering, what is
going on here. It's got to be leading somewhere." But it wasn't. Henry also
marveled at the defense's lack of discretion with witnesses. "You had a person
[Almand] who was acclimated to prosecutions where you're questioning
witnesses who are drug dealers and prostitutes, and you can be a bully, you can
get away with it; that's what the jury wants you to do. But when you're
questioning faculty members, even when you don't like what they're saying,
you have to take a different approach; and he had no experience at all in that
kind of thing."

Certainly Almand didn't help the university's reputation when he conceded early in the trial that athletes did indeed receive special treatment. "We
do not contest that to the slightest degree," Almand told the court. Claiming
that Georgia was only operating like other major athletic powers, he said that
if it did not, "it would be like unilateral disarmament in sports. Athletes would
go somewhere else and the sports program would go down the drain." It is
possible that universities do operate unethically in accepting athletes and
keeping them eligible, but they don't usually admit it to a federal court. And,
violating a cardinal rule of cross-examination—never allow yourself to be
surprised by an answer—Almand asked Kemp how much money she hoped to
win in the case. Her slam-dunk response: "Money has never been my primary
motivating force. Had it been, I never would have become a teacher."

A succession of witnesses for the plaintiff testified to preferential treatment
for athletes, in support of Kemp's free-speech claim that she was demoted and
fired for protesting the preferences. One instructor in Developmental Studies
swore that an athlete was allowed an extra quarter of remedial work because
he had scored the winning touchdown against Georgia Tech. Another conceded that she had agreed to give two women track athletes a D instead of an
incomplete to keep them eligible for Olympic trials. Another said she had been
told not to ask how a football player's sociology grade changed mysteriously
from F to C although he had attended only two lectures. Kemp's witnesses also
spoke positively about her ability as a teacher and her care for students. Kemp
herself testified that her boss, Ervin, had screamed at her because she had
refused to order another teacher to change the grades of student athletes who
had failed an English course. She also said that when he saw her working on a
grammar textbook he told her that Developmental Studies was "not a research
unit."

A former UGA professor produced devastating evidence in the form of a
tape recording she had made surreptitiously at a faculty meeting. According to

the transcript, Director Ervin said, "I know for a fact that these kids would not be here if it were not for their utility to the institution." In statements not disputed by the defense, he said, "There is no real sound academic reason for their being here other than to be utilized to produce income. They are used as a kind of raw material in the production of some goods to be sold as whatever product, and they get nothing in return." Further, the tape revealed a discussion about establishing a literacy program that would precede even Developmental Studies. "We're talking about creating a second- or third-grade curriculum and working those kids on up from there," Ervin said, according to the transcript.

As is frequently the case in touchy lawsuits like this, the central figure, Jan Kemp, is no Joan of Arc. She was considered by many to be abrasive; one couple who knew Kemp and her husband socially years before the trial said they ended the acquaintanceship because of the Kemps' repeated thoughtless behavior. Kemp discussed from the witness stand her divorce and psychiatric treatment. The defense exhibited faculty evaluations indicating that Kemp was moody and took out her frustrations on students. Defense witnesses, who said Kemp had trouble getting along with faculty colleagues, called her "elitist" and said she "demoralized" students who were in trouble academically. Others who say they were once her friends tell stories of anger and what they characterize as paranoia. Henry, who seldom sees Kemp, observed that her erratic behavior tracks the anguish suffered by many government "whistle blowers." (After the trial, Kemp gave a huge chunk of her settlement to her fundamentalist church, then lost much of her remaining money in an angry and losing child-custody battle with her former husband.)

On the witness stand, the highly placed academics Trotter and Ervin appeared unsettled dealing with Henry. Trotter conceded that their status as football players had something to do with her decision to promote nine students from Developmental Studies to the regular curriculum, and she admitted that a parent's political status "would be an appropriate factor to consider" in how a student was treated. A decade later, Trotter recalled the trial as one of the worst experiences of her life. "I've had a few things happen in my life that have been difficult, but I think this was one of the most difficult," she said. "My husband was killed in World War II, and I really thought that was the worst thing that could happen to me. I'm telling you, I think this was almost as bad. It's just like some . . . you grieve almost like it's a . . ." She stopped.

During the trial, "I had a very hard time with myself," Trotter said, "and [with] the attitude that the president took. I felt like he really had thrown me to the wolves. That was the worst part, and I really had to get that sort of straightened out. But I got it straightened out. One thing that helped me, and this is just personal, just me, is that I absolutely told the truth. I've never had to stop and think about what I said or not, because I told it just like it was. And I knew that I was right. That helped me a lot. You see, I didn't have to feel like I was apologetic, or that I was trying to cover anything up. Now, I didn't tell some things I could have told." Why not? "What I tried to do was to keep from [hurting the university]. At that point in time, I thought we were all in this together and that we were trying to help the university and get out of this mess we were in." Only later, she said with a sad laugh, she discovered "we weren't all in it together."

Plainly, Trotter, who was forced from her position as vice president after the trial and retired two years later, remains bitter about the treatment by her closest colleagues. "[Davison] says he didn't know anything about any of this until after the fact. It's not true. I met with him three times, at least two times a week. I had agendas where we could talk about some of these problems. . . . [Our meetings were] just one-on-one, and [in court] he said we never talked about those [things] when we were together." Did you talk about it? "Sure. Why would you not talk to him about it. It was a problem. That was my job, to keep him informed. . . . I mean, it doesn't make any sense [not to tell him]."

Trotter said she didn't realize that everybody wasn't singing from the same hymnal until a meeting the evening before Davison was to testify. "I had a list of things I wanted him to be sure and mention. The fact that we had regents' permission to give these athletes another quarter. That I had kept him informed all the way. . . . And he said, 'I don't even know what you're talking about, Virginia. I knew nothing about this until after the fact.' . . . Well, I just got up and walked out of the room, is what I did. . . . I couldn't stay there and argue. It was just so ridiculous, and I was so shocked. I was really just as shocked and surprised as I've ever been about anything. It never occurred to me that I wouldn't have the backing of the president. How naive could I be."

Davison's memory of Trotter's incumbency is very different. First, he suggested that she wasn't a strong vice president. Trotter had been hired in 1977 after serving the Ford Administration as assistant secretary for education in the Department of Health, Education, and Welfare, which at the time was the top education job in the federal government. "I ran an institution in which the deans were my field generals," said Davison, "and this committee of deans, I am fairly confident, decided that they were going to get me a vice president they didn't have to worry too much about. . . . [In regard to Trotter], the committee said, 'Gee, we kill all the birds with one stone. She's got the background; we've got an entrance into Washington;' and it did look good [that she was a woman]. . . . Virginia would have functioned much better in a more bureaucratic kind of administration than the [lean] one I ran."

He also remembered conversations differently than she did. "This is the kind of problem I had with Virginia. I can't remember the time, [but] she came into the office, and it had to do with something about a football player. My position always was if they don't pass, fail them, get them out of there. I can't remember exactly, but something came up about [a player who had gone to Georgia Tech]. I made a comment that I don't know how Tech . . . gets their students eligible to play. Virginia, in later conversations, I have heard indirectly, took that to say, 'Virginia, you find a way to get our people eligible to play.' That's the way Virginia would take it. To me, I was making an observation. I wasn't making a charge of anything else."

A person who has worked with both Trotter and Davison accepts both versions. "I can absolutely believe it. . . . Virginia probably felt like people were running at her. She felt like Fred let her hang out. Fred probably was saying [to Trotter in the meeting before he testified at the trial], 'It's a tough thing I have to do, but I'm not going to say, yes, Virginia, you were saying all these things, and I was winking and nudging.' Fred Davison was absolutely a hard liner when it came to the notion of excelling in the classroom. . . . Probably he was saying [in the meetings with Trotter before the crisis erupted], 'Where are the rules? What does the NCAA say? Does it say we can admit this student? Can we? All right, you have the discretion to make a call on this student.'"

Since the only defendants were Trotter and Ervin, the president had in general remained above the fray. But the potential impact of his testimony was eventually considered important enough for the defense to insert him directly into the trial. "I thought it was the worst idea I had ever heard," said one university official about the decision. "Because up to that point the strategy had worked in one way; it had kept Fred Davison out of the limelight. The big players were Trotter, Ervin, and [Coach] Dooley, and it was all focused on athletics. It was believable that maybe [Davison] didn't know to what extent this was going on. I remember thinking that day, you're giving him the responsibility for it all now, by putting him on the stand."

When he testified as the last witness, Davison defended both the preferences for athletes and for students with political connections. He said that he had worked within the NCAA to raise academic standards for athletes, but that until standards were raised, Georgia would not "unilaterally disarm." Blaming high schools that produce students who cannot read or write, he said, "All the university does is accept the problem. It doesn't create it." He also saw no harm in enrolling unprepared students. "I can see absolutely no damage done teaching a student how to read and write."

The fact that Davison took the witness stand highlighted a dilemma faced, ironically, by both the university's and Kemp's counsel: It was in their mutual interest to protect the president. If lawyers hired for the university had been intent on clearing only Trotter and Ervin, who were, after all, the named defendants, they might have appropriated a version of the "Nuremberg defense"; that is, contended that the clients were only taking orders from their boss. But to succeed, they would have needed to spread the blame to Davison and his administration, as well as to Coach Dooley and the athletic department, whom the lawyers seemed more anxious to protect. On the other hand, Henry believed all along that Davison and Dooley were those ultimately responsible. But Henry lacked evidence strong enough to prove that, and had he attempted to blame them, the defense could have moved for dismissal on the grounds that he was suing the wrong people.

Vince Dooley was a special case. One of the most prominent football coaches of his era, he won a national championship and six Southeastern Conference championships in 25 years at Georgia, and was elected to the college football Hall of Fame. At the time he gave up his football coaching assignment in 1989, remaining as UGA athletic director, he was so popular in the state that it was expected he would run for governor or United States senator and would be favored to win. But Dooley never pursued elective politics; instead, he concentrated on protecting and building UGA's athletic program. And more than most football coaches, he is conscious of the big picture. He personally led a $1 million campaign for library endowment, which enlisted a number of contributors unaccustomed to supporting the library; the campaign eventually raised more than $2 million—including a $100,000 contribution from Dooley himself.

Dooley is also the only person prominent in the trial who survived in his job at the university, a fact he acknowledges with a laugh. It is a tribute, associates agree, to his achievements, his political savvy, and his down-home yet polished style. Unlike some others, unreconstructed a decade after the fact, Dooley takes a relentlessly positive approach to the Kemp case. "It might have been an unfair experience in a lot of ways," he began, "but yet there are certain things that you can always improve upon in a program. And there were things that we needed to improve. And we did. Every part of our body was split open, and a flashlight was shining in the cracks of our body. Finally, after awhile, I said, 'Look, if this program is on a solid foundation, we're going to survive these strong winds of criticism. So let's stand tall and take advantage of this as an opportunity to make this program better. . . . We may have a black eye, we may be bruised a little bit, but in the final analysis, our program will be better.' And that is what happened. We did survive, because the program was solid. And we're a better program as a result of it."

Dooley maintains that national academic standards for athletes are only now returning to the level they were when he came to Georgia more than three decades ago. He blames lower standards accepted by the NCAA in the 1970s and the decreasing quality of secondary schools. He also calls it ironic that UGA was publicly shamed, noting that President Davison, a supporter of meaningful academic standards for athletes, had years earlier convened a private meeting on Sapelo Island, off the Georgia coast, invited such recognized sports leaders as football coach Joe Paterno of Pennsylvania State University and basketball coach Bob Knight of Indiana University, and produced a statement that led to the NCAA's famous Proposition 48. This rule, which allowed for the admission of athletes who fell below certain academic standards but denied them immediate athletic eligibility, became the cornerstone of NCAA academic reform rules.

Dooley believes that his program suffered in two ways from the Kemp trial. It hurt competitively. After the trial, UGA became the first big-time sports institution to announce publicly that it would not accept any "Prop 48s," some of whom attended universities whose teams Georgia played. It also hurt credibility with the faculty: "It just knocked us for a loop. . . . Anything that looked like there might be something irregular, there was a red flag. Even though maybe the student body as a whole may have been doing the same things student-athletes were doing, because they were student-athletes, there was a report written about it. [But] a lot of people who questioned us got to know this program better, and I think the respect for it and the credibility has been restored."

Suggesting that administration "stonewalling" exacerbated the difficulties, Dooley cites his own different handling of Jan Kemp. Long before the lawsuit, she wrote him a nine-page letter chronicling her complaints about Developmental Studies and athletes' places in it. Dooley invited her for coffee, "several cups of coffee," at a Howard Johnson's to talk about the program. He told her that she was wrong about half the complaints but that he would look into the rest. He then called to inform her that some of the problems could be dealt with only by Developmental Studies but others, which were of concern to the athletic department, he would do something about. "The point I'm trying to make is, because of at least listening to her concerns, and trying to address those concerns, . . . [we made sure] her focus was not a personal thing about Georgia athletics. . . . The real focus was a vendetta against Developmental Studies, against [Ervin, Trotter, and Davison]."

Nevertheless, the athletic department, "because we were so high profile, became the focal point. Our 'trial' really continued long after the Jan Kemp trial, because what that did was to trigger all of these other inquiries. We had a faculty committee that looked into the situation. We had the board of regents that looked into the situation. We had the attorney general's office that investigated the situation, not to mention the newspapers. Every day there was some allegation, or accusation. . . . It was like throwing all these things up against the wall, all this mud, and there was a little bit of it sticking. A lot of it was coming off, but there was enough there that you could point to something. We spent all our time trying to defend each new allegation. . . . So it went on for years. . . . There's still a little bit out there." Then, the confidence shows through. If Georgia had really run a dishonest program, "I don't think we would have survived this. Had it not been pretty good overall, I really don't believe we could have survived."

Fresh from the bicentennial celebration of scholarly excellence, the trial and its aftermath attracted more national attention to the academic program at the University of Georgia than any other event in its two-century history. The *New York Times*, which two years earlier had said UGA was "muscling [its] way onto the list of prominent institutions," referred sarcastically in its trial-verdict story to "Georgia, situated in the town of—as Socrates rolls over in his grave—Athens." A Detroit paper headlined, "Georgia Defends Using Illiterate Athletes," and a Baltimore paper printed, "Georgia's a loser with its shameful policy on athletes." Hundreds of newspapers and other news organizations from *Sports Illustrated* to National Public Radio reported regularly on the trial; the *Los Angeles Times* played the jury verdict on its front page; both the *New York Times* and the *Washington Post* ran front-page stories on the board of regents' subsequent audit report.

But perhaps the most scorching, and poignant, judgment came from closer to home, from Frederick Allen, the respected political editor of the *Atlanta Constitution*, the most influential newspaper in the South:

> It may be that Sanford Stadium would be empty on Saturday afternoons if Georgia 'unilaterally disarmed' and accepted only athletes who met the same academic standards that are applied to other students. It may be that the public knew that Georgia bent the rules to accept and keep athletes. It may be that other universities do the same.
>
> But no one knew that Georgia took kids who couldn't even read. This one realization swept away all defense. Perhaps the kindest thing to say is that the university's leaders have been so close to the situation that they lost perspective. 'If they leave us being able to read, write, communicate better,' Georgia President Fred Davison said of his university's student-athletes, 'we simply have not done them any damage.' Here was a university president saying, in so many words, that his institution accepts illiterate students, sees nothing wrong in doing so, and has no intention of doing otherwise unless every other school goes along. Here was a university president inviting—demanding—ridicule.

Former Dean Beaird insists that the regents could have won a reversal had they appealed the jury verdict. Whether or not he is correct, neither the regents nor almost anyone else in authority at the university or in state government had any stomach for an appeal; they wanted the matter over with. "I don't want to hear the name Jan Kemp again for the rest of my life," one high-level state official said at the time. The authorities faced a dilemma. If they appealed successfully, it would mean a new trial with the attendant publicity—perhaps more publicity than the first time. And the plaintiff's case

might be even stronger: The regents' post-trial audit of Developmental Studies furnished Henry with new information, including conflicting stories from
President Davison and Vice President Trotter. "We only had the tip of the
iceberg in the first trial," Henry suggested with a devilish smile. "I would have
put Fred Davison on the stand as a character witness for Virginia Trotter."
After Judge Ward reduced the damages to $600,000, Henry announced that
he was prepared for another trial. But he never had to commit himself formally
because Attorney General Bowers hastily settled for $1.1 million.

The end of the trial set off a series of rapid events that changed the face of
higher education in Georgia. Almost instantly the board of regents took what
appeared to some to be a face-saving action. Declaring that it was shocked by
revelations about the university's academic enterprise, it announced an audit
of Developmental Studies programs at all of the more than 30 institutions
within its jurisdiction, even though everyone knew that the University of
Georgia and the other athletic powerhouse in the state, Georgia Tech, were
the targets.

However athletes might have benefitted, Developmental Studies had been
created in the 1970s largely to serve two groups. One was black students,
many of them products of segregated, and unequal, elementary and secondary
education, who were, for the first time, allowed to attend the university; the
other was rural whites, many of whom were guaranteed admission to the
university by virtue of their high class standing in small, impoverished high
schools.

While the audits were pending, the regents said, they would postpone the
annual one-year contract extensions of all the institutional presidents, which
were usually renewed automatically. In an astonishingly short time for an
academic study, the auditors reported in less than a month that, sure enough,
the other schools' programs came up essentially clean, and the presidential
renewals went forward. But to give them more time to examine the UGA
audit, the regents delayed President Davison's reappointment to his 20th year.
This was a humiliation he didn't deserve, Davison decided, and he angrily
announced his resignation.

The official UGA Developmental Studies audit, which appeared little more
than a month after the Kemp trial ended, proved devastating. It cited exceptions made for numerous students in the program, listing as the reasons
"request of regents," "request of music," "political family," but most often
"athlete." Trotter and Ervin, whatever their stance had been at the trial,
obviously intended to protect their own reputations as best they could in
speaking with the auditors. The report declared:

> Dr. Trotter and Dr. Ervin state that on numerous occasions, beginning as
> early as 1980 [six years before the trial], they attempted to show the

President that many athletes were too weak to attend the University and could not be handled through the Developmental Studies Program.

All major exceptions for athletes which involved Dr. Trotter's office were according to them discussed with the President in advance. . . . On one and possibly two occasions, he allegedly indicated that failure to allow selected athletes to exit Developmental Studies would place the University of Georgia in a non-competitive position in football, leading him to say, "What do you want us to do? Play high-school football?" . . . According to Dr. Ervin, if he appeared reluctant to make such arrangements, he would be told that Coach Dooley would get his way whether in Ervin's office or the Vice President's office or the President's office. Dr. Trotter, in turn, indicated that although she was always reluctant, she felt that the pressure from the Athletic Department and the President left her without alternatives.

In its conclusion, the report stated "Neither Dr. Trotter nor Dr. Ervin denied their responsibility for decisions that resulted in preferential treatment for athletes and selected students in the areas of admissions, additional time in Developmental Studies, and administrative exiting from Developmental Studies. . . . Allegedly because of pressure from the Athletic Department, Dr. Ervin and Dr. Trotter made numerous exceptions to university and regents' policies."

Davison was furious. His own staff analysis of the findings produced a lengthy refutation of almost every point in the report, and the president prepared to go public. "We had reviewed the audit, we knew how wrong it was, and I had decided to just go over and tell [the regents] what I thought," Davison said. "But the chairman of the [UGA foundation] was a friend of mine, and he said, 'Look, you've resigned; there's no need to upset the whole system. If you can bring yourself to do it, just say, here's the refutation, and if you'll do that, I'll guarantee that [Governor] Joe Frank Harris will come out and say great things about how it was handled, and what a great job you did.' [Harris] never said a word. . . .

"We agreed that it would do more damage to the university than it would make me feel good. . . . I [had spent] 19 years trying to make it a great university. I said [to myself], 'Gee, you'll probably hurt the university worse than you'll hurt the regents.' It wasn't worth it." So Davison released an abbreviated version of the response, citing relatively few errors and eliminating, among other things, references to behind-the-scenes political manipulations.

The trial further set off an enormous upheaval in the public-relations functions of the university. Because the Kemp case had become such a serious embarrassment for the university and the regents, it was easier to use "bad PR" or "the media" as an excuse than to blame the Developmental Studies program, undue influence from the athletic department, the university administration, or wheeler-dealer Atlanta politicians—any or all of which might have contributed to the public fiasco.

"Bad PR didn't cause the Jan Kemp scenario," said Tom Landrum. "If there's any lesson that is to be learned . . . it is that an open and two-way public discourse would have helped a lot. . . . When you need the press to give you a break, it may not be now but it will be at some point in the future. You can't come in when you need that break and ask the press to give you a break, unless you've had some relationship with it before that happens. . . . There was not a proactive [system] in good times, keeping the lines open [to the press] with the administration and the president."

After Davison's resignation, the regents persuaded Henry King Stanford, the longtime president of the University of Miami, then living in retirement in Americus, Georgia, to guide the university until they could find a new leader. One of Stanford's first actions was to commission a communications audit from Gehrung & Associates, a New Hampshire-based firm that specialized in advising colleges and universities on dealing with the media. Its conclusions were harsh. It condemned the department's managers; the staff, of whom there were too few; and top university administrators, who gave the department too little power. One of the recommendations executed immediately was to change the name of the office from "public relations," which seemed tainted with a promotional sense, to "public information."

A year later, the new president, Charles Knapp, brought in a new vice president for development and university relations, Nicholas Edes, who promptly cleaned the public-affairs house. Barry Wood, who, as director of public relations and then associate vice president, had evolved into Davison's personal spokesman more than the university's, was again assigned to Davison, who had claimed his tenured professorship in the school of veterinary medicine. (Wood also accompanied Davison when in 1989 he became president of the National Science Center Foundation in Augusta, Georgia.) Landrum, who had succeeded Wood as director of public relations, was moved to Edes's staff (and subsequently to Knapp's, where he became assistant to the president, preparing speeches and managing the office budget and personnel).

To run the reorganized news operation, Edes hired Tom Jackson, a UGA graduate and television newsman. "We talked about what it would take to rebuild that office, because the office was truly decimated," Jackson recalled. "With no reflection on [my] predecessors, they had been neutralized in their ability to function simply because of their close involvement with the Kemp situation." The staff was a "shell," down to eight people, of whom four eventually left. It has now grown to 22, responsible for the news bureau, broadcast, video, photography, publications, and, recently, campus tours, with a budget six-fold higher.

"There was not a culture of questioning the president," Jackson said of the Davison era. "Good public relations is avoiding group think, making sure you ask the questions that [the media] are going to ask. I try to approach this job as if I were a reporter. . . . I think we've been able to build an atmosphere on campus where this office has the credibility that deans, directors, and department heads call us when they see certain situations, call asking for advice. . . . They're relying on our office in dealing with public issues. In my first couple of months here, I was watching 60 *Minutes* one night, and one of our faculty members comes on. He was a board member of a camp for disturbed children that was somehow involved in [a coverup], being interviewed on 60 *Minutes* [and] identified as a member of the University of Georgia faculty, interviewed right in his office. I didn't know 60 *Minutes* had been on the damn campus. It is inconceivable to me that could happen today."

Jackson credits much of the progress to "the culture brought in here by Donald Eastman," who took over as vice president for development and university relations in 1991. "Don formalized what I was doing from my gut feeling. I was doing it because I knew it worked as a reporter and from my experience. He was educated and experienced in the administration of it. He came in and said, 'This is a smart way to operate, we need to do this, [and] we need to ask these questions,' and he gave me the authority, the marching orders, to carry it on to a higher level and [to] be more forceful in doing it. Prior to having his backing, if I ran up against a brick wall, I'd back down, with a department head or a vice president, if they'd say, 'We don't want to do it that way.' Now I'll argue my point and not worry about retribution, because I'm not going to get retribution, because I have his support.

"Public-relations people, in my mind, often have to be a much larger part of managing the issues, not glossing the issue, but managing the issue. . . . [In recent years] this office has put forth solutions in a number of what could have been public relations issues that never became issues because we saw a problem and got it fixed." Jackson offers an illustration. "There was a very good reporter, with the Athens daily paper, who was asking a lot of questions around campus. I was beginning to get phone calls: 'He's asking questions about the art we hold, wants to know about the inventory, what the maintenance and care is, [and] how we keep track of what we own.' I started asking these people, 'You got any problems with the art?' 'Yea, well, this [piece] is damaged; I don't have enough money to keep this up.' I got to the campus inventory people. They said they didn't know: 'The museum keeps up with the art inventory on campus.' The museum said, 'We only inventory what we hold. There is art all over this campus, presumably held by central inventory.' The reporter was right on to the story.

"I [could just see] this story going statewide: The University of Georgia has all this art, nobody knows who's responsible for it, [it's] not being taken care of, [and it's] being damaged. . . . Dr. Eastman [and I decided to ask] the department heads who held art and [university property control to] put serial numbers on it. In a meeting or two we worked out basically a new protocol—actually we had a protocol that was not being followed—on how we acquisitioned art, maintained, and inventoried it. We set up a process by which the museum would advise other art holders on campus on the maintenance and display of art, about sunlight and humidity.

"We put out a story in the faculty and staff newsletter about the university instituting art control and inventory measures [and] let the internal people know that this was now policy. The reporter called and said, 'You preempted my story.' I said, 'What was your purpose, to blast us statewide or improve art-control measures at the University of Georgia? If it was the second purpose, it has been achieved.' A couple of months later, he did a nice Sunday piece, with color, a positive story, on the difficulties of managing an art collection the size of the University of Georgia's."

As with embarrassing cases at other institutions, UGA can provide evidence that the damage caused by the Kemp trial was limited. Applications for admissions held firm or increased. Fund raising did not fall off, especially among football loyalists who felt the sports program unfairly maligned. "People rallied to the side of their great, injured mother university," one UGA leader said. But the football team's record slumped, partly because UGA would no longer accept "Prop 48" athletes as its rivals did, and partly because those rivals not-so-subtly suggested to high school stars that their academic records would be scrutinized more severely at Georgia than elsewhere. When a larger number than usual football recruits failed academically, some Bulldog fans blamed university officials for going overboard in their effort to rebuild the post-Kemp academic reputation.

"I thought it was uniquely important [when I arrived], without making any judgments, to spend absolutely a minimal amount of time looking backward," said President Knapp (who left UGA in 1997 after a decade to become president of the Aspen Institute). Knapp said he believed the university survived the debacle in part because of particularly fortunate years for the state: "We have had the wind at our back—demographic change, a robust economy, [and] six years with the best higher education governor in the country [Zell Miller]."

No one doubts, though, that the university suffered. The trial embarrassed UGA, and its impact continued for months through post-trial motions and settlement negotiations, to say nothing of Jan Kemp's sympathetic appearances in *People* magazine and on morning network news programs. But at least these blows came from a terrier of a teacher and a bulldog of a litigator. The Developmental Studies audit punished the university even further, a hurt inflicted by its own governing body, the board of regents. It is impossible to judge how much damage was done to faculty recruiting, either immediately or over the next several years. More than a decade later, people new to the state of Georgia still hear about the Jan Kemp case.

Vice President Eastman, a former professor of literature who considers the university fortunate to have a man with Dooley's interest in education as athletic director, does not bemoan the reality that football will always be critical to an important segment of UGA's friends. "I think people are pre-pared to believe that you can have a good athletic program at an institution with first-class academic credentials," he said. "I don't think that if Berkeley wins football games, or Michigan, or Duke in basketball, that people see it as a contradiction. I suspect that the people who think about it at all assume that there are special considerations being given to [athletes], but universities are supposed to be tents with many mansions."

Eastman believes that one positive legacy of the Jan Kemp case is a "license" to "tell the truth, tell it as quickly as you can, get it out ahead of the story, and move on." Too many institutions think that "good PR is not telling the bad news," which is ultimately self-defeating. "We can use a challenge to fix a problem, rather than say, 'There's not one,' because there are problems. I think that if a university can avoid being defensive about it, a reasonable person would not be surprised to know that if you have a place that's got a $750 million annual budget, and 10,500 employees, and 30,000 students, each of whom has a parent or two, that there are going to be some problems. There are problems all the time. What you try to do is fix them."

CHAPTER 4

"The Students Were Wonderful"

The Holocaust Denial Advertisement at Queens College

Editors of the *Quad*, the student newspaper at Queens College, had drifted back from winter break to their crowded little office in the student union, where they shared vacation experiences and sifted through a stack of mostly junk mail. One envelope had stood out, Andrew Wallenstein, who was the editor-in-chief, remembered, "because it was a pink envelope from an address I did not recognize." As he glanced at its contents, something struck him as familiar. Sure enough, on the bulletin board where staffers posted articles of common interest, he found a recent story from *Time* magazine about a man named Bradley Smith, who purchased ads in college newspapers to question the authenticity of the Holocaust. Smith had sent a check for $240 to buy a half-page ad in the *Quad*. Its headline was "A Revisionist Challenge to the U.S. Holocaust Memorial Museum."

Andy Wallenstein was an Orthodox Jew, having attended Yeshivas (Jewish parochial schools) since nursery school, and all but a couple of the nine members of the *Quad* editorial board were Jewish. Jewish students made up about 20 percent of the enrollment at Queens College, the academic jewel of the City University of New York and the pride of the Borough of Queens, the most ethnically diverse county in the United States. This was a student body energized by eager immigrants and first-generation Americans, large numbers of Asians and Asian Americans, West Indians, Latin Americans, and Eastern Europeans. But the college represented something special to its Jewish students.

Queens College was founded in 1937, the year before the Crystal Night smashing of Jewish property in Germany and two years before the start of World War II, as Jews in increasing numbers sought haven in America from

Nazi persecution. A considerable number attended Queens or sent their children there. After the war, many survivors of concentration camps, nearly all of whom had lost relatives to genocide, tasted American higher education at Queens College. Several members of the Queens faculty were Holocaust survivors or children of victims. And the Jewish community in Queens, as well as some of the college's Jewish graduates, who were among its strongest supporters, were extremely protective of it.

Wallenstein had heard a lot about the Holocaust in his Yeshivas, but he was born in 1974, so the full import of the ad to his college did not sink in immediately. At first he planned to ignore it. Still, he was drawn to do some research and "gradually it dawned on me that there were reasons to print it." A few days later he mentioned the issue at an editorial board meeting, telling his editors that he was still "checking it out."

He called peers at other universities, who offered conflicting advice. A family friend gave him a book by Emory University Professor Deborah Lipstadt, *Denying the Holocaust: The Growing Assault on Truth and Memory*, so he called her; she urged him not to publish the ad. He called Nat Hentoff, the New York journalist and staunch defender of First Amendment rights; Hentoff advised him to publish it. Then Wallenstein spoke to professors and administrators, fellow Jewish students, and a rabbi at Queens College, where "pretty much everyone urged me not to" run the ad. But now he had in effect gone public: "I think the words 'Holocaust' and 'denial' just rang alarm bells for a lot of people," he said ingenuously.

The pressures soon escalated. Wallenstein received a call from the CBS News program *60 Minutes*, which was reporting a piece about Holocaust deniers with Mike Wallace as correspondent (Bradley Smith had mentioned Queens among other college newspapers to which he had recently submitted ads). The producers also informed Ron Cannava, the college's director of public relations, which, says Cannava, "quickly threw everybody, including myself, into a state of panic." (Corporate public relations officers share a little joke. Question: What do you do when *60 Minutes* calls? Answer: Update your resume.)

Soon Wallenstein received a call from the college's dean of students inviting him to a meeting with the vice president for student affairs and the legal counsel. "Right off the bat, they were urging me not to do it, and going into the reasons why. They were perfectly blunt about the fact that it would be terrible public relations for the college [and] that it could hurt donations. But I wanted them to understand that the *Quad* was an independent newspaper, and what was best for Queens College wasn't necessarily best for the *Quad*." It was a point that many outsiders never grasped: The *Quad* was an independent entity, and college administrators had no authority to tell its editors what to do or what not to do.

Meanwhile, Cannava, the veteran public-relations officer (whose background is Roman Catholic), was conducting his own research. "I contacted friends in the Jewish community at Queens to get their reactions to this thing. They formed immediate judgments, and there was almost universal condemnation of Mike Wallace. They knew him by reputation and they were very suspicious. They said, 'Even though Wallace is a Jew, he's dangerous to Jewish thought, and he's out to destroy Queens College.'"

Despite the anxiety among people he liked and trusted, Cannava thought that Queens could benefit from this kind of attention if it handled itself well. Cannava's boss, Ceil Cleveland, the vice president for institutional relations, endorsed cooperation. "If we didn't work with 60 Minutes," Cleveland said, "we would set up a defensive, adversarial relationship, and that is almost always harmful. If Mike Wallace and 60 Minutes want information, they are likely to get it, and I wanted them to get their information through us."

As a final check, though, Cleveland and President Shirley Strum Kenny wanted Cannava to determine if 60 Minutes could be dissuaded from using Queens as its centerpiece. "I discovered that they were really intent on going ahead, mainly because it was so dramatic, a school so heavily influenced by Jewish thought," Cannava said. He was also impressed by the young producer the program had assigned to the story. "I said to him, 'You know, you can hurt us. If we cooperate with you, we can be doing something that would really be bad for the college, given our constituency.' They said, 'To the extent that we can give you any assurance, we are not out to make Queens College look foolish.' 60 Minutes could easily have done a story about a callow young man who had blundered into this situation."

Kenny recalled long sessions with Cleveland and Cannava, and occasionally with others in the administration: "We would sit together and strategize about what would work, and play it back and forth, and look at it from a bunch of different perspectives, so that by the time a decision was made to do something, everybody was in the loop, which is the way I work with my administrators anyway. One of the reasons we were able to get through this is that there was open communication."

Once the top administrators approved, Cannava recalled, "They said, you work with them. Do everything you can to make the story not hurt Queens College. That was my assignment. I became the 60 Minutes contact on campus. They did nothing without working with me. It was quite true that if Queens College had not made me available, it would have made the job more difficult for 60 Minutes. But it would also have placed the job totally out of Queens College's control."

The actions over which she had no control were clear to Kenny from the start. "I don't think there was any single right answer here. There were lots of possibilities. Any kind of good decision could go wrong, if it were picked up wrong by the newspapers, if it were represented wrong. You do your very, very best, and then you need luck. Because in something as volatile as this, anything can bounce wrong. You do everything you can, but then there are these quirks of what happens in public life.

"For example, you know that 60 *Minutes* is interviewing these students, and that is something you totally cannot control, you can't spin, you can't do anything. The risk of that kind of national coverage on something as hot as this is enormous, but sometimes you've got to take risks. You should take intelligent risks, but sometimes you've got to jump in there and hope that it comes out right. In this case, the students were wonderful."

Kenny did try to persuade Wallenstein to withhold the denial ad, and the two of them had several serious conversations. "I had a very good relationship with President Kenny," Wallenstein said, "and throughout all this, it never, ever got hostile. I really respected how the administration handled it, but they made clear their position. I respected the president a tremendous amount, so what she said carried weight." But not enough to change his mind. When he held out, Kenny signaled her appreciation for the independence of the *Quad* by purchasing her own ad to rebut the deniers. "I thought it was important for me to express my point of view to all of our constituencies, while also expressing my conviction that the students ought to be able to do what they wanted," she said. "There was nothing to keep me from putting in an ad if Bradley Smith could."

Kenny, herself a Jew, understood the importance of maintaining communication on this issue with the influential Jewish community in Queens (one of five boroughs of New York City); with organizations such as the Anti-Defamation League of B'nai B'rith, which provided background on similar episodes at other institutions; and not least with members of her own faculty. "You have to realize that a lot of these faculty members lost their families in the Holocaust, and a number of them are survivors—they have physical proof, and I don't mean just numbers on their arms, but visible scars. You can imagine the passion they would feel about this. They have lived it and survived it and created a new life and found a haven in Queens College. Then it looks as though these unthinking kids, some of them Jewish, are going to do this unthinking thing."

To lessen the risks, Cannava, who thought "Andy was a terrific kid," began to serve as his unofficial advisor. (Wallenstein calls Cannava "my press agent.") "I was shocked at first about the ad," Cannava says. "My thought was, this is dynamite, and they don't know what they're handling, so I had to educate myself to what was going on in the students' minds. The suspicion was that Andy was trying to aggrandize himself and didn't care how dangerous it was. Well, it wasn't too long before I knew, that doesn't fit Andy. He's a journalist. He's almost intuitively a journalist. And the depth of his concern made the issue different."

As tense days passed, the atmosphere within the *Quad* editorial board heated up. "I was waxing, wavering, back and forth, almost daily on what to do," Wallenstein said, "depending on who had given me the guilt trip that day." Most of the board supported Wallenstein's increasingly strong view that the ad should run, including Managing Editor Chris Ferraro, one of the two non-Jewish members. "I first thought that we should not give it any credence at all," Ferraro said. "Then I realized we shouldn't turn a blind eye. We can't pretend that certain things don't exist; [we] can't pretend that people aren't out there saying things like this."

But two women on the board, devoutly Orthodox Jews, continued to protest, believing that Wallenstein didn't understand the pain he would cause. Someone who was close to the deliberations remembers the culture clash. "Andy was Orthodox too, but it was a different degree. Andy would wear a baseball cap and not a yarmulke. Andy would hold hands with his girlfriend. These women weren't allowed to touch their boyfriends until they got married."

Wallenstein admits, with a little embarrassed grin, that he was being seduced by the attention the *Quad* was getting. "We knew there would be a controversy on campus, but we did not see the media coming into this. When they did, I would be the first to admit, the media definitely fueled our desire to publish. We were a little starstruck. When I heard *60 Minutes* was on the story, I wanted them to do it at Queens. I told them, we're going to set the precedent here." In the meantime, the influential New York paper *Newsday* discovered the story, "and the snowball started picking up speed," Wallenstein said. "The Jewish papers and the local Queens papers were in a feeding frenzy. The *New York Post* managed to write an editorial without speaking to us about it and got all the facts wrong."

Cannava was now at work with *60 Minutes*. "One of my assignments was to locate Holocaust survivors on the faculty and staff. Sam Heilman, the sociologist whose mother was one of the *Schindler's List* people, has written major books about ultra-Orthodox life in Israel. He is insightful and tolerant, but he was so acerbic in this incident. He seemed intolerant of any possibility that the mass media, and particularly Mike Wallace, could be fair. He dismissed Wallace as a lowlife. He was used on the program as the one person who called into question their motives."

60 Minutes interviewed President Kenny and a number of Queens faculty, most of whom Wallace charmed, but he focused on the students. Cannava remembered Wallace manipulating the students before the interview, "telling them that what they were doing was noble. But Andy didn't buy that. The kids were healthily suspicious of everybody. They were trying to find, as young people will do, a real answer for them. The most impressive scene was the kids."

Wallace failed in his attempt to interview Bradley Smith, the person buying ads in college newspapers. Smith had decided he would make only live television appearances because of how taped interviews could be edited, so 60 *Minutes* finally settled for bites from an earlier CBS News broadcast. When I called Smith for an interview, he said he would agree only if he could tape-record the session himself, to make certain that nothing he said was taken out of context. I told him I did not use statements out of context and he was welcome to record the interview. With that ground rule, we agreed to meet.

Bradley Smith lives in a modest house in a modest neighborhood in the modest town of Visalia, California. He greeted me wearing jeans and a sport shirt, then apologized for leaving for a few minutes to drive his college-student daughter to a friend's house. He is 66 years old, has gray-white hair, and a blue-collar manner that would fit your teammate on the factory bowling team.

This is the man who relishes toying with the minds of students at some of the nation's best colleges and chortles at the anger and frustration he arouses in some of the nation's leading scholars. He says he has modest goals, intellectual goals; but they are much more far reaching. He is, after all, denying—or, in his view, "revising," the occurrence of what Winston Churchill called "the greatest and most terrible crime ever committed in the whole history of the world."

Smith has dealt with interrogation about his beliefs and his motivation often enough to deflect what he does not want to answer.

JKF: What is your motive for doing this?
BS: The attack on me is always the same. I hate Jews. I want to destroy Israel.
JKF: Those are not your reasons?
BS: I don't think they are.
JKF: What are your reasons then?
BS: Well . . . I don't think you ever get to the bottom of motive. For instance, what is your motive for asking me that question.
JKF: To get your answer for my book.
BS: Wait a minute. Your answer has to satisfy my standards of motive.

Then I appear to win a round:

JKF: Because readers will want to know your motive.
BS: That's fair. I buy that. . . . But the thing is, you're in a special category here because you're carrying out a professional assignment, with a certain idea [writing a book] in mind.

We played word games like this for nearly four hours. Smith appeared to trust me. A few minutes into our interview, his tape recorder stopped working. I offered to wait until it was operating again. He said it didn't matter, we could go ahead.

Smith said he had grown up in a working-class family in South Central Los Angeles, had never gone to college, had always wanted to be a writer, and was working at a construction job in the late 1970s. Outside a Libertarian Party political meeting in 1979, someone handed him a leaflet containing a translation from the French of an essay raising questions about the Holocaust. This moment changed his life.

"It had never occurred to me to doubt the Holocaust story. . . . What really struck me was that by reading an essay by a man I didn't know, that a crack in this lifelong belief could occur in a space of 20 minutes. . . . It was a very shocking, deeply moving experience. . . . I understood that there was a taboo, that to ask these questions would be breaking a taboo. And I knew immediately what was ahead of me, if I ever took this thing seriously. I knew I was in the center of a taboo and that I would pay dearly for that. . . . I was deeply disturbed. I was put into an emotional turmoil inwardly."

Looking for more information, Smith came upon a book by Northwestern University Professor Arthur Butz that claimed the Holocaust was a hoax. He said that after having read one passage, "All of a sudden, at that moment, at that night, it was New Year's Eve 1979, I knew then I was going to do something about this. I didn't know what."

What he did was produce a short essay that he distributed to, among others, the Institute of Historical Review, which Smith calls "a revisionist think tank," a sort of command central for Holocaust deniers. Here Smith made the connection that was to provide him financial support for many years in exchange for serving as the institute's media spokesman.*

After a decade in which he had gained little attention, Smith decided that "It was hopeless talking to adults about this. . . . If any adult talks about this, my experience is, you lose your job, you lose your social circle, you lose your income, your life is destroyed, literally. . . . There are too many entities who identify with the story. . . . Veterans identify with the Holocaust story, especially European veterans of World War II. This gives them good reason for having gone through what they did. . . . Everybody has got an investment in this story."

---

*The institute was long bankrolled by Willis Carto, a notorious racist anti-Semite who supported David Duke for president and runs the infamous Liberty Lobby. For reasons not relevant to this story, Carto and the people who operate the institute had a bitter falling out over money and are now suing each other. Because of the fight, the institute has fallen on hard financial times.

Except young people, Smith decided. "I wanted to find a way to talk to young people, whose minds are still open. . . . The kids are more likely to read this stuff, without being afraid, than adults are." He shrewdly figured out something else: "College is a community of itself, and a newspaper published there speaks to the entire community." It's also cheap to buy advertisements in college papers.

So, in 1989 Smith bought a few one-inch ads in student newspapers, inviting anyone interested in information on "revisionist theory" to write him. He got little response from students, but, he says with glee, "I got a very strong response from faculty and administrators. . . . Academics got very nervous." In April 1991, he bought his first full-page ad, in the *Daily Northwestern*, the newspaper at Northwestern University where Butz taught. "The proverbial firestorm descended. All of a sudden, you know what, I finally found out how to get somebody's attention."

The next academic year, 1991-92, his full-page ad, titled "The Holocaust Controversy: The Case for Open Debate," was accepted by student newspapers at more than a dozen major universities, including Cornell, Duke, Georgia, Howard, Michigan, Ohio State, Vanderbilt, and Washington University in St. Louis. Two years later, the next major ad, "A Revisionist Challenge to the U.S. Holocaust Memorial Museum," appeared in student papers at about three dozen more universities, including Georgetown, Maryland, Michigan State, Notre Dame, and Pennsylvania State. Smith says that about twice as many student papers rejected his ad as accepted it.

Smith does not deny a Holocaust—that is, he concedes that Hitler's persecution of the Jews, beginning in 1933, occurred, that Crystal Night, for example, occurred. What he denies is the genocide, "specifically the gas chambers. I don't believe the genocide took place. Because the genocide means, essentially, it means this: that there was a state program for the murder of all the European Jews. And that it was largely carried out. I don't believe that there was a state program for the murder of the European Jews. . . . I think the Germans killed a lot of people, but there was no state program for it. And I don't believe they used gas chambers."

Legitimate scholars on the Holocaust refuse to debate Smith, or usually even deign to respond to him, but Michael Berenbaum was willing to speak to me on the subject. Berenbaum is the director of research for the U.S. Holocaust Memorial Museum in Washington, D.C., a professor in the Department of Theology at Georgetown University, and a graduate of Queens College. He, of course, finds Smith's contentions both ludicrous and exasperating. "We have direct evidence of deportations from the ghettos of Warsaw to these death camps, and we have eyewitness accounts, both from perpetrators and victims, of the gassings taking place at each of these killing centers [including] . . . statements by the commandant of Treblinka [and] the recorded statement of Heinrich Himmler speaking to his troops. What more documentation do you want?

"We have documentation from about 14 different countries. We have the outlines of the gas chambers and the construction of the crematoriums. We have the zoning permits for this. We have death lists, we have deportation lists, we have plans for the gas chambers, we have statements on the shipping routes of gas, we have labels. [Smith's] statements, on their face, strain credibility. Why is it the killers didn't deny what they were doing. They documented it. They photographed it. The Germans never denied it. The Austrians never denied it. Eichmann didn't deny it.

"I think the question becomes, Are the inmates that we have interviewed lying? Are the perpetrators lying? And what would be the stake of the perpetrators in lying about their goal. You have statements from the commandants of Treblinka and Auschwitz, you have physical evidence, archeological remains, ruins. You have the intersecting of documents—bills that were issued by, for example, the people who made the gas, invoices that they sent, copies of payments that were sent to them for these chemicals, like Zyklon B. It's discussed in myriads of places, in multiple elements of documents. You have the intersecting of information, all of which coheres and tells an essential story. There's no way in which you could create a conspiracy so wide to prove this in so many different locations."

To demonstrate how Smith has twisted the facts, Berenbaum explored certain of Smith's hypotheses. For example, Smith claims that there is no evidence that gas chambers existed at Auschwitz, except material introduced by the Soviet Union at the Nuremberg trials: No American troops liberated any death camp, only the Red Army. "American troops did not liberate the camps in which the killing centers existed, that's 100 percent correct," Berenbaum agreed, "and the [Holocaust] Museum presents no testimony [that they did]. The six [death camps] were liberated by Soviet troops. But there were American reporters with the Soviet troops. The *New York Times* had a front-page story on the liberation of Majdanek [including the reporter's statement, 'I have just seen the most terrible place on earth.']. And there is ample evidence aside from Soviet eyewitness accounts."

When I suggested to Smith that historians' refusal to acknowledge his position is analogous to the reluctance of scientists to debate "creationists" about the origins of life on earth, Smith's response identified him as anti-intellectual in ways he doesn't even understand. "There's a real subjective difference," Smith replied. "Remember, we're talking about scientists. A historian is not a scientist, just to start with. Writing history is an art more than science. History is not a science. We know there's a difference between hard science and social science."

Smith has it wrong at both ends. He clearly doesn't grasp the intellectual discipline required of a legitimate historian, or any scholar in the social sciences or humanities. And thinking that "hard" science is cut and dried, he apparently doesn't understand the analyses, the judgments, and the interpretations that these "hard" scientists must apply to what the untrained mind assumes to be indisputable data.

For much of our conversation, Smith portrayed his campaign as a widely applicable intellectual exercise. Then, gradually, his description of the illegitimacy of the Holocaust and the resistance he has encountered took on a disconcerting new element: the centrality of Jews, not as victims of genocide, but as perpetrators of myth.

"Tens of millions of people died [in World War II]. Some of them were Jews. There's a political issue involved here. This is the real problem. Why are we so sensitive to the sufferings of Jews? . . . At the beginning it was not a Jewish story, but it's become a Jewish story now because the Jewish lobbies, they took it over. All of the energy comes from the Jewish lobby. But in a Gentile environment. After all, this is a Gentile country, by and large, it's not a Jewish country. But, nevertheless, Jews in the media and in academia are extremely influential, far beyond their numbers, you know that."

Smith recited a litany of things he thinks Jewish scholars have done to make him look bad. "Because [they believe] I'm a hater, they feel they can do anything. They don't have to have any ethical principles whatever." He refers to a racist quote attributed to him in a Midwestern student newspaper. It's not his quote, he says, and he can prove it, "though it makes no difference to what I have in [the ad]." Then, he volunteers this thought: "Just because you're a racist doesn't mean that everything you say is wrong."

Near the end of our discussion, I observed that Smith's railing against Jewish intellectuals, Jewish lobbies, and Jewish academics sounds a lot like anti-Semitism. Not to him, Smith said. I asked, "You are not anti-Semitic? Is that what you're saying?" He replies, "No. That's right." I confirmed, "You are saying you are not?" He replied "Yes. Uh-huh." I continued, "All these things that involve Jews? It's just coincidental." He replied by naming some scholarly opponents who are very likely Jewish.

"Is the U.S. Holocaust Museum Jewish?" he asked. "That's the national government," I responded. "Is it run by Jews?" "I don't know." "It is. It's run by Israeli Jews."

A few moments later, Smith said, "When you talk about the [Holocaust] story, you have to talk about Jews. It's a Jewish story. So if you talk about Jews [it's assumed] you don't like them."

Let me offer another analogy, I began. "Don't tell me," he interrupted, "If it walks like a duck, quacks like a duck." "Exactly," I agreed. "What's your answer?"

"I talk about Jews, and I address Jews. . . . Look, I'm interested in a subject that's run by Jews. Jews have a particular interest in me. I'm associated with Jews, interested in Jewish . . . [voice trails off]"

"I won't carry this further," I said.

"Good, good," he said. We went on to a different subject.

According to Berenbaum, "These guys [like Smith] essentially are engaged in what is clearly part of a larger picture, the establishment of a white supremacist nation in the United States and elsewhere. If the Holocaust didn't happen, then everything they want to say about anti-Semitism is true, and there's an international Jewish cabal that goes on all over the place."

But Berenbaum expressed little anxiety about their threat. Smith bought himself "a very successful couple of years, a lot of attention on the cheap," Berenbaum said. "He was going from college newspaper ads to the front pages of major newspapers, from the University of Miami to the front page of the *Miami Herald*, to *U.S. News & World Report*, to *Time*, to the *New York Times* and the *Washington Post*, so it was a very successful use of a tactic from his perspective, because what he wanted was the noise associated with it.

"But whether he's convinced anybody, we have no evidence of that. I don't think [Smith and those like-minded] are threatening. What they say is essentially nonsense. And the Holocaust is being widely taught on college campuses. Ph.D.s are being given. There's enormously wide student interest. We have yet to see any serious evidence that he's changed anybody's mind, aside from a lunatic fringe."

When I observed to Smith during our interview that many of the universities at which he advertised appeared to have significant numbers of Jewish students, he said that he was targeting the better universities, which Jewish students attended in disproportionate numbers. Notable among the student newspapers that accepted the Smith ad were the *Judge* at Brandeis University, the most important Jewish-affiliated university in the nation, and the *Hurricane* at the University of Miami, located in a community that is home to a great many Jews and perhaps the largest number of Holocaust survivors in the United States due to its significant retirement population.

Student editors at the University of Miami published the ad less than two months after the Queens episode, contending in an editorial that "as journalists, we have an ethical responsibility to educate students and allow everyone's ideas to have a forum." University President Edward T. Foote II, who, unlike Kenny, held the authority to overrule the students, chose not to do so. "The best antidote for error is not to suppress it but to expose it to the truth," he said in a public statement, and the "best human hope for avoiding another Holocaust lies in freedom and knowledge." A former newspaper reporter himself, Foote found the *Hurricane* decision "within reasonable limits that should be allowed student editors." He told me, "I wanted to persuade people of the benefit of freedom of expression in a university setting, and this was a wonderful opportunity to show the value of it."

The university's trustees weren't pleased. Only after what one person called hours of "intense and emotional debate" did they come up with a public statement expressing "full confidence in President Foote and his leadership" and "respect for his integrity on this issue." They also ordered a change in the rules governing the school paper, so that "hate and misleading advertisements" would be rejected.

The fallout also included the withdrawal of a $1 million pledge to the university's art gallery and cancer research center by Miami philanthropist Sanford Ziff. Foote, almost needless to say, spent a great deal of time "respectfully explaining my position" to Ziff. A few months later, Ziff reinstated the pledge, deciding not to punish the university financially.

The city's powerful newspaper, the *Miami Herald,* took a mixed view. It called Foote's decision "admirable" and said it "reflects well on him and UM." But it said, too, that the *"Herald* wouldn't have published it, because we don't publish anything that we know to be false." Smith's "sly plea for 'free inquiry' is specious," the paper said. "And clever. Very, very clever. For a quarter-page ad's $288 fee, the Holocaust revisionists 'bought' more than three pages of space in yesterday's *Hurricane."*

At Duke University, the faculty of the Department of History were so incensed that student editors bit at Smith's fallacious line that they bought a full-page ad of their own in the *Chronicle* to teach students what "revisionism" really means and to turn an unspeakable claim into a true learning experience.

The History Department Responds to Holocaust Ad

The Duke History Department wishes to state that the assertions made in [the Holocaust] advertisement do not constitute "revisionism" as scholars understand the term. . . . Nothing in the ad except the layout and language suggests that these false assertions deserve the name "scholarship." The scholarly pretensions of this advertisement were effective enough to deceive *The Chronicle's* editor, who believes that these fraudulent claims fall within the range of normal historical inquiry. "What the revisionists are doing is reinterpreting history, a practice that occurs constantly, especially on a college campus," she wrote.

That historians are constantly engaged in historical revision is certainly correct; however, what historians do is different from this advertisement. Historical revision of major events (e.g., the American Revolution) is not concerned with the actuality of these events; rather, it concerns their historical *interpretation*—their causes and consequences generally. There is no debate among historians about the actuality of the Holocaust. Scholars may discuss detail and nuance, but there can be no doubt that the Nazi state systematically put to death millions of Jews, Gypsies, political radicals, and other people.

The appearance of historical interpretation in this ad is a very clever deception. Its "good news of Holocaust Revisionism" is surely not that six million Jews thought to have been killed in death camps are really alive and well (which would be a factual revision). Rather, its "revision" suggests that Jews (and their sympathizers) have conducted a forty-five year, world-wide conspiracy to elicit unwarranted support and sympathy. The advertisement is, thus, a restatement of the old, anti-Semitic charges of Jewish conspiracy and control, enshrined in such notorious documents as the forgery, *Protocol of the Elders of Zion*. The "revisionism" in this advertisement is not really meant to rectify an historical error; rather, its aim is to hurt Jews and to demean and demonize them.

The Chronicle editors make a serious error when they confuse Holocaust deniers with historical revisionists. Whatever one thinks about the right of *The Chronicle* to accept this advertisement, as historians, we deplore the effort to use the language of "scholarship" to distort and obliterate an event which, to our everlasting shame, did occur. We urge all members of the Duke community to treat such advertisements with the contempt they deserve.

At Queens, as the date approached for the *Quad* to publish the Holocaust denial ad, the heavens opened. In the worst winter ever known to New York City, another among a score of brutal ice and snow storms began on a Wednesday, paralyzing transportation to this commuter college and forcing cancellation of classes on Thursday and Friday. The student union building, which held the *Quad* office, was officially closed, and the student editors were told to leave. This meant they couldn't use their computers to produce pages to send to the printer over the weekend. So, they simply postponed the most anxiously awaited issue in the history of the *Quad*.

Cannava was angry. "I couldn't believe it, after they had gone through what they had. It struck me as gross irresponsibility. They had an obligation, it seemed to me, to do something. Everybody assumed it was going to appear that Monday, and there was this tremendous suspense. Mike Wallace had already been there. The whole thing was a go. Nobody could believe that a little snowstorm could have stopped them. I called Andy, and he said, 'Well, we couldn't get to the office.' He didn't seem terribly concerned. Later, I decided it was kind of cute. Andy and some of the others were suburban kids."

What the intervention from above did was give the students some breathing room. They sanded their stories. "A lot of the stuff that we had put together was a mess, including my editorial," Wallenstein said, "and we polished everything up. There are [still] mistakes in it, and we still could have done a better job, but it was improved."

The students also made two critical editorial decisions. First, they decided to return Smith's check. Originally they had planned to donate the funds to the Holocaust Museum, but they were persuaded that it was tainted money.

Second, they took the advice of some professional journalists to eliminate the bottom of the proposed ad, which contained the address at which Smith could be reached. "What we really did in the end wasn't printing the advertisement," Wallenstein said. "It was taking the advertisement and using it as an editorial illustration. Not printing it along with the editorial would have been like printing a wanted poster without a picture of the culprit. I wanted people to see it for what it was."

The February 22, 1994, issue of the *Quad* devoted its first 5 pages and 7 of the first 13 to the subject of Holocaust denial. The right side of the front page contained the Smith "ad," with his address eliminated. A long editorial by Wallenstein began on the left side with the words, "The reader would be hard-pressed to find [facts] amidst the devious logical leaps, unfounded assertions, half-truths, and outright lies." A second editorial, headlined "A Man and His Lies," began on page 3, ending with a bibliography of a dozen books about the Holocaust.

The Holocaust package also included a first-person account by a *Quad* editor who had visited the death camps in Poland, an interview with a former GI who had helped liberate Buchenwald, a sidebar about Deborah Lipstadt's book on denial, a question-and-answer with students on what they knew about the Holocaust, and a news story on a Holocaust seminar held at the student union, which featured Michael Berenbaum. Page 2 of the paper contained the ad purchased by President Kenny (she said it was particularly hard to write because it was due before she knew exactly what the students would publish). This is what it said:

> To the Campus Community:
>
> I have been informed that the *Quad* will carry an advertisement by Bradley R. Smith, a Holocaust denier from California who claims to speak for a "Committee for Open Debate on the Holocaust." The advertisement is an example of the hatemongering aimed at college campuses now with ever increasing viciousness.
>
> Printing the ad is not a matter of freedom of the press. All newspapers may and do use editorial discretion about whether to accept an ad based upon its content without violating the First Amendment. The *Quad*'s masthead attests to its right to turn down questionable material.
>
> But the *Quad* is an independent newspaper, and we have the solemn responsibility to protect its freedom to make such decisions, right or wrong.
>
> I believe the *Quad*'s decision to accept the ad was wrong.
>
> The *Quad* is not the first student newspaper to be offered this specious ad. [Kenny here discusses, with examples, how some other student papers handled the issue.]

I am both angered and saddened by the appearance of the ad in the *Quad*—angered that persons such as Bradley Smith would prey on the good intentions of young student editors, and saddened that our *Quad* staff, after long, earnest, and well-meaning consideration of whether to accept the ad, decided to print it.

In its disregard for truth, this advertisement is an insult to all members of our community. Queens College is home to faculty, staff, students, and alumni who are survivors or children of survivors of the Holocaust. Many lost family members in the Holocaust. The offensive lies and distortions of the Smith ad, passed off as scholarly inquiry, are hurtful and derogatory not only to all these people but to the entire Queens College community.

We live in a time when the whole world is smoldering with ethnic and racial strife, when growing anti-Semitic, anti-Black, anti-gay, anti-everything hatreds are flaring and even getting out of control on some college campuses.

Please not here.

Queens College belongs to all of us. Every member of this campus community. Every American, native or naturalized, and every future American wherever born. Every international student. From every religion and every country of origin. Queens College belongs to all of us, and unless we speak out for decency and humanity for all of us, the haters will win.

We cannot let that happen here.

Shirley Strum Kenny, President

N.B. After I sent this letter to the campus community and the *Quad,* I learned that the *Quad* editors later decided not to accept Smith's submission as a paid advertisement but rather to write a news article about it. Although I have not seen the finished article, I commend the editors for this decision. — SSK

When the week-late *Quad* finally appeared, "It was crazy," Chris Ferraro remembered. "People were in our office in seconds wanting copies, demanding copies. Hillel [the Jewish student organization] wanted 100 copies; the president's office wanted 100 copies. We needed a second print run. It was getting out of hand."

But the important fact was that the students pulled it off. "There was enormous surprise that what the kids said they were going to do, they did, because nobody thought they could," Cannava said. "The idea that they could have the sophistication and the industry to deal with the issue in a way that looked respectable. I think it was more than respectable. It was very, very impressive. The issue came out as a condemnation of Smith and an educational opportunity. That's what they said they were going to do, and that's what they did."

Wallenstein was proud of the work. "We felt, given the way other student newspapers had handled it, that we had a responsibility to expose Bradley Smith. It was very much about setting a precedent. We wanted people to know about him, but we also wanted student newspapers everywhere to look to what Queens College did. I'll say it right now: I think we did that."

Newsday also thought so. In an editorial headlined "Handling Hate: College Editor Does It Right," the paper said, "These hatemongers exploit the idealism of young editors who are philosophically inclined to put *all* ideas on the table and aren't always equipped to vet material before they print it. But [Wallenstein] didn't fall for this ruse. . . . He took a bold approach . . . to print Smith's propaganda along with an editorial repudiating it as 'hazardous to your head.' And he returned Smith's check." With this immediate support for the *Quad,* most of the Jewish weeklies and Queens neighborhood papers fell into line, praising the students, albeit sometimes grudgingly.

Having been postponed, the *60 Minutes* piece on Holocaust deniers did not appear until mid-May, almost three months after the *Quad* issue was published. Cannava said he waited for it "with my heart in my throat. All the stuff I had said, how we had done the right thing. If it turned out to be an embarrassment to Queens College—some kid could have said the wrong thing—I figured that could be my job. But Wallace did what he said he was trying to do, to nail the insanity of those people." The piece included the recycled interview with Smith, as well as another denier, comment from Queens sociologist Heilman, and Wallace's interview with the *Quad* editorial board, which portrayed Wallenstein as a thoughtful young man and his colleagues as serious about their responsibility.

Cannava could now relax. "My training, which I'm going to claim has been validated by this particular case history, says, you work with people, you don't close the door in their face." He took away another lesson, which concerns the importance of the news officer's status as a reporter on campus. "You report to yourself. This convinced me that the best way to serve a president is to make no assumptions about anything—to go out and find out what's going on."

And what did the Queens student editors understand that student editors at some other universities didn't? Among other things, their responsibility, on an issue this consequential, to research the subject thoroughly, to think long and hard about it, to seek the advice of elders whom they respect. President Kenny's advertisement in the *Quad* underlined the value, even in excruciatingly painful circumstances, of mutual respect between the leadership of an institution and its students. The issue of the *Quad* demonstrated to a suspicious community how thoughtful Queens students could be—not a bad recommendation for a college.

CHAPTER 5

The Pied Piper of Columbia

James D. Holderman's Presidency at the University of South Carolina

Perhaps it was the visits from Ronald Reagan and George Bush. Perhaps it was the days that Helmut Schmidt and Henry Kissinger arrived to give speeches. Or maybe the commencement at which Walt Disney mogul Michael Eisner and British composer Andrew Lloyd Webber received honorary degrees. Or the times Bill Cosby, Danny Kaye, William S. Buckley, Jr., Alex Haley, and Carl Sagan dropped by to pick up their honorary degrees.

No. The highlight of James D. Holderman's presidency must have been the moment when Pope John Paul II stood on the "Horseshoe," the verdant quad studded with live oak and magnolia that is the historic heart of the campus, and proclaimed, "It is wonderful to be young and a student at the University of South Carolina."

It was an exhilarating ride, those years, from 1977, when Holderman arrived with a pledge that he would turn this homely institution into a world-class rival of Berkeley and Cambridge, until that day in 1990 when he resigned in the face of public humiliation—to be followed by years of personal humiliation that included the disgraceful collapse of his marriage, bankruptcy, and criminal convictions.

The two-century-old university, the city of Columbia, and the state of South Carolina had survived William Tecumseh Sherman, had come to terms with "Pitchfork Ben" Tillman and "Cotton Ed" Smith, had reveled in the achievements of Jimmy Byrnes and George Rogers, but they had never dealt with anyone quite like Jim Holderman.

Holderman operated like many an ambitious new university president. He shook up the faculty; concentrated on a handful of promising academic opportunities; wooed community business leaders and politicians; flattered celebrities; and dispensed gifts and other favors to those he thought might enhance his reputation and that of his university. He did much of this on the strength of his enormous personal charm and with largely private funds parked in university foundations for just such purposes. Most university presidents have funds similar to Holderman's at South Carolina; they just don't dispense them as profligately as he did. And most university presidents don't have the personal charm that he did.

According to people in South Carolina who knew him, friend and foe alike (and years after the worst about him became widely known), "He had an inimitable way of handling people and crowds. . . . He was extremely witty. . . . He had verbal agility that you just simply had to admire. . . . One on one, Jim Holderman could be one of the most charming people I've ever seen. . . . It was this ability to sell refrigerators to Eskimos that convinced [many people] that the institution was going somewhere. . . . He made you feel like you're the only person in the room if he wanted to do that. . . . He had a dynamic personality, with what appeared to be great intellect and vision."

Small wonder that Holderman swept so many South Carolinians off their feet when he blew in from Illinois, accompanied by a classy wife and three bright young daughters, promising, almost literally, the world. There are those in Columbia today who believe that Holderman got a bad rap, or at least an unbalanced one, that his stimulation of the university and its community was worth the price in ridicule. Then there are those who think that he, and some of his associates as well, belong in jail, their legacy a public mistrust and loss of political capital from which the university is taking years to recover.

Governor David Beasley, who as chairman of the higher education sub-committee of the South Carolina legislature was one of the first politicians to stand up to Holderman, believes that the revelations damaged the university severely. "It really did hurt, no if's, no or's," Beasley said. "Any time a portion of the system falters, there is a reluctance within the entity that powers that system to give it more money, to give money to a system that abused authority." What's more, "To this day it is still having an impact. There has been a lingering concern regarding the higher education community's ability to have a focused agenda. . . . Even though most people don't think everyone acts like a Jim Holderman, there is a concern that the university system is not as accountable and efficient as it should be, which is a concern that I have."*

---

*In 1996, the General Assembly approved a law that could make South Carolina the first state in the country to make all legislative appropriations to its public colleges and universities contingent on how well the institutions are judged to be performing. Reviews are to be based on 37 "performance indicators" contained in the law. A year later, the legislature and higher education administrators were still quarreling over the fairness and appropriateness of these formal rules, especially as applied to different kinds of institutions.

In retrospect, it is easy to wonder how Holderman could have so dominated the university, and to a significant extent the capital city and the state, for a decade. But he plainly brought excitement and enough visible evidence of progress to mesmerize associates. Holderman energized the faculty with grandiose plans, captivating them by seldom missing a meeting of the faculty senate, whatever his travel schedule, and continually reminding them of the importance of faculty prerogatives. He added departments and graduate programs, making the university more comprehensive than it had ever been. He identified targets of excellence, notably the business school—much to the delight of the Columbia business community—and in particular strengthened its international program, which was seen as a signal that USC could take on the world. The city cheered when *U.S. News & World Report* rated the master's program in international business as the best in the country. A medical school was founded and an engineering center constructed, both positioned to gain major research grants. Programs in public health and marine science grew. South Carolina College, a small honors program within the university, attracted quality students.

The South Carolina power structure was awed. Columbia's business and society leaders, of course, but even more so, members of the university's board of trustees and the state legislature, a number of them rural lawyers, store owners, and farmers who had not imagined themselves drinking and dining with James Stewart and Michael Keaton, shaking hands with Mark Hatfield, hearing Sarah Brightman sing Andrew Lloyd Webber. An invitation to the president's house became the hottest ticket in town. He handed out tasteful little gifts, such as a quaint glass tree ornament for each guest at a Christmas dinner party. He never overlooked the opportunity to perform a thoughtful favor: Bob Sheheen was speaker of the South Carolina General Assembly and his brother Fred was executive director of the state Commission on Higher Education in 1987 when Pope John Paul II came to call. Since they were Roman Catholic, Holderman made certain not only that they met the pope but that their elderly, devout parents did as well.

On the other hand, when Holderman was challenged, he could respond cleverly or fiercely. Fred Sheheen remembered clashing with the president over the existence within USC of a vestigial two-year program, similar to a junior college, which Sheheen thought didn't belong at the flagship university; Holderman called it invaluable for non-traditional and struggling students, among whom were some star football players. Sheheen thought he was winning until George Rogers, who in 1979 had become the first Gamecock to win the Heisman Trophy as the nation's outstanding college football player, was invited to address the state legislature. Sure enough, Rogers devoted a significant portion of his short speech to the importance of USC's two-year college and how it had helped him; an exuberant legislature approved its continuation. Sheheen doesn't believe that Rogers wrote that speech himself.

Governor Beasley, no wimpy political infighter, recalled how difficult it was to resist Holderman when he was riding high. "If you went to criticize him," Beasley said, "he would attack you personally, cause political fear in your heart, and cause personal anguish until you thought, well, maybe I was wrong. When I went on the offensive [against Holderman] . . . I had to make the decision that it could very well end my political career because of the political clout that he had. . . . I was merely a [state] house member at the time. . . . I was threatened politically, phone calls, letters, you name it. . . . He had beguiled the people of South Carolina."

How long, or whether, Holderman could have carried on unscathed can still be debated in South Carolina, but like a night watchman's finding a taped door lock during a third-rate burglary, Holderman's downfall began with something beneath his notice: one undergraduate's tuition charge.

Paul Perkins grew up mostly overseas as a Department of Defense civilian brat, dropped out of several colleges, and bummed around Europe, where he met a woman who was a native South Carolinian and moved home with her about the time Holderman became president of the university. After the couple broke up, Perkins spent five years in the Merchant Marine, but he liked South Carolina so much that he returned to enroll as a full-time student at USC in 1984. He worked two jobs to support himself, as a clerk-typist at the School of Government and International Affairs and as a weekend manager at an apartment complex. One weekend at poolside, he met Cheryl Forest, a USC law school graduate practicing in Columbia, and before long they were living together.

By this time Perkins had completed a full academic year at USC, had considered himself a South Carolina resident for 10 years, and had every intention of remaining in the state, so he decided that he was entitled to the lower in-state tuition. When one administrator after another turned him down, Paul was furious. Cheryl remembered well his screaming in their living room: "I really want to make someone pay for this, I'm going to cause chaos here, they're going to wish someday that I got my in-state tuition."

Of course Perkins had no idea how he would make the University of South Carolina pay for hurting his pocketbook and his feelings. Then one day while pursuing his secretarial chores at the international school, he became curious about what the university was paying Jihan Sadat, the widow of Egyptian president Anwar Sadat, for her once-a-week teaching stint. He considered writing a free-lance article that he thought maybe *Parade* magazine would buy.

But nobody would tell him. So he and Cheryl drafted a request for Sadat's salary under the South Carolina Freedom of Information Act (FOI). On the last day permitted for response, they received a letter from President Holderman containing Sadat's letters of appointment. But the salary figures were blotted out, the president's office explained, because of an exemption for personal information. Her expenses were also not reported, the letter continued, to protect her privacy and because of potential security dangers. "The first thing Cheryl does is count the spaces under the white-out," Paul remembered. "She turns to me and says, 'Well, we'll just have to sue the university.' And my mouth dropped open."

Perkins and Forest sued, in June 1986, the same month they got married as it happened. Since then a lot has changed in their lives: Paul finished college and graduated from USC law school; he and Cheryl both practice law in Columbia; they have three children. But Holderman's life has changed a lot more.

The day after the suit was filed, the *Columbia Record* did a story about it. Before long, people were phoning the Perkins's apartment anonymously, encouraging them to keep it up, and a debate began in the student newspaper over Sadat's remuneration. In September, 47 students arriving for the first session of Sadat's class, "Women in Egyptian Culture," learned that she had decided not to teach any longer at USC. Despite the university's legal resistance, a state judge approved the Perkins claim in October 1986, holding that Sadat's salary and expenses should be public information.

The university reluctantly reported that it had paid Sadat $313,000 in salary and expenses to teach one class for three semesters. She had received $50,000 in salary the first semester and $75,000 in each of the next two. Among her expenses were $10,000 for three first-class round-trip air fares to Cairo and $94,000 for 44 round-trip charter flights to Washington, D.C., for her and her security personnel. It was not clear if or how much USC had paid her assistants, translator, or security force. "She helped the university achieve national attention way beyond our capacity to reimburse her," Holderman told reporters.

If paying Jihan Sadat that kind of money was Holderman's idea of building the university's reputation, how else was he utilizing its resources? Over the next three years, reporters for the *Charlotte Observer* and the *Greenville News* pulled aside one curtain after another. They discovered that he stayed in $700-a-night suites at the Madison and Willard hotels in Washington, with staff assistants and student interns occupying adjoining rooms. They found that a university foundation had been leasing a Beechcraft jet, which the president used not only for his own trips but to shuttle celebrities to and from Columbia. Holderman also operated a personal scholarship program, awarding USC scholarships without public notice or competition, frequently to the children of prominent South Carolinians or of national politicians such as Oregon Senator Mark Hatfield and Secretary of State Lawrence Eagleberger.

The newspapers reported that he traveled to Mexico and to Europe, sometimes with an entourage, and once took his family on a Hawaiian vacation for which a university foundation budgeted $15,000. His travel, entertainment, and other expenses, closely guarded by university foundations until they were forced to open their books, ran into the hundreds of thousands of dollars annually. He gave President Reagan a $3,000 Steuben sculpture, paid for on the university's charge account with Steuben, and gave away enough Boehn porcelain to earn a discount from the maker. "You know, I think it was the glass that did it," a South Carolina politician ruminated one day. Passing out elegant bric-a-brac to celebrities somehow demonstrated Holderman's contempt for the ordinary folk of South Carolina and their tax money, "and they didn't like it."

It is hard to conceive of a public-affairs crisis at any institution that does not concern in important ways the media, but South Carolina's circumstances were qualitatively different than most. The press was not an enemy the way people under fire usually think of it—"They're out to get us" or "They're unfair." This was a case in which the press was literally a part of the story. News organizations were not merely reporting, and doggedly investigating; they were filing law suits against the university. And they were scrapping for turf and defending their honor against each other. A veteran South Carolina political hand, Russ McKinney, onetime press secretary to former Governor Richard Riley and now director of university affairs at USC, opined resignedly, "[Holderman] was not only a huge public relations problem, which most universities at some point in their histories are going to encounter, but the media were direct players in it. So it was kind of different from what most universities go through."

The principal journalistic players were the *Charlotte Observer*, a Knight-Ridder newspaper considered one of the brighter lights of American journalism; the *Greenville News*, the second largest and one of the best newspapers in South Carolina; the *State* of Columbia, the largest and most influential newspaper in South Carolina, and the Associated Press (AP), the giant news-gathering organization that serves most of the nation's newspapers and broadcast stations.

The *Charlotte Observer* had long maintained a significant South Carolina presence and a bureau in Columbia, but it was nonetheless an out-of-state paper, based in a dynamic North Carolina city just above the border. The *Greenville News* was in-state, to be sure, but an "up country" paper suspected in Columbia of divided loyalties because of its location, midway along the bustling Charlotte-Atlanta corridor, and near Clemson University, USC's great rival. Although both papers were read by leading politicians and power brokers in Columbia, their tough stories might have gone relatively unnoticed in the rest of the state without the impact of the Associated Press. Typically, when investigative reporters John Monk or Henry Eichel produced a story for the *Observer* about Holderman transgressions, by 10 o'clock that morning the

AP's South Carolina bureau chief John Shurr had picked up the details, added information, and filed a similar piece to dozens of small-town newspapers and radio stations throughout the state. As a result, politicians like Beasley began to hear from their constituents in rural areas like Darlington County: "What's going on with this Holderman fellow anyway?"

The Columbia establishment saw the *Observer*, the *News*, and the AP as outsiders trying to embarrass a driving leader who had brought unprecedented attention to USC. The *State*, however, was the voice of the capital power structure. Locally controlled when the Holderman exposés began, the paper was purchased soon afterward by the highly regarded Knight-Ridder chain, but, as one journalist put it, "Its central nervous system remained intact." The *State's* longtime publisher, Ben Morris, and the executive editor, Tom McLean, continued to ignore the Holderman story except to rail at the perfidy of their out-of-town rivals. After the other two papers had described Holderman's expensive gifts to public officials, for example, the *State* wrote nothing for two days before leading a story: "University of South Carolina President James D. Holderman scoffed Friday at news reports of gifts that he has given state officials." The *State* also declined to join FOI suits against the university; Morris is said to have explained privately that since the newspaper had long supported the university and its president, it would be inconsistent to sue them.

In February 1987, four months after the original court order in the Sadat case, the *State*, and its smaller afternoon sister, the *Columbia Record*, assaulted their rivals in synchronized editorials. First the *Record* snarled at "the jackals— journalistic and otherwise—who are snapping so voraciously and voyeuristically" at the president. The next morning, the *State* was blunter: "A number of prominent friends of the university are convinced that certain newspapers are out to get Dr. Holderman through their relentless reporting and commentary. Most cite the Greenville *News*; some add the Charlotte *Observer*. The *News* particularly has shown an anti-Columbia bias in many ways over the years."

The Greenville paper wasted no time accusing its Columbia foe of a cover-up: "Except in the sense that public ethics are influenced by press indifference, the *State* has influenced no one in the matter of President Holderman's unusual activities. The *State* pressed not at all for disclosure of Holderman's spending records, and it editorially praised as sufficient each of the reluctant steps he has taken toward fuller disclosure." Somewhat distanced from this particular fray, the *Observer* produced an amused story about the "spat" between the South Carolina papers, calling it "highly unusual" in the "polite world of South Carolina journalism."

The response in Columbia to criticism of Holderman can be easily understood, said Arthur Smith, who served for two years as provost of USC under Holderman and then as acting president after Holderman's resignation. (Smith subsequently became president of the University of Utah, as discussed in Chapter 2. He is now president of the University of Houston.) The newspapers were in a "feeding frenzy," Smith said, but "it was also the competition between [the cities of] Columbia and Charlotte, and Columbia and Greenville. . . . [The news stories were] seen as an attack by rival cities. . . . There's a defensiveness in Columbia that is manifested in a number of ways, not just in the way the *State* handled the Holderman situation." McKinney put it slightly differently. "When the university feels pain, the Columbia area feels pain," he said, "because we're just too big a part of this place. So business leaders and community leaders in Columbia reacted to the fact that the up-state Greenville paper and the out-of-state Charlotte paper were driving this thing." McKinney also suggested a commercial explanation. "The *State* was in an awkward position at times because their advertisers were part of that loyal base here in Columbia."

The press war changed dramatically, however, in April 1990, when Knight-Ridder brought in, as executive editor, Gil Thelen, who had edited newspapers in both Carolinas. The first thing he did was call a staff meeting to announce: "We are going to cover the [Holderman] story aggressively, fully, and fairly, and from this point forward, we're not going to be beaten by anybody." The emancipated *State* reporters and editors pursued the story with vigor, warming up the leftovers and using their own good contacts to break news. Thelen thinks, in retrospect, that the *State* overdid some of its stories, a condition attributable to the pent-up energy of the reporters.

On May 30, 1990, less than two months after Thelen took over at the *State*, Holderman resigned the presidency of the university. The timing was probably not coincidental; with the *State* having joined the *Observer* and the *News* in pursuit, Holderman had no place to hide. He said at the time to an executive of the *State*, "If I don't have you guys [on my side], I can't survive." *

Shortly after his resignation, Holderman sought help at the USC Medical School, where he was diagnosed as manic depressive. Both the psychiatrist and Holderman himself observed that, given his schedule and longtime behavior patterns (standard 17-hour work days, 15 telephones in the presidential mansion), the diagnosis should have come as little surprise.

---

*The relationship between the *State* and Holderman reached a level of conflict of interest that would make most journalists shudder: The sons of both Publisher Morris and Executive Editor McLean served as personal interns for Holderman. In a long story published in the *State* after Holderman's resignation, McLean conceded errors of judgment at the newspaper. "We should have pursued stories more aggressively," he was quoted. "But senior management at the newspaper was giving support to Jim Holderman. I was part of senior management." Asked by an associate if he had considered resigning on principle because he wasn't allowed to pursue the Holderman story, McLean responded that he wasn't sure he could get another job if he quit.

His mental state could not have been improved by the newspaper investigations, which only increased in intensity. Early in 1991, the *Greenville News* and the Associated Press won a Freedom of Information Act lawsuit that forced the university's two foundations, which had been tightly controlled by Holderman, to display their records. Faced with a state supreme court order, foundation officials announced that almost half the pertinent documents had been sent accidentally to the county dump during a renovation. The *News* found the student who had discarded the boxes, and with him as a guide, two reporters, wearing rubber boots, stomped through the stinking dump until they found more than two dozen cartons of foundation material. The newspaper later established that the records had been deliberately dumped.

Studying documents opened by the FOI lawsuit, the *Charlotte Observer* discovered evidence of a typical Holderman deed—arranging a favor for an important friend—that this time had led him to overstep legal bounds. The McNair Law Firm of Columbia, led by Robert McNair, a supporter of Holderman and a former governor of the state, had a client who had been jailed in the Dominican Republic on cocaine charges. Holderman dispatched a prominent USC faculty member of Cuban descent to the Dominican Republican to intervene, and the McNair client was released. The law firm sent what it later called "a charitable contribution" of $25,000 to a USC foundation, but the money wound up in Holderman's pocket.

Shortly after the *Observer* story appeared, Holderman was indicted on a misdemeanor charge of misusing his office for personal enrichment, then on a felony count of state tax evasion. He pleaded guilty to the misdemeanor and no contest to the tax charge. At the sentencing, the chairman of the USC board of trustees, Michael Mungo, testified as a character witness on Holderman's behalf. The judge praised Holderman's work at the university, adding, "You broke the laws of the state of South Carolina, but you are no criminal." Then he sentenced the former president to five years of probation and 500 hours of community service, which Holderman largely fulfilled by writing a motivational course for prison inmates. The next day, driving back to Jacksonville, Florida, where he then worked, Holderman totaled a company car in a three-car collision. His new employer, a prominent real-estate developer and USC contributor, soon fired him because of his criminal record. (The developer later went bankrupt, without fulfilling millions of dollars in commitments to the university.)

To this point, despite the turmoil at the university and his acknowledged criminality, Holderman had retained considerable sympathy among Columbians, especially the most financially and socially prominent. But in late May 1991, a year to the day after he had announced his resignation with his

wife Carolyn at his side, Carolyn Holderman filed for legal separation, prepara-
tory to divorce.

It might be impossible to find anyone in Columbia, no matter how they felt
about Jim Holderman, who would utter a negative syllable about this winning
presidential spouse. Carolyn Holderman was described as "gracious," "charming," "wonderful," "an absolute princess"—characterizations that made her
statements in official court documents shocking, especially to close friends.
She charged that she had been violently abused, both physically and with
hurtful words, and was the victim of dishonesty and deceit. Her husband had
"failed to engage in the normal acts of intimacy between husband and wife for
the past 10 years." After the divorce, Carolyn Holderman retained the sympathy and affection of Columbians, while living single in the city and working for
the state's public-broadcast system.

While the divorce action was proceeding, the *Charlotte Observer* broke a
story in its Sunday edition of October 20, 1991, that illuminated Carolyn
Holderman's accusations. The front-page headline read:

> Interns: Holderman made sex advances
>
> Some students in USC's exclusive intern program say the university's
> former president suggested they could be the "son he never had." On out-
> of-town trips, several say, they were asked to share his bed. Holderman
> denies any sexual advances.

The story, by John Monk, an *Observer* reporter who had spearheaded the
Holderman investigations, described the president's relationships with the
male student interns he kept constantly at his side, on campus and on his
frequent trips: "Holderman overwhelmed them with travel, cash, scholarships
and gifts. They say they kept the advances secret for years, except for a few
trusted friends and professors, because they are not gay and were embarrassed
by the overtures. They feared no one would believe their word over that of
Holderman."

The story offered specifics. One student reported being assigned to a room
adjoining the president's "at the Madison, a deluxe Washington hotel. . . .
Holderman was lying in bed. . . . Holderman asked if he could turn out the
light and if [the student] would spend the night beside him. . . . 'I got the hell
out of the room.'" On another occasion in another Washington hotel, a
different student reported being summoned to the president's room. "Holderman
said, 'come lay by me and give me a hug,' the student recalled. Holderman
patted the bed at the same time." In response to the story, Holderman's lawyer
said that his client "denied making any sexual advances," but the former
president himself would not discuss it.

Shortly afterward, with Holderman insisting that he still intended to claim
the tenured position in the USC political-science department that he had not

given up with his presidency, the new president of the university, John Palms, instituted a tenure-revocation procedure. A week before the report was due, Holderman surrendered his tenure.

Only then did the board of trustees, which upon his resignation had awarded Holderman the honorific "distinguished president emeritus," withdraw the designation. Holderman had resigned under pressure, yet even then, for the board of trustees, "president emeritus" wasn't good enough; he was designated "*distinguished* president emeritus." To the end of his presidency, Holderman's nominal bosses, the trustees of the university, had kept the faith, despite evidence of his inflated spending habits and allegations of sexual misconduct. Governor Beasley condemns the board for dereliction of duty. "Here was an administration, in theory elected by a university board, which had been elected by the legislature . . . never once realizing they were not fulfilling their fundamental and primary obligation, which is general oversight of the university, particularly the president." According to the governor, the board was primarily bought off by favors, "football tickets, meeting Andrew Lloyd Webber, being wined and dined. And the president, through his wining and dining, blinded through political drunkenness those who should be truly providing leadership and oversight. Not management, but oversight."

Trustees have portrayed themselves, however, as naive victims of either the president's charm or his intimidation. Holderman's supporters dominated the board, some trustees claimed, making it difficult to question any of his decisions. On the rare occasions that his presidential actions were challenged, Holderman complained that he was the target of a smear campaign led by out-of-town newspapers. His enemies would stop at nothing, he told board members privately, even to intimate that he was homosexual. People are "spreading rumors that I'm a queer, for God's sake," he told one trustee. "Do you think I'm queer?" Administrators who worked for him assured the board that there was nothing untoward about the intern program, either financially or personally.

Only a few days before Holderman's resignation—with the board of trustees clearly not expecting it—board chairman Michael Mungo had finally gone to state legislators for their approval in requiring the president to cut back on his embarrassing spending. Yet even as the board took this moderate step, a group of civic leaders, including two former governors, McNair and John West, as well as the Columbia Chamber of Commerce, announced a campaign to support Holderman, praising his success as a USC fund-raiser and a builder of the city's economy. West, also a former U.S. ambassador to Saudi Arabia and not an unsophisticated man, seemed adulatory: "A group of businessmen supporting the university might want to say, Holderman, go to it. A $700-a-day hotel room may be a little excessive, but if that's what it takes for you to do your job, do it." On the Sunday after Holderman resigned, a group of Columbia business leaders bought a full-page ad in the *State* to affirm their faith.

Holderman had clearly persuaded his pals that in higher education like business you had to spend money to collect money. These supporters pointed to a jump in the university endowment from $3 million in 1977 to $35 million in 1990. But the cost of raising funds was extreme. In his final year on the job, 1989-90, Holderman collected a salary of $117,900, which made him the highest paid public official in the state, and an income supplement of $78,000 plus $96,500 in expenses from the two university foundations. His home, including the upkeep, and cars were essentially free. And he received a discretionary expense account from the university of $533,000, presumably for "donor cultivation." In that year, 1989-90, USC raised $22.6 million in private contributions for endowment, capital construction, and operating needs. By comparison, Max Lennon, the president of neighboring Clemson, received $32,000 from a discretionary account, and Clemson raised, excluding gifts to the athletic program, $34.5 million. Why neither the trustees nor the business-people of Columbia noticed this remains unclear.

A significant portion of the university faculty stood by him as well. Arthur Smith, who had become acting president, recalled that at the first faculty meeting after the resignation, Holderman "received the longest standing ovation that I've ever seen any president receive—a long, loud standing ovation." And the week after the resignation announcement, Holderman was sent a letter signed by USC's Dean of Humanities and Social Sciences, Carol McGinnis Kay, and 18 department chairs. It read:

> We write to express our deep appreciation for your visionary leadership for the past thirteen years.
>
> You encouraged us to think more ambitiously than we had before. We thank you for helping us to move towards being a major research and teaching institution and towards having many programs that are in the top ranks nationally. You fought consistently and determinedly for better salaries for the faculty, for better state funding and for better private funding—and we are in your debt.
>
> We fully support your concept of the mission of USC. We will miss you, but we pledge our continued pursuit of the vision we have shared.
>
> USC is a stronger university than it was when you arrived. Please know that your entire family will always have a special place in our history and hearts. We wish all of you much joy in your new undertakings.
>
> Cordially and gratefully,

Despite this display of support, the faculty had been bitterly split for months. Holderman's contrasting effect on his professional associates is no-where better illustrated than in the attitudes of two of the university's most prominent faculty members, Peter Becker and Gunther Holst. Becker and Holst have been best friends for half a century, having met as high-school students in Germany, while both worked for the American occupation force following World War II. They emigrated to the United States six months apart and both served in the U.S. Army. Becker, a historian whose specialty is the Nazi period, came to South Carolina in 1966 and essentially created the German history program. He alerted Holst to a position in German literature at USC a year later. Both have taught at the university ever since and both have chaired their departments. Holst, who was serving as faculty senate chair at the time of Holderman's resignation, calls himself one of the "fairly late holdouts" for the president. Becker, who was then on the senate steering committee and succeeded Holst as chairman, does not have a single good word to say about Holderman. What effect did this have on their friendship? "It didn't have any," said Holst. "After all, we go back to 1946. We knew that we disagreed on a few things. Peter and I didn't talk a lot about it."

Holst pointed to the aura Holderman brought to the university and sympathized with his more recent tribulations. "I don't think it can be denied that Jim Holderman put this university on the map," Holst said. "He made it well known. He used everything that you could, he used the international board, the advisory board, he brought in people like Helmut Schmidt, he pulled it off, it's amazing." More, Holderman worked to bring "excellent faculty to the campus. He wanted a higher academic standard." Holst still feels regretful. "There was in this man a heap of talent," he said slowly. "I thought, what a waste, what a tragic waste."

Becker, too, cheered Holderman's arrival. "I thought, here was a new breath, someone who had energy, enthusiasm. He wanted the university to become better, which is something we all wanted." Several years later, Becker began to think that Holderman's aspirations "were in no proportion to what was actually happening." As chairman of the faculty welfare committee, he saw compensation falling behind comparable institutions, leaving the university to struggle in the national market. As Becker remembered it, Holderman first spoke about making USC one of the 10 best universities in the world, then continually redefined his goals—the top 10 in the United States, the top 25, then public institutions, then multi-campus public systems, heading, Becker said, toward institutions of "many campuses and enrollment of such and such, which would have defined it so closely that we would indeed have been number 1."

Becker dismissed the sanguineness of many faculty leaders and Columbia businesspeople. "Most of [the faculty] came from decent universities and they do not like to be teaching in an academic backwater, so if they cannot get to a top institution, then at least they prefer to think that they are at one. The same thing applies to the businesspeople. He could tell them what they wanted to hear, and they were taken in by these great promises, and how this great university was going to make it a much more comfortable and pleasant climate for business development."

Perhaps Holderman thought that having Columbia's power structure and the local publisher and editor in his pocket was enough, but it seems odd that a person so conscious of public image appeared to misunderstand so much about how the media work. He could maintain the university's image single-handedly with the big fish—businesspeople, politicians, major donors, and national celebrities. Yet he never attempted to deflect dogged reporters with flattering one-on-one interviews and off-the-cuff tidbits.

The only person with direct authority over USC public affairs was Holderman's closest associate, Chris Vlahoplus, an old friend from the Midwest who held a succession of important jobs at the university and its foundations, always at the president's right hand. (As titular head of a USC foundation, Vlahoplus later argued that its records should be considered private and separate from the university's; but, as one observer put it, "in the media's minds, Vlahoplus and Holderman were joined at the hip, so when the foundation claimed privacy, the media just wouldn't buy it.")

Whether in times of crisis or everyday operations, someone has to answer basic questions from reporters, and the USC public-affairs service was almost totally ineffective. News staffers were not privy to the president's thinking; reporting lines were blurred. During the height of the crisis, the department's chief operating officer was a woman whose background was in printing and publications, not news. She reported to Vlahoplus, the Holderman confidant, who had a lot of other things to worry about. As pressure intensified, starting with the 1986 lawsuit, the university made it increasingly difficult for reporters to get answers. After awhile they grew accustomed to waiting hours for responses to routine questions and to filing FOI requests for more consequential information. This approach may have slowed the news gathering, but it couldn't stop it, and inevitably it spurred reporters to greater efforts.

McKinney, the practiced South Carolina political spokesman who was brought to the university late in the game, dates rock bottom in its press relations to a 1988 legislative audit on spending practices and USC's relationship to its foundations. In response to the audit, the university opened its books wider than ever before, making "far-reaching changes, very, very far-reaching." The systemic changes, made with Holderman's acquiescence (two years before his resignation), were announced quite publicly by the chairman of the board of trustees at a press conference. "But the reaction [from the press]," McKinney said, "was, you're just doing more of the same, we don't believe you." So suspicious were the media that reporters and television crews began to cover even routine committee meetings of the board, trying to make sure that nothing slipped past. That, McKinney said, "was when I realized our credibility was completely shot. . . . By this point, attention on Jim Holderman personally overshadowed our changes. By his operational style he was such a lightning rod."

After Holderman's departure, the university leadership realized that rebuilding the public-relations operation was an important part of regaining public trust. Acting president Smith reorganized the department and gave McKinney greater freedom to deal with the press. He could now "call these guys and say, 'You don't need those [FOI suits], just tell me what you want,' like you would normally do. There were basic things. If they wanted to talk to the president, they talked to the president, talked to him quick." Although press relations began to improve, "There was still so much smoke in the air that people couldn't see over this battlefield. It started to lift, and then John Palms came in, and it continued to dissipate. It's still not gone, but you can make out the battlefield."

To McKinney, the loss of credibility was a critical hazard. "As *the* University of South Carolina, the flagship public university, that is an untenable position to be in. . . . Credibility can't be gone in the legislative quarter, if you're a state agency, it can't be gone in state government, and it can't be gone in the court of public opinion. I mean, how can you function?"

As nearly as his former associates can tell, Holderman didn't understand that. Smith, who arrived at USC in the late 1980s as provost, attributed this blind spot to the president's self-confidence. "He had supreme confidence in his oratorical skills, his ability to sway an audience. He was supremely confident, right up until the end, that having overcome as many threats as he had, he would still be able to dodge any bullet that came this way. . . . He always saw the danger. But I don't think he ever believed that the danger would get to him, because he always believed he could talk his way out of it."

The University of South Carolina is a different place now, on a more even keel, everyone agrees, but hardly as exciting. New president Palms, a physicist who had been president of Georgia State University and provost at Emory University, has concentrated on institutional openness and accountability. He has been criticized for being personally less visible and active in the community than his predecessor, but, as one Columbian said, "He had to get the patient healthy." The university can point to steady financial contributions and student applications, and in this academic seller's market it has little trouble attracting faculty or graduate students from around the country, many of whom have never heard of Holderman and don't care about him anyway as long as they get a job.

Fred Sheheen, who directed the higher education commission, believes that the university has continued to improve academically since Holderman departed in 1990. But he thinks that it benefitted during his tenure as well, because the president sparked enthusiasm, then went about his worldly enterprises while more serious scholars pushed educational change. Smith, who was Holderman's chief academic officer at the end, confirmed that he was largely left alone to run the academic shop during their two years together. Sheheen also believes that many faculty and others in the community "yearn for the flash and verve of the Holderman era, the fireworks, and shooting stars, and Roman candles." Another well-placed South Carolinian worries that the university has "lost energy, lost momentum, lost leadership, and has been drifting. I don't think they've had a good sense of direction and mission. How do we preserve the best of the momentum that Holderman established and also restore a sense of competence and faith, inherent decency, and goodness, and credibility to the institution."

To look at the big picture, the Holderman scandal was part of a series of coincidental events that irrevocably changed South Carolina higher education in particular and South Carolina government in general.* A major factor hardly unique to the state was a serious recession, during the Holderman crisis, which damaged funding for education just as it did for other elements of government. The recession gave legislators an additional excuse to punish wastrel university administrations. About the same time as the Holderman revelations, for instance, many South Carolinians were annoyed at the state's other major university, Clemson, which spent about a million dollars to buy out the contract of Danny Ford, a football coach who won games but cheated, and a couple of years later spent $600,000 to buy out his successor, Ken Hatfield, who didn't win enough games. (It can hardly be blamed on Holderman, but USC's erratic record on the gridiron also soured potential supporters. "There isn't much wrong around here," one university official said with a slight smile, "that a 10-win football season wouldn't cure.")

The university plainly feels better about itself. "We are probably the most scrutinized, and open, agency in this state," McKinney said. "It's almost like we put ourselves through a cleansing, a healing." McKinney recalled that about the time of Holderman's resignation a media-crisis specialist conducted a seminar in Columbia. "I told her I thought it was going to be 5 years before we can ever get things back right. She said, 10. I really thought that was too long, but she was probably closer to it." McKinney sees reasons to believe, though, that the university is on the road to public credibility. How can he tell? "The reporters and television people don't bother to show up at all the board meetings like they used to."

After Holderman severed his official ties to the university in 1991 with the resignation of tenure, he continued his downhill slide of Candidian proportions. He moved to Charleston the next year, completing his community

---

*Independent of the universities, scandals erupted in other state agencies, the department of social services and the highway department prominent among them. Ironically, these events collectively may have benefitted the state of South Carolina. They created a political force that brought about a restructuring of the state government, which resulted in relatively more authority for the full-time governor and his professional executive branch, and less for the part-time legislature. The reading so far is positive.

service by folding hospital gowns and preparing sterile packages for surgery at a VA hospital, and took a job working on international projects for another loyal USC alumnus. But his financial behavior continued to be disastrous in almost inexplicable ways. He signed a book contract with Random House and pledged his prospective earnings to at least three different creditors; the publisher eventually rejected his manuscript as not "adequate or sufficient" and demanded its advance returned.

Despite the fact that he had commanded upwards of $1 million some years in salary, income supplements, housing and other perquisites, and personal expense accounts; and despite his apparent access to an inherited family trust; and despite tens of thousands of dollars in deferred fees and pensions from a directorship with BellSouth, Holderman ran out of money not long after his presidency ended. Asked what could have happened to the money, a number of people who knew him well responded uniformly that they wondered the same thing themselves. Holderman filed for bankruptcy protection, amending his legal position under the bankruptcy code and his financial statements several times. After the U.S. Department of Justice told a federal court that Holderman had "repeatedly provided misleading or untrue information throughout the case," he agreed to the imposition of a bankruptcy trustee to control his assets and debts. It didn't help. In 1996, he pleaded guilty to eight counts of bankruptcy fraud and was sentenced to a year in federal prison.

To measure the full effect of the Holderman presidency on the University of South Carolina, one must ask, "Compared to what?" Some smart people in Columbia, and at the university, are prepared to argue that the institution is a far better place for his having been there, for the sense of progress he established, the decade of excitement unlike anything USC had known, and the academic advancements he set in motion. No one doubts, though, that USC suffered enormous pain in those four traumatic years, 1986 to 1990, from the point at which Jihan Sadat's salary was disclosed to Holderman's resignation; and perhaps has suffered more from revelations that postdated his departure. It is still recovering.

CHAPTER 6

Due to Circumstances Beyond Our Control

Brown University and Prostitution

Bob Reichley said it is something you do only once in your career: Call a press conference to denounce the press.

"I was angry. I made no effort to hide what my emotions were. I said, 'I'm going to stay here as long as any one of you has questions. And you get your questions out. Because you guys have blown this, and our reputation is at stake. And so is the reputation of these two young women, who have been convicted of nothing.' And I stayed there for over an hour, answering questions for everybody."

At that press conference, Robert A. Reichley also issued a statement on behalf of Brown University, of which he was vice president.

> The purpose of this press conference is not to reveal sensational new information, but to correct a substantial amount of misinformation and unjustified conclusions as to Brown's role in the current police investigation in Providence.
>
> I approach this conference with a sense of undisguised anger.
>
> Undue emphasis has been placed on Brown's role in this investigation. Wrong and unsupported conclusions have been drawn in the media and elsewhere about Brown students. And about the university itself.

The police investigation to which Reichley referred concerned prostitution, and Brown, one of the most distinguished universities in the nation, had been identified as a "School for Scandal" by the shabbiest mainstream newspaper in the country, the *New York Post*. Inevitably, the tabloid press feasted on this scrumptious story about illicit sex at an Ivy League university. But it was also covered by the television networks and newsmagazines, the *New York*

Times, the *Boston Globe,* and dozens of other newspapers and television stations. "The second call I got on this story," Reichley remembered, "came from the London *Times.* I do not know to this day how they found out. But at that point, it was over. It was very clear that this thing was out."

Two senior women at Brown University had been arrested and charged with pandering for prostitution. It was a charge that might be filed against 1,000 women a day across the nation, but pictures of these two would appear on the three network news programs and in newspapers as far away as Thailand and the Soviet Union. The Providence Police Department later confiscated photographs of 46 other women from the apartment of a prominent Providence man, whom the two Brown students had identified. Six of those pictured were current or former Brown students; none was charged with any crime. From that set of facts, Brown received more international publicity than for any other story in the more than two centuries of its existence.

One lesson to be drawn from this experience is that there are certain unnerving events from which no university can protect itself. Especially if, like Brown, you have rapidly gained a reputation as an outstanding academic and student-friendly institution—in the vernacular, a "hot college." The turning point in its fortunes came in 1969 with the introduction of a flexible liberal arts curriculum that became a model for colleges across the nation. In the early 1980s, Brown drew more freshmen applicants than Harvard; its selectivity rate today is below 20 percent (i.e., it admits fewer than one of every five applicants).

This stellar academic reputation also brought a surprising kind of celebrity. At one point in the 1980s, Brown appeared to be educating the next generation of the Democratic Party: John F. Kennedy, Jr., Amy Carter, William Mondale, and Donna and Laura Zaccaro (daughters of Geraldine Ferraro). Or the next generation of *People* magazine cover subjects: Vanessa Vadim, Jane Fonda's daughter; Cosima vonBulow, Claus and Sunny vonBulow's daughter; and the son of the king of Jordan. University officials say with some pride that they—and the culture of Brown itself—deflected attention from every one of those students while they were on campus, except Amy Carter, who got herself arrested in sit-ins and eventually left school. "We couldn't do anything about her," said one administrator.

Newsweek noted Brown's celebrity status in the lead of its story about the prostitution arrests: "By ancient tradition, Americans delight in discomfiture among the ruling classes—never so much as when it springs from a scandal of the flesh. So it was last week, after the revelations [at Brown.] . . . This wasn't Arizona State, where last year a professor was convicted of pandering in connection with a massage parlor staffed in part by students. This was Brown; not just Ivy League but the 'hot' Ivy of the 1980s. . . . The press rose to the bait, led in luridity [sic] by the *New York Post* . . . ."

The only episode to rival prostitution for attracting national attention to Brown had occurred less than two years earlier. A small group of earnest students, anxious to alert the world to the dangers of nuclear war, traveled throughout Rhode Island carrying orange-and-black bomb-shelter signs, which were intended to mock the worthlessness of the shelters built in the 1960s. When the campaign received almost no notice in the media, the anti-nuke students, looking for a better publicity stunt, sought to piggyback their cause on a campus election in the autumn of 1984. They circulated a petition calling for a place on the ballot, stating: In the event of nuclear attack, Brown University would, on request, dispense suicide pills from its health service. Before the university could respond, CBS News queried an official in the health service, who said the request was ludicrous but, "if ordered" to dispense suicide pills, he would not do so.

The Brown administration almost came unstrung. Obviously the university would not dispense suicide pills—"Who the hell would order him to do it?" one high-level official shouted at the time—but the fact of a health service staffer's taking the absurd suggestion seriously enough to respond ignited the story. Just before the suicide pill referendum—it won in a close vote—the organizers held a press conference in the student center on the campus green which Reichley interrupted. He took the microphone out of a student's hand and said, "Ladies and gentlemen, I want to make one thing very clear. Brown University takes the threat of nuclear war very seriously. We admire these kids for finding a way to get this before the public, which you're now helping them do. But in no circumstances will this institution ever issue suicide pills. It is antithetical to what we do as an institution. Period. We don't care how the referendum turns out. It will not happen."

That did not quell the story. The students appeared on *Today* and *Donahue*, and were interviewed by countless newspapers and magazines in the United States and beyond. They had underestimated their power to influence the media, and it made them a little nervous. For his part, Reichley, the official university spokesman, followed them around, like Sancho Panza with Don Quixote, the *New Republic* said of him. "Everywhere they went, every inter-view they gave, I gave another one," Reichley said, "to commend them for their concerns, but to say, 'No way.'"

From each story, he polished his performance. "I learned not to say first that Brown takes potential nuclear war seriously. I reversed the order of the sentences, starting with, 'We will under no circumstances ever issue suicide pills.' We said that we admired these kids for their dedication to this point— our own research showed fear of nuclear war to be high among their genera-tion. We said they were very inventive and bright students who have found a way to get this up on the national agenda. But we do not approve of their means or the circumstances they are laying out." Brown took criticism from some commentators for not condemning the students or disciplining them. Students at a few other campuses tried similar plans. Before the story flickered out, the university had collected more press clippings than for any other single story in its history. That record lasted until the two women were arrested.

Brown set in motion the scandalous events by being a good citizen. In the fall of 1985, an undergraduate woman told university authorities that she had been pressured to engage in prostitution, and that other women were involved, some of them high school girls who may have been taken across the Massachusetts state line. The dean of students office immediately alerted the Providence police. It is not clear how seriously police pursued the investigation for the next few months; there is no evidence of any action having been taken. Then the break came with a classified ad in a Providence underground newspaper: "INDULGE YOURSELF . . . Experience unparalled [sic] pleasure in the form of two Ivy League blondes. Generous gentlemen only."

The two women turned out to be Dana Smith of Avon, Connecticut, and Rebecca Kidd of Orange, Connecticut; both were Brown seniors, 21 years old, and living in their own off-campus apartments. The ad had given only a post office box, but someone tipped their phone numbers to Inspector Malcolm Brown, a Providence undercover cop. He called each of the women separately, telling them he was an out-of-town businessman "looking for some entertainment." Each made an appointment with him. According to the inspector, one of them met him at a coffee shop called Penguins near the Brown campus, took him to her apartment, accepted $150, and started to take off her clothes. He arrested her on a misdemeanor charge of prostitution. Almost immediately, the inspector said, he went to the other woman's apartment. There, according to the police report, after she set a price of $250 and stripped to black lace, she was arrested.

Informed by the women, police the next night raided the carriage-house home of Stanley Henshaw III, a 43-year-old insurance agent and member of a prominent Providence family, whose father was a Brown alumnus. Their search turned up about 150 photographs of 46 different women (none of them Smith or Kidd), some nude, some partially dressed. Richard S. Tamurini, who then directed the Providence police plainclothes unit and later became deputy chief of police, recalled with a smile that they were "excellent photographs. He was a good photographer." But not much more. "He didn't charm them," Tamurini said. "He was a little fat guy who looked harmless, and he paid pretty well."

Of the 46 women, 6 were identified as current or former Brown students. Two were found to be students at Johnson & Wales College in Providence; another was a 17-year-old girl from Rhode Island; one was a 14-year-old girl from Massachusetts; several were married. Police interviewed all of the women they could locate (including five of the six with a Brown connection; the other was out of the country), but none expressed any complaints about Henshaw and none admitted doing anything other than posing for him. None was charged with any crime.

The Brown students Kidd and Smith provided a different tale. On the Monday following their arrest, after what was almost certainly a police leak, their story broke on a Providence television station (the call to Reichley from London came even before the television report). By the next afternoon, dozens of reporters and television technicians had climbed the hill to the historic Brown campus, where authorities said nothing except that they were cooperating with the police. On Wednesday, Providence Police Chief Anthony J. Mancuso gave the story new legs by calling a press conference to discuss the "widening vice investigation."

Years later, a high-level Providence police official said he could not explain why Mancuso called the press conference. The chief may have been overwhelmed by the number of reporters in town or pressure from top city officials, or he might have been infected by star fever, a chance to get his picture on front pages and on national television. Mancuso talked freely about the two Brown students who had been arrested and Brown students in the photographs, but he never mentioned what police already assumed: No Brown students except those two had been implicated in prostitution and no Brown-related prostitution ring existed. Brown authorities asked Mancuso after the press conference why he had not provided a simple exculpatory statement as he had promised. He forgot, he told them. Tamurini insists now that aside from the press conference Providence police "did what we normally do. We went where the evidence led us. We have excellent relations with the university, and we had full cooperation from them on this case; no problems. But I had the feeling they were pissed off at us." He is right.

After Reichley began a counterattack with his own press conference (nearly 70 news organizations were represented), Brown continued to make its position known as widely as possible. He and Eric Broudy, the associate vice president for university relations, followed up by giving individual interviews to any media organization that asked. "We were going to talk to every single news person, individually, for as long as it took," Reichley said. "I personally did 98 in a period of about two weeks. I talked with everybody from the *Times* to *Hustler*—which didn't run a story, by the way." Nasty and often inaccurate newspaper stories were met with letters to the editor. After a lively internal debate about whether it was the right course, Reichley agreed to appear with the editors of the student newspaper, the *Brown Daily Herald,* on the ABC television program *Good Morning, America.* It was "a clear risk," Reichley knew, but Brown administrators considered David Hartman "a fair and experienced host." The segment lasted four minutes—an eternity in television time—giving the university a chance to tell its story at some length to an audience in the millions, and Brown was more than satisfied with the result.

But the university worried most about the reaction from its core off-campus constituents, alumni and parents of students. So two weeks after the news became public, President Howard Swearer wrote a two-page, single-spaced letter to the "Members and Friends of the Brown Community."

> I am writing to make direct contact with you concerning the recent arrest of two Brown undergraduates on a morals charge and the torrent of media publicity that attended this sad development. Those of us here at Brown who are close to the facts of the case have been stunned at what seem to us as grossly sensationalized media reports of the regrettable circumstances facing two of our undergraduates. Perhaps this is the inescapable price of national reputation and visibility. In any case I want to share with you— the Brown family—the actual chain of events, and the facts as I know them today. [The next paragraph summarized the facts of the case.]
>
> With the investigation still underway, shreds of information were leaked to the press—apparently more in the interest of generating publicity than in protecting the rights of the accused. While the investigation has focused on the activities of the male Providence resident, media coverage has concentrated unfairly on many women who may not be guilty, and on Brown itself which not only initiated the inquiry but also is no more than marginally involved.
>
> When all the evidence from the police investigation comes to light, I believe it will become apparent that a number of people have in fact violated no law, but nonetheless the reputations of many may be jeopardized by selective leaks and sensational press accounts. . . . [T]hose who are guiltless are entitled to have their reputations protected from rumors and public speculation.
>
> In the meantime, what of our responsibilities? I believe that those of us who are close to Brown will consider that the welfare of all our students (the overwhelming majority of whom have nothing to do with the case) must be of primary concern. We have moved quickly to protect any who may have been coerced or victimized.
>
> All students who enroll at Brown sign and thereby subscribe to Tenets of Community Behavior, beginning with a commitment to "personal integrity and self-respect" . . . The overwhelming majority of our University community—decent and honorable men and women—have made this commitment a part of their daily lives in the past, and I am confident that together we will exercise leadership to do so in the future.
>
> Finally, and just as important, we should never forget the fundamental reasons for the pride that we all feel for Brown. Our University is attracting some of the finest students and faculty in the nation, and it is embarked on an ambitious program of intellectual leadership and public

service. Most members of the Brown community have demonstrated repeatedly that they care deeply about upholding the highest personal and professional standards, about maintaining the civility of discourse, about engaging in the great issues of our time. So it is not surprising when members of our community endeavor, often in dramatic ways, to make a difference on important issues, from the nuclear arms race to racial injustice in South Africa. And it is fitting that our University engages in open debate of these issues, and that mutual respect only increases despite the differences of view.

Many students and parents, faculty and alumni, have shared with me their concerns over the past few weeks. Without exception, they express pride in Brown and in the behavior of the thousands of admirable people who comprise the Brown community. They know that the high reputation of our University is well deserved and cannot easily be tarnished. We join with them in a determination to uphold the name of Brown—without apology and with an unflinching concern for justice and fairness to each member of the community.

Judged by their backgrounds, the two women seemed almost prototypical Brown students, and hardly women who would have dipped into prostitution because they desperately needed money. Dana Smith lived in a big red-brick house just off Lovely Street in Avon, Connecticut, and attended a well-regarded suburban high school, where she was editor of her senior yearbook, a member of the National Honor Society, and one of the two National Merit Scholarship semifinalists in her class. Her high school counselor was quoted as saying that Dana was the kind of kid you love to see in school. But at Brown, some friends reported, she had trouble adjusting. She bounced around different extracurricular activities; her behavior patterns changed unexpectedly; she was shy around men; and she was needful of praise.

Becca Kidd was the youngest of four children in a close Orange, Connecticut, family, who prepped at the Hopkins School, where she sang in the chorus, played varsity soccer, and won a National Merit Society letter of commendation. A stellar pianist, she was a quiet, serious student, who chose an unusual major at Brown, semiotics, the study of signs and symbols. One reporter found a corps of loyal friends who spoke "lovingly and protectively" about her and described her as "patrician-looking."

Facing conflicting pressures, police and prosecutors seemed uncertain how to proceed against the women. A month after their arrests, prosecutors dropped the charges of prostitution without explanation. Then Smith was indicted on charges of inducing Kidd into prostitution; Kidd was never indicted but was named an unindicted co-conspirator. By summer even the indictment against Smith was dropped in exchange for her testimony against Henshaw. Thus, neither of the students ever faced a trial or the need to negotiate a plea. Dana Smith left Brown with a leave of absence after the arrest. Becca Kidd returned to school almost at once and graduated magna cum laude less than three months later; she skipped the commencement ceremony, a family member explained, to avoid "a media circus."

Henshaw was another matter. A member of an important Providence family and stylish Providence clubs, and a onetime president of the Rhode Island Association of Life Underwriters, he appeared to have been carrying on a parallel life unknown to his society and business associates. A month before the two women were arrested—and unrelated to the prostitution case— Henshaw had been charged with insurance fraud. He was convicted a year later of faking a burglary and selling items he had reported stolen, for which he received a two-year suspended sentence and two years' probation.

While the insurance case was moving through the courts, Henshaw was indicted on 16 counts stemming from the Brown arrests (9 were dropped before trial). In her sworn statement to police, Smith said that Kidd had introduced her to Henshaw. Smith claimed she was told that Kidd posed for nude pictures and had sex with Henshaw; eventually, Smith did the same. Henshaw later asked for her Brown class album "to look for new prospects." She said he "explained his rating system" for prospects, but she never met anyone he might have called. She also said she felt threatened when he told her he was keeping nude photographs he had taken of her.

Not until 21 months after the arrests did Henshaw go to trial, and both Brown women returned to testify against him. But the women received a special dispensation from the judge, who barred the press from photographing their testimony. "I might find myself frozen," Smith was quoted about her request, noting that she was engaged to be married and attending graduate school abroad. "I feel that having my picture taken would do considerable damage to me," Kidd was quoted, saying that she had taken a job in publishing in New York and had entered therapy after the arrest. A third woman, Maria Picciano, asked for equal treatment, testifying that her mother in New York had a rheumatic heart and "knows nothing of this." But the judge allowed photographs of Picciano, who had not attended Brown.

Apparently Smith and Kidd were not persuasive witnesses. Henshaw was acquitted on all seven remaining counts: two counts of persuading Smith and Kidd to become prostitutes, two counts of committing oral sex with Smith and Kidd, maintaining a common nuisance at his condominium, soliciting Smith to help him recruit other women, and conspiring with Smith to procure sex for pay from a Massachusetts woman. (Henshaw was convicted, however, of possessing marijuana and cocaine, and although first-time drug offenders like him usually received probation, the judge ordered him to jail for three months.) A woman who served on the jury told a reporter for the *Providence Journal* that she did not think either Kidd or Smith were "victims." "They weren't forced" to pose nude or have sex, she said. "They were educated girls. They knew what they were getting into." No evidence even remotely suggested the existence of a prostitution ring connected with Brown.

Presumably it's a coincidence and not something about the air on the Hill, but Brown seems to attract women who find sex in one form or another to be lucrative. Heidi Mattson, who was valedictorian of her high school class in Maine and graduated from Brown in 1992 with a degree in English, published a book in 1995 called *Ivy League Stripper* (the cover shows her twice: in a Brown sweatshirt and on the job in high-heeled leather boots, a G-string, and sequined halter). Mattson described her three years of stripping at a Providence club called the Foxy Lady, where a half-dozen or more Brown women had worked in recent years, some while students, others while on leave. As one might expect from Brown students, the strippers spent a lot of time contemplating whether they were exploiting their male customers or were being exploited by them. "If my image is a sex object, it's in someone else's head. It's in their head, what's in my head is mine," Mattson told an interviewer for a student magazine. Brown would ordinarily shrug off nuisances like this, but the Mattson episode festered into a lawsuit and public recrimination about her financial aid; Brown officials claim that her editors made "substantial changes in her book" after university lawyers had reviewed a draft.

The risks of misinformation are more obvious when an institution is dealing at the upper echelons of journalism. The university still recoils at the memory of a 1993 cover story in the *New York Times Magazine* on campus crime. "[The writer] came here because Brown had done such a good job," Reichley said. "We have an effective police force, which is unarmed, and a good record on campus security. We cooperated. We allowed them to shoot pictures. If you can't trust the *New York Times*, who can you trust?" The magazine story focused on other institutions, while largely praising Brown's safety record and anticrime effort. But the cover photograph showed an unarmed Brown security officer—his shoulder patch identified him clearly—speaking with a frightened-looking young woman at night. The cover line read: "Crime Turns the Campus into an Armed Camp." "[The picture] looked like a rape, or sexual assault case," Reichley said. "You should have seen this place. Calls coming in from alumni. Calls coming in from parents." Brown had to settle for a short letter of protest to the editor.

Not long after being burned by the *Times* on crime, the university declined to cooperate with a *U.S. News & World Report* story on campus racial issues. But the caution did it no good. The story contained a file photograph of a black student carrying a placard during a Brown march, with a caption labeling it a racial protest. This time the university sent the magazine a seething letter noting that the photograph had been made during a Take Back the Night demonstration, in which blacks and whites together marched on behalf of women's safety, and had nothing to do with race. It could do nothing more.

Experiences like that are hard to explain to a university community, either on campus or outside. "Even the most knowledgeable administrators still wonder why you can't do something," Reichley said, "why you can't get out like a traffic cop, put up your hand, blow your whistle, and say, 'Stop!'" A lot depends on the president. The late Howard Swearer, who led Brown from 1977 to 1988, did not enjoy dealing with reporters and didn't trust the media. On any significant public issue, Swearer and his senior staff, of which Reichley was a part, would develop a position, then hand the dissemination responsibility to Reichley, as the official spokesman for the university, and to the news bureau led by Broudy.

The contrast could hardly be greater with Swearer's successor. Vartan Gregorian, a historian, rose to become provost at the University of Pennsylvania and was bitterly disappointed when Penn's presidency went to Sheldon Hackney in 1980. So he quickly took a consolation prize, the presidency of the New York Public Library, then a down-at-the-heels victim of New York City's 1970s financial crisis. Imaginative and determined, Gregorian badgered the city's politicians and charmed its philanthropists until he had returned the fusty library to its place as a major civic resource and made himself one of New York's most visible party guests in the bargain. (In 1997, Gregorian resigned the Brown presidency to become president of the Carnegie Corporation of New York.)

The lively, cherubic-looking Gregorian is more than comfortable dealing with reporters and is well connected at the highest levels of New York journalism. So although Reichley remained the university's official spokesman, the president himself took on some of the biggest issues. When Brown became enmeshed in a legal and political struggle over Title IX of the Education Act of 1972, related to its intercollegiate athletic program for women, Gregorian elected to personally testify before Congress. But even the media-savvy Gregorian has been burned occasionally. When Brown expelled a male student who had drunkenly shouted anti-Semitic and racial slurs outside dormitories, Gregorian gave a long interview to an ABC News reporter, patiently explaining that the student had repeatedly violated the university's code of community behavior. He found himself quoted for three seconds on *World News Tonight,* as part of coverage that essentially labeled the action "politically correct." (Reichley once had six seconds on *World News Tonight* giving Brown's position in the complicated Title IX athletics lawsuit.)

With confidence in his media sophistication, and his historian's instinct for getting the facts on paper, Gregorian believed the university should issue official statements on newsworthy matters. In that way, Brown's position could be understood both within the institution and by the media. The news bureau, however, found the process cumbersome. "There's nothing wrong with having things on the record," Broudy conceded. "It's the number of statements we issue. We're constantly issuing statements where I think we could be handling the issues in a less complicated way. The fact that it is going on paper requires that not only the writer gets involved, but the lawyers are reading it, the financial officers. There are group editing sessions that turn an easy statement into a speech."

Unexpected and fast-breaking stories create a different problem. Brown learned a hard lesson in the suicide pill episode when an off-the-cuff response from a university staffer gave the story national legitimacy. "In a crisis situation, having a university spokesman is the best way to respond," Reichley insisted. "The media have got to know that there's somebody they can call." He reported with satisfaction that he was one of the first people to know about critical university decisions that could affect the public, "but it's more than knowing about it." The spokesperson must be trusted at the highest levels of the institution: "It's knowing the university well enough to be able to say that this is what we ought to do." That person must be acknowledged to be trustworthy by the media as well: "I have never in my career—ever—been asked to say anything that's wrong—never—not in 25 years; it's never been asked, never been insinuated. For obvious altruistic reasons—but also because it never works."

Broudy said he still cannot quite grasp why the prostitution story took off as it did. Obviously sex was an attraction, as well as Brown's "hot college" image and Ivy League prestige. But after a media flurry that appeared to exceed any reasonable expectation, sending the story to an audience estimated at 800 million worldwide, the university decided that it needed its own disproportionate reaction. "The big decision, the crucial decision," said Broudy, "was whether to go after the press, and we decided that we would do it. . . . We needed a dramatic way to kind of yell 'No!' to the press, that they were on the wrong track by calling it a Brown prostitution ring; let's set the record straight. Talking to individuals here and there wasn't going to do it, because each media outlet picked up the stories of the others and just repeated the error that this was a Brown ring." Broudy and Reichley saw evidence that the press conference tactic worked because the flow of stories associating the university with the arrests stopped almost immediately.

"The first thing I took out of [both the suicide pill and prostitution cases] was the notion of speed," Reichley said. "Not at the expense of accuracy, or at the expense of going so fast that you've said the wrong thing, but we must move fast." He worries that universities instinctively want to make measured responses; the problem is, such responses may never catch up with an unpleasant story. Journalists work with different deadlines than academicians. "You have to get across to your academic colleagues," Reichley said, "that this is not a term paper, this is not a thesis. Your opponents are out there with their story, and theirs is the one most likely to drive the coverage because they're the first ones there. We have got to be part of that first story." Speed has become even more important in these days of fax and e-mail communication for press releases and other official statements.

Still another, perhaps more consequential, message concerns the relationship of an institution to its students. "In trouble, or disagreeable publicly as they may sometimes be, students are *ours*," said Reichley. "We took great pains to accept them while turning down thousands of others. Brown will survive the future far more easily than will the reputations of young people who err as they first find their voices on a college campus. Except in a few situations when candor is absolutely necessary for the welfare of all of our students, laying the blame for the transgression of a few of them does not distinguish us as a great university."

Reichley says he is "very proud" that Brown supported the daring of the anti-nuke students while dismissing the fantasy that it would issue suicide pills. Brown even supported the two young women who appeared to be acting solely on their own behalf. "Our first act could have been to distance ourselves from them," he said. Instead, the university immediately provided on-campus housing for the women to help protect their privacy and always began its statements with the reminder, "We are first and foremost concerned for the privacy and welfare of these two women and their families."

Reflecting a decade later about the two cases, Reichley spoke regretfully of a vivid change in the public affairs atmosphere, one that flies in the face of university culture: the tabloidization of news. Obviously the prostitution arrests were a natural for cheap-shot reporting. But Reichley, who joined Brown in 1968 and was executive vice president at his retirement in 1995, finds today's coverage in general to be looser and nastier. "The situation has gotten so much worse, with trash TV and talk radio. I probably would not follow today the policy we followed in the prostitution case, talking to everybody." What would you do? "Maybe we would release a short statement, so everybody had it, and had no excuse that they didn't know. Then we would probably talk to those places that we normally talk to, that we consider reliable."

Yet in this era, what is reliable? Brown certainly knows what it is like to be burned by the nation's most respected publications. And as national events of recent years illustrate, mainstream news organizations can find themselves forced to follow stories driven by supermarket tabloids. University administrators may want to yell "Stop!" and Reichley demonstrated that it can be done, however rarely. But certainly some events are beyond the control of universities. In such circumstances, a well-prepared public-affairs unit—and confidence—become the best hopes.

CHAPTER 7

Town v. Academical Village

Drug Raids at The University of Virginia

J ust off Jefferson Park Avenue in Charlottesville, the University of Virginia (UVa) began work in early 1993 on a new parking lot behind the Woodson Institute for Afro-American and African Studies. One day a workman maneuvering a grader over the lumpy turf noticed what seemed to be unusual rocks and chunks of metal. He had the good sense to stop and call his bosses, who, after examining the chunks, had the good sense to call in academic authorities, who decided that Jeff Hantman ought to look at the find.

A UVa archaeologist, Hantman immediately identified a headstone and other artifacts from an old gravesite. As it turned out, a most unusual gravesite: the family plot of Kitty Foster, a mulatto freed slave, who bought the land three decades before the Civil War. The property had been handed down from mothers to daughters for three generations before being sold to railroad speculators early in this century. The dozen coffins discovered there almost assuredly belonged to the Foster family.

Quickly the university set up a joint committee with leaders of Charlottesville's black community to consider what might be done about the find. They decided to turn the site into a scientific dig, supervised by university archaeologists and anthropologists, with UVa students and local black teen-agers volunteering to help and learn. The scientists and their interns discovered in that first summer fragments of a doll and children's teacups, broken plates and bottles, and marbles and buttons. Later genealogical detective work, again with the help of volunteers, traced descendants who hadn't known about their Charlottesville roots. Upon the recommendation of the university-community committee known as the Venable Lane Task Force, the university postponed indefinitely plans to develop the site and continued to conduct archaeological research.

There was a day, many people in Charlottesville believe, when the powers that be at the University of Virginia might have ignored a freed-slave burial ground and sent the graders and pavers back to construct the parking lot; certainly they wouldn't have consulted the local black community. There was a day, everyone knows, when students brought their slaves with them to Mr. Jefferson's academical village and a day, not so long ago, when the only blacks associated with the university made the beds and cut the grass.

Those days are gone. In 1986, UVa president Robert O'Neil, understanding the fragile nature of town-gown relations, in particular the skepticism of Charlottesville's black community, joined with the mayor of Charlottesville and the county executive of Albemarle County to create a Planning and Coordination Council. The leaders and their top advisors now meet regularly to discuss mutual problems and opportunities, such as traffic, noise, public transportation, and volunteer programs.

But a cooperative leadership council couldn't help UVa on the first evening of spring in 1991, when a task force of city, county, state, federal, and university officers swept without notice into three fraternity houses, arrested nearly a dozen Virginia students on drug charges, and seized the houses as drug-related booty. Among the principal reasons for the raid, Charlottesville police chief John DeKoven (Deke) Bowen conceded, were complaints from the city's black residents that police regularly arrested local blacks on drug charges while ignoring similar malefactions by rich white boys on the hill.

The raid tainted the lives of several students and led to lawsuits over the seized fraternity houses. It caused students to rethink their recreational choices and campus authorities to set new standards of conduct. It troubled alumni and allowed politicians to shoot off their mouths. It also embarrassed UVa, in its state and, because this is a famous university, across the nation— a public nightmare that authorities at many colleges and universities probably think themselves fortunate to have escaped.

This is a legitimate thought, because the University of Virginia was unlucky, a victim of local circumstances, unusually determined law enforcement, and, not least, its own fame. Not that UVa was drug-free; illegal substances were known to be available many places on campus, especially in fraternity houses. But everyone familiar with the university, students and administrators alike, believed that the use of illegal drugs had fallen significantly since they had first become a rage in the late 1960s.

Alcohol was the drug of choice at UVa, as it had been for more than a century and a half; and if there was illegality in its use, it was because alcohol was available to students below legal drinking age and because it often led to boisterous behavior and dangerous driving under the influence. Almost any male graduate, no matter his era, can spin tales of alcohol-fueled carousing—as UVa President John T. Casteen III said, "Some stories told as current truth I heard as a student here 30 years ago"—which have given the university a reputation as one of the nation's great "party schools." (Like much about the institution, this reputation can be traced back to the founder. His biographers have written that Thomas Jefferson went to his grave worrying about the rowdiness of the young gentlemen he had personally chosen to fill the first class at the university.)

The highlight, as it were, of drunken partying was an annual spring festival known as Easters, a 72-hour binge that made Rugby Road dangerous and sharply boosted aspirin sales. It was generally noted by Charlottesville's black residents that nothing remotely like it on their part would be tolerated by city police. But Easters is gone, having been eliminated by the university in 1982. And while no one doubts that drinking at UVa, as at most other universities, remains an important part of the social fabric, alcohol consumption appears to have slipped in recent years. In the face of these ameliorated conditions, the university suffered through the searing raid that changed conclusively its administrative operation and its relationships with its fraternities.

Early in the evening of March 21, 1991, television vans and reporters began cruising the Rugby Road fraternity neighborhood. Yes, television vans and reporters, before the police arrived; there is disagreement about whether they had been alerted by federal drug enforcement officials or local police. Shortly afterward, in an eerie atmosphere lighted by television floods and police spots, officers armed with search warrants knocked on the doors of three fraternities, announced the prospective confiscation of the houses, and made a number of arrests.

During these very moments, down the street, in the Rotunda that Mr. Jefferson designed as the centerpiece of his academical village, members of the Board of Visitors, the governing body of the University of Virginia, and their spouses were having dinner on the eve of their regular spring meeting. As dinner ended, President Casteen and Executive Vice President Leonard Sandridge, who had learned the day before that police action was imminent, asked the board to convene for a short emergency session. As the spouses nervously waited in another room, the wives of Casteen and Sandridge assured them that the president was neither resigning nor being fired. Board members listened in silent shock as the president outlined what had occurred and what the administration was doing. Then the chief of university police, Mike Sheffield, was called in to brief the board. It "was very orderly, somewhat subdued, but not overly emotional," Sandridge remembered. "These were people, obviously, who had dealt with crises before."

A few minutes later, Louise Dudley, director of the UVa News Service, received a telephone call at home from the Associated Press, asking for university comment on the raid, to which she replied, "I beg your pardon?" She hadn't known about the raid. Her next phone call was a summons to a meeting at the president's home at 7 o'clock the next morning, at which the university would begin to plot its response. The administration did nothing further that night, nor did she, Dudley said, because there was nothing they could do. "It was not really our story in the beginning. The federal people had conducted this raid, they were in touch with the media, they were the ones who had the facts, whatever they were, at their disposal. . . . This was something that was kind of happening *to* us in a way, or happening to these fraternities that happened to be attached to us."

"We were simply trying to behave responsibly with regard to a wide range of issues," Casteen said of the administration's reaction. "It's not altogether customary to have to deal in compact fashion with potential conflict of various legal and regulatory entities, and here we had them all on deck at the same time: student-run discipline systems; university, local, state, and federal police officials; involvement of a U.S. magistrate in Roanoke, Virginia, a couple of hours [away], and a substantial media presence—[federal officers] were actually leading a kind of bus tour for reporters through the area."

The 7 a.m. meeting brought together Casteen, Sandridge, Dudley, and representatives from other concerned offices: student affairs, liaison with the fraternities and sororities, legal counsel, and security. First they shared their bits and pieces of information; then they talked about their immediate responsibilities. Dudley arranged to have UVa's Institute of Substance Abuse Studies provide context on college drug problems, both at the university and nationally. Then she headed downtown to join reporters at a police press conference, since that was the only way she could gather information the university needed. For example, although most stories referred only to UVa students, one man arrested was a former student, one was a former part-time student, and one had never been a student at the university. She gathered up documents handed out by police and took them back to her office to be copied, so that the university could distribute them as necessary. But the news office was not overwhelmed in the opening days, because reporters were dealing mostly with the police.

The president responded to reporters' questions for a half hour the first day, then did not meet with the press again for about a week. He wanted to deal first with his Board of Visitors, who were still on campus. "The issue was to get enough information to inform the board, but to keep this from being the central point of the board meeting," Casteen said. "The board took a hard look at it, but [this was] a classic task for administration." He also downplayed the significance of the event. "This was not a congressional investigation; this was a drug raid involving three fraternities. This was not a pattern-setting event; it was a severe test of local institutions that have to do with the regulation of student conduct."

Casteen remembered being annoyed that the student newspaper, the *Daily Cavalier*, immediately editorialized that the image of the university, and thus the value of their degrees, would be tarnished. "We didn't see this as a matter of image. We saw it as a matter of community responsibility, an obligation to deal candidly and quickly with issues. . . . I think the short-term [student] reaction was pretty immature, this business of the student paper crying into its beer about our image. . . . They kept asking us, 'What are you going to do to protect our image?' The answer, which was deliberately flippant, was to suggest that you stop doing drugs in the fraternity houses."

The story exploded in Virginia newspapers and the *Washington Post* the morning after the raid, made the national television news broadcasts that evening—complete with pictures of the Lawn and the Rotunda*—and soon was carried in newspapers across the nation. The *New York Times* climbed all over the story with a reporter who had been a college classmate of Charlottesville police chief Bowen. Politicians expressed shock, shock like Captain Renault, the most ludicrous being Virginia Governor L. Douglas Wilder, who speculated about mandatory drug testing for college students. UVa became a kind of "poster child of the war on drugs," Dudley said. "There's a certain incongruity between Mr. Jefferson's beautiful academical village—people know it has high academic standards, a certain reputation—and the idea that if you can find drugs here, imagine what you can find other places."

Not until he got a call the morning after the raid from NBC News did Robert Canevari, UVa's longtime dean of students, "realize this was a little larger than I thought it was." Later that day, a CNN reporter arrived on Grounds to interview him; after congratulating Canevari on how well he had handled the questions, the reporter mentioned casually that he had a daughter in high school who was interested in UVa. Canevari smiled as he recalled his 15 minutes of celebrity. He appeared on a nationally syndicated morning talk show. When NBC's Jane Pauley visited Charlottesville to interview him about how the university communicated with parents of students, they chatted about one of Canevari's favorite people, *Today* co-anchor Katie Couric, who

---

*The Lawn and the Rotunda are terms special to the University of Virginia. The Lawn is the grassy center section of the university campus as designed by Thomas Jefferson; on most campuses, it would be called the quad. It is rimmed by the Rotunda, the original main building, and connected Pavilions, in which faculty have lived since the university's founding, as well as interconnecting rooms for about 50 outstanding senior students. At Virginia, the campus is called Grounds, without an article. Students are not called freshmen, sophomores, juniors, and seniors, but rather first-years, second-years, third-years, and fourth-years. In this chapter, Virginia terms and more common terms are used interchangeably.

had been a member of the residence staff program for three years and head resident in coveted Lawn housing as a fourth-year. "I don't think I fully comprehended why [the raid] was such a big deal," Canevari said. "Here the feds had spent six months looking into this campus, and the only thing they could find was three baggies of marijuana. I wish the perspective had been a little bit better."

A month after the raid, a reporter for the local newspaper, the *Charlottesville Daily Progress*, ran a search of how the nation's major newspapers, including the *Washington Post, New York Times, Chicago Tribune, Los Angeles Times*, and *USA Today*, among others, covered earlier drug busts on campuses. Two years before, more than 100 people, including students and staff, at West Virginia University, had been arrested in Morgantown; no coverage was noted outside the state. In 1988, 27 people, including 18 students at California State University, Chico, had been charged with sales of cocaine and marijuana; a single four-paragraph story appeared in the *Los Angeles Times*. That same year, four members of the Sigma Alpha Epsilon fraternity at the University of Alabama were charged with distribution of cocaine; that case merited one paragraph in a 1,300-word article on fraternity problems in the *Los Angeles Times*. In 1987, a drug seizure and the arrest of four students at a fraternity house at the University of Maryland, located in the heart of the circulation area of the *Washington Post*, resulted, astonishingly, in a single four-paragraph story in the *Post*, which did countless stories on the Virginia case.

O'Neil, who left the presidency a year before the raid, still marvels at the attention that UVa receives, far more, he observed by comparison, than the University of Wisconsin, which he previously served as president. "This is a very visible institution," he said. "[The visibility] does good things and sometimes it also does bad things. It exposes everything that goes on here." Now president of the Thomas Jefferson Center for the Protection of Free Expression in Charlottesville, O'Neil suggested that the Virginia raid was used "to serve notice to higher education that drug use on college campuses is taken seriously. . . . I cannot help but feel that the high level of media exposure and interest contributed to whatever process this was part of. Somewhere beyond Charlottesville, a conscious decision was made [to focus on] this institution of exemplary quality."

Beyond its importance as a signal, one other factor called particular attention to the Virginia raid. It marked the first exercise on a university campus of a 1987 federal law that allowed authorities to seize property used in drug trafficking. Congress intended the law to strip organized drug dealers of their ill-gotten buildings, trucks, and fancy cars; the confiscated property was to be sold and the profits returned to the war against drugs. Here the law was invoked to seize fraternity houses where a few students were mostly peddling tiny quantities of marijuana.

The confiscated properties, like most fraternity houses at UVa, were owned not by the university but by private corporations, usually formed by the chapters' alumni, which leased them to the chapters. The three of them were collectively appraised at $889,000 for tax purposes, which in theory could have been the amount the government demanded from the owners for the return of the property, and early news reports suggested the possibility of just such a drug-fighting windfall. But the chief trustee of one house, a local fraternity called Phi Epsilon, demonstrated in negotiations with the government that he had repeatedly warned the members that drug use was forbidden in the building; it was returned to the landlord corporation without ransom. The other two alumni corporations, which held title to the Delta Upsilon and Tau Kappa Epsilon houses, eventually settled with the government, paying an estimated $20,000 to $50,000 each for their return. The corporation for Tau Kappa Epsilon, whose chapter was having trouble finding members, quickly sold the house to a women's resource center and purchased a smaller one.

More than a year passed before all the dozen criminal cases were completed, and the results were remarkably different. Eight of the 12 men were charged with federal crimes, which under the new and tougher drug laws required prison sentences, even for first offenders, without shortened terms for good behavior except in the most unusual circumstances. In the first of the trials, Ernest Pryor, Jr., a 19-year-old sophomore engineering student from suburban Richmond, pleaded guilty to selling three-quarters of an ounce of marijuana and a bag of hallucinogenic mushrooms, which was exacerbated under the law because the sale came within 1,000 feet of a public elementary school. The judge expressed his dilemma. "I find this to be one of those instances which falls outside the mainstream of drug cases," he said at the sentencing. "It tears up the court's conscience in a case like this. But if I am to be true to my oath, I have no choice but to follow federal directives." He sentenced Pryor to 13 months in prison without parole and two years probation upon his release.

Jamie Graham, a 21-year-old former Eagle Scout, received a similar sentence for selling about $5 worth of LSD to an undercover officer. Graham had been attending a Grateful Dead concert in Washington, D.C., at the time of the raid and turned himself in when he learned the police wanted him. He was "kind of bitter" about the experience, he told the student newspaper later, complaining that college students were singled out unfairly, both as targets of the raid and inside prison. "Jamie Graham was a pawn on behalf of the government's propaganda campaign that they are not racist and went after some white middle-class people," his lawyer said after the sentencing. "The criminal sanctions in this country are cockeyed and destructive and Jamie Graham is a victim." Three other students, Mark Croy, David Freelund, and Andrew Schwaab, all were sentenced to 13 months, the minimum allowable, on federal charges.

But despite the judge's lament in the Pryor case, the federal sentencing guidelines were soon sidestepped. Prosecutors told a federal judge that Matthew Evans, who had pleaded guilty to distribution of marijuana near a school, had provided "substantial assistance" to authorities in their drug investigation. So, apparently for the first time since the sentencing rules had gone into effect in 1987, an exception was made: Evans received seven weeks in prison and four additional months under supervised house confinement, then reentered the university that autumn. Another student, Peter Schaeffer, went to trial on a felony charge for drug sales, but when prosecutors lost faith in their star witness, they negotiated a misdemeanor plea of marijuana possession, with no jail time. Eric Heller, the last student to go to trial, received the lightest sentence, two years of unsupervised probation, for what federal authorities said was important cooperation. Finally, Pryor, whose mandated sentence tore up the judge's conscience, ultimately served only a couple of summer months in prison before the judge decided that he had also provided "substantial assistance" and reduced the sentence to an academic year of house arrest except when he was going to classes.

Four of those arrested in the raid faced state rather than federal charges. James Hottle III, who was attending a community college, not UVa, pleaded guilty to cocaine sales and went to jail. Patrick Hanrahan was sentenced to two years in prison, but the state judge suspended all but four months and ordered that Hanrahan serve time between semesters and on weekends. Stephen Marvin seemed to personify the sophistication of the UVa students about drugs. He hoped to reduce his sentence for LSD possession by becoming a police informant. But when police turned him loose on the street, he didn't know how to buy crack and couldn't make purchases even after they tried to teach him how. So he served six months in jail.

James Carter II was the only UVa student acquitted after trial. Although Carter admitted that he had used cocaine, everyone assumed that the jury was primarily punishing the police for their reliance on an informant named Tamir Noufi. Carter testified that he had never used cocaine before Noufi introduced him to it, and that Noufi repeatedly urged him to find drugs. Noufi, who had once been a part-time UVa continuing-education student, was arrested the summer before the raid for possession of more than three pounds of marijuana, and police offered him a deal if he would inform on UVa students. When Noufi himself went to trial on federal charges of selling marijuana and a hallucinogen, with several students testifying against him, it took a jury 30 minutes to vote conviction.

The critical informants against UVa students, more or less unintentionally, turned out to be a number of black citizens of Charlottesville. Deke Bowen, now retired but then the city's chief of police, said flatly that their complaints played an important role in the raids. Given the limited resources available, police were devoting most of their antidrug efforts to the inner city, Bowen explained, because "crack cocaine was distributed openly on the streets; [there was] violence and certainly fear of violence. . . . Citizens from those neighborhoods were begging for some relief." At the same time, "We had information coming to us that there was pretty open, blatant marketing and use of drugs at the university, through the fraternities. . . . [P]eople [had been] stopping me on the streets, telling me about what was going on [with] powdered cocaine." Much of the information was coming from black residents, Bowen said. "You see, they work up there [at the university]. They work up there cleaning those houses; they work up there cooking in those houses; and they know what goes on in those houses, better than we know. . . . Not only are we getting some of the information, but the community's getting that information because they tell their friends."

The raid grew out of a joint effort among police forces of the City of Charlottesville, the County of Albemarle, the State of Virginia, the U.S. Drug Enforcement Administration, and the University of Virginia. Although their campaign had previously produced a few arrests, including charges against Barry Word, a former UVa football star, it reached few students and no one in the fraternities. In the summer of 1990, when police decided to focus more intently on the fraternities, Chief Bowen wrote to every fraternity, reminding them of the illegality of drug use and the fact that their houses could be confiscated if found to be involved in drug trafficking. (Bowen said he heard complaints from blacks that no such warnings were issued in the inner city. He replied that warnings were unnecessary, since inner-city residents could see drug arrests around them almost every day.) Some of the fraternities took the letter seriously and discussed it in meetings and with advisors. Some responded to the chief with a "How dare you?" attitude, in effect telling him it was none of his business. Some ignored the letter.

Over the next few months, using at least one informant and at least one undercover officer, police worked to make cases in the fraternities. To this day, Bowen believes that they failed to nail some of the worst offenders, largely because most fraternities did what they should: control the doors to their houses. If fraternities only admitted members, guests of members, or those on invitation lists for parties, undercover cops were effectively barred.

All this time, the man in the middle was Mike Sheffield, chief of the university police. He defends the decision to align his department with the drug task force. "I felt it was important to be part of it. If I were a parent and had a student here, I would feel it would lessen the impact if the institution was involved, and not just outsiders. We can either be a part on the front, or we're going to be a part on the end." As a unit of the task force, the UVa department was committed to cooperating with the other police authorities in making drug cases, even against university students on Grounds. At the same time,

Sheffield was torn by his loyalty to the university and allegiance to his bosses. He kept his immediate superior, Executive Vice President Sandridge, loosely informed about the task force's progress. (For his part, Sandridge said, "There are two people whose confidence I simply can't afford to violate. One of them is the chief of police.") Then, early in the week of the raid, Sheffield met with Sandridge and President Casteen to alert them that important action was imminent, without providing many details; he was accompanied by federal drug officers who were not keen about giving the university special treatment. The date of the raid had been chosen for no particular reason, and Sheffield said, "I probably panicked when I found out the Board of Visitors was going to be here." Shortly after the raid began, he notified Sandridge and was invited to the Rotunda to brief the board.

Sheffield, who had been a UVa police officer for more than two decades and chief for six years at the time of the raid, had grown up in Charlottesville and understood the mixed emotions that residents of the city, both black and white, felt about UVa. As a young man, he, like his neighbors, "always looked up to the university" and aspired to work at the elegant institution. Yet he knew that many in the city felt the students were not held accountable for their actions the way Joe Citizen was. "You go back to the Easters years ago; there's thousands of people in the middle of a city street, blocking the street, drinking and partying. But we [the ordinary citizen] can't do it downtown, or we can't do it in our part of the community. So when that happens, it just adds fuel to the fire, [it] continues to build, it builds in every issue.

"We probably as an institution didn't do a good job over the years educating people in the community about the makeup of the student population, how many were getting financial aid, these types of things. The student population has become more and more involved in the community—volunteer work, [helping to alleviate] drug problems, athletes getting involved. They can make an impact in someone's life, but at the same time they are carrying the message around that, 'Hey, we're really people, my background may be just as tough as yours. If you want to go to school, you can get help.'" But, Sheffield reflected, "I'm still certain a segment of the community is always going to feel that they've been cheated and wronged."

The police forces of Charlottesville and the university have developed a remarkably cooperative arrangement, which has been copied in Richmond with Virginia Commonwealth University and in Norfolk with Old Dominion University, and draws inquiries from university police officials around the country. Although it took a long time, the teamwork eventually developed from the dictates of Charlottesville geography. The principal Grounds of the university, which in its early years was separated from the town by open fields, is now subsumed in the city, its facilities mixed with private property, and its thoroughfares unidentifiable from city streets. A significant portion of the institution lies in the surrounding County of Albemarle, a separate jurisdiction.

In the mid 1980s, Charlottesville chief Bowen and university chief Sheffield won state court approval of an agreement to make UVa police "special officers" of the city. Recruits to both forces now attend the same police academy, and UVa officers now have jurisdiction in about half the city, the parts adjacent to university Grounds. It is a practical solution that avoids some potential dangers: for example, a university officer driving through the city to reach a UVa facility can stop to assist someone without risking jurisdictional questions. Typically, the city and the university jointly operate a police substation at the Corner, a UVa business hub adjacent to Grounds. Officers of the two forces may share a walking beat, a patrol car, or a horse patrol. And the city can save considerable money since university police maintain order on sometimes rowdy party weekends.

Police long ago learned how to deal with fraternity parties, and the UVa administration had learned to live with them, but the drug raid raised the stakes and led to significant changes in the relationship between the university and the fraternities. To the uninitiated, fraternities at the University of Virginia seem to be an integral part of Grounds, their houses occupying a central position abutting university facilities. But except for a handful, all of the privately owned houses lie on private property. Although Greek-letter organizations have long played a disproportionate role in campus affairs for their membership (about 30 percent of undergraduates), the administration has worked hard in recent years to make clear that the fraternal groups are not official arms of the institution.

A turning point came in the early 1980s when some fraternity men driving a rented trailer crashed on a hill in southern Virginia. Among the outcomes of this accident were a host of lawsuits, including one against the university, although it eventually extricated itself on the grounds that it had no culpable connection to the accident. Nonetheless, President O'Neil and other top administrators decided that they needed to clarify the institution's position vis-a-vis fraternities. Thus was born the Contracted Independent Organization (CIO).

Each year, student organizations, now known officially as CIO's, are required to sign a carefully drawn contract with the university. The rules currently apply to about 350 organizations—although none of them, including sororities, give the university anything like the problems caused by fraternities. The development of the formal CIO contract caused considerable debate within the UVa administration. On the one hand, the contract could be understood as the university's voluntary surrender of whatever degree of control it held over the fraternities. (Certainly many residents of Charlottesville, including municipal officials, believed that the university was abdicating responsibility, especially over loud parties, abuse of alcohol, and perhaps drugs.) But the prevailing arguments within the administration were that the contract both relieved liability pressure on the university and reduced its *in loco parentis* role; students would now be treated as adults. A fraternity can refuse to sign the contract; to do so, however, would cut its ties with the interfraternity council, intramural sports, organized rush, and a multitude of other university-related activities. As evidence that the university does retain a considerable measure of power, no CIO has ever declined.

Immediately after the raid in 1991, UVa stiffened the CIO contract. The revised preamble states:

> Fraternal organizations are defined for the purposes of this document as organizations comprised of University students, which are traditionally governed by an all-greek black fraternal, interfraternity or intersorority council, and which offer educational, service, and social opportunities for its members. Various fraternity organizations comprised of University of Virginia students wish the University to provide the fraternal organizations with certain benefits. Without necessarily approving or disapproving the goals or activities of particular fraternal organizations, the University recognizes that the availability of a wide range of opportunities for its students tends to enhance the University environment. . . . [T]hose benefits should not be misinterpreted as meaning that those fraternal organizations are part of or controlled by the University, that the University is responsible for the fraternal organizations' contracts or other acts or omissions, or that the University approves of the fraternal organizations' goals or activities. The University does not use the concept of "recognizing" fraternal organizations.

In subsequent clauses, the revised contract states:

> The parties understand and agree that this Agreement is the only source of any control the University may have over the fraternal organization or its activities, except . . . matters covered by the University's honor or judiciary systems. . . . The fraternal organization understands and agrees that the University . . . will not be liable for any of the fraternal organization's contracts, torts, or other acts or omissions. . . .

> [F]or fraternal organizations with residential facilities, the house shall be permanently and completely free of illegal drugs, use of such drugs, and transactions involving them; . . . the chapter's sponsored events shall be completely free of illegal drugs, use of such drugs, and transactions involving them as well as the consumption and possession of alcoholic beverages by underage persons and the provision of such beverages to underage persons by the chapter. . . . The [fraternal organization] shall include detailed means of demonstrating compliance with the foregoing chapter commitments and related University rules and regulations with particular emphasis on measures of self-monitoring and enforcement.

In other sections, the Greek organizations commit themselves to educational programs on drug, alcohol, and sexual abuse.

Since the drug raid occurred in late March, shortly before new CIO contracts were to be signed, the revisions were quickly dropped into place. Beyond this new agreement, which applied to all fraternities, the three fraternities affected by the raid faced extra responsibilities. Each was required to prepare an additional detailed plan intended to ensure that neither its property nor any of its members would be involved with drugs or other illegal activities. The plans were compiled in loose-leaf notebooks and negotiated over a period of weeks with Dean of Students Canevari before the university would agree to reapprove the fraternities. "We worked pretty hard with them," said Canevari, a Virginia graduate who has been dean of students since 1970. "These are our students. We are an educational institution. They're supposed to be learning."

Ironically, members of the fraternities who faced criminal penalties for their involvement with drugs escaped any direct university punishment because of a bureaucratic snafu. UVa regulates student behavior through two principal systems, which have in common that they are student-operated. One is the legendary Honor Committee, which dates almost to the founders and treats cases of lying, cheating, and stealing with a single sanction for guilt: expulsion from the university. The other is the Judiciary Committee, which resembles systems found in scores of other institutions. Functioning under standards of conduct first formulated in 1970, the Judiciary Committee deals with violations of assorted university policies, such as disorderly conduct, property damage, and assault (a separate branch has been established to judge sexual assaults), and can impose sanctions ranging from "oral admonition" through "probation" to "suspension" and "expulsion."

After the raid, law enforcement officials, who controlled all the evidence in the case, wouldn't share it with Canevari, who wanted to institute university judicial proceedings against the students. After being rebuffed on several requests, he finally collected some evidence by July and filed complaints against individual students. The Judiciary Committee rejected the complaints on the grounds that he had missed the 45-day statute of limitations. "I said, 'Wait a minute, I did not know for sure that a crime occurred until I had evidence.' They said, 'You should have known; it was in the papers.' So we got into this procedural thing. They denied me the ability to file complaints. It really, really took me by surprise. But [the accused students] did not have to answer in our court, although they should have." New procedural rules allow a complaint to be filed and held in abeyance until evidence becomes available.

The drug raid led to other changes at the university—including the development of new crisis-management procedures. A plan prepared to cope with student protests in the 1960s had been forgotten by this time, so after its ad hoc response to the raid, the administration set about creating another one. "I think we learned a lot from the drug bust," said Executive Vice President Sandridge. "We learned first of all that we could serve ourselves a lot better if we didn't approach these issues timidly, [and] we recognized that there was a lot to be said for having sort of a response team. That response team changes depending on what the issue is, [but] there were some components of that team that were always going to be the same." Although the president partici-pates when necessary, Sandridge, as the principal operations officer, takes charge of the crisis team. Its membership almost always includes the university relations director and the university counsel, and, as required, the dean of students, a business officer, a medical officer, the chief of police, or anyone else whose area of responsibility is involved.

From her perspective, Louise Dudley, who has since been promoted to director of university relations, emphasizes the value of keeping the crisis managers regularly in touch with each other. "What we learned, starting with the drug raid," she said, "was how important it is to get the players together, not just one time, not just the next morning, but to continue to have this team of people who are involved in their own separate areas get together regularly, to have a system where we know how to check with each other, how to share information." A newly developed plan has been invoked in several instances of lesser or greater import, ranging from a stripper performance at a fraternity party to a sexual assault in a fraternity house.

The first notable test came only two months after the drug raid when the National Collegiate Athletic Association (NCAA) placed the university on two years probation for "lack of institutional control" over its sports program, which had allowed interest-free loans to student athletes. The university itself announced the probation publicly. "Just to show you how we progressed and what decisions we made," Sandridge said, "we were quite formal and struc-tured in how we went about it. We had lists of assignments. We tried to identify which ones of our constituents were most likely to be affected by the bad news, who should be responsible for notifying them, talking to them, who should receive letters of explanation, who should receive phone calls, how should that occur, [and] how should we be dealing with the press."

In particular, the administration has learned the importance of having a public information official in the loop from the start. "We want the public relations person not to be the second or third person called, or not to be called in just when an issue has become an issue," Sandridge said. "But we want to have a person who is skilled enough—and I think this is a difficult assign-ment—skillful enough to have the confidence of the media as being objective and open, careful enough and skillful enough to understand early in a situation that something was happening, so their advice and counsel could be sought." Dudley is not an official member of the president's cabinet, Sandridge conceded, "but other than the boring parts, I would hope there's not much that the cabinet's involved in that she's not aware of."

The University of Virginia has created an unusual public affairs model. In most institutions, the chief news or public relations officer is a vice president, reports to a vice president for public affairs or development, or reports directly to the president. At Virginia, Director of University Relations Dudley reports to Executive Vice President Sandridge. "Vice presidents for development are hired and fired on how much money they raise," Sandridge contended. "They are not typically the ones most aware of potential embezzlement in the business office or a patient's problem in the medical center, or student athletes about to be charged with shoplifting. . . . They are not involved in those operational issues. . . . I do think ours is better than the development model, [but] it's awfully hard to say that there's one size that fits all. . . . So much of what we do in higher education is a function of the team you put together." Virginia likes its current team; it will be instructive to see if the model survives with a new president and principal deputy.

Sandridge said that university authorities understand the impact of "extraordinary bad news" like the drug raid. "[There is] always a segment of the population who perceive it as lack of control. So I would be less than candid if I didn't say that there were certainly some short-term reactions [from this population]—young people are out of control, and the colleges and universities are simply a haven for that." But he considers the long-term damage "minimal." The first piece of evidence came from the admissions office. Since the drug raid and its attention-getting aftermath occurred at the height of the admissions season, UVa protectively increased the number of acceptances it offered. The result was one of the university's largest first-year classes ever, since the yield rate didn't fall. Sandridge likes to think that issues that "bring attention to a place like this, and cause people to learn more about it, soon [lead them to] focus on the good things here."

Good things like the continuing care lavished on Kitty Foster's gravesite, which helps bridge the historic chasm between gown and town: Academic specialists are now pursuing their disciplinary research, and community volunteers still participate in summer digs under the guidance of a doctoral student in anthropology. "I would say the historic relationship was one of lack of communication, remoteness, a sense of the university being what it was, which was an all-male, all-white enclave," Dudley said. Originally, about two miles of open country separated the city and the university, "but even in more modern, twentieth-century times, as the city has filled in, there still was a sense of somewhat geographic, but also psychological, social, and economic isolation, some of that having to do with race, but not entirely. The university itself was not welcoming. There aren't many signs on buildings, for example, so it creates the impression that if you don't know where things are, we don't really care."

"The community dynamic has always been complicated and probably will be for a long time to come," former president O'Neil agreed. He said the community-university coordination council grew out of plans for a research park to be developed by the university, which the city and county seemed determined to resist. O'Neil was told, "'You want our blessing for your university real-estate foundation, with authority to acquire land for things like research parks, we'll need to work out a whole new relationship.' I said, 'Fine,' so we negotiated, the city, county, and university, for some time, and in due course worked out an agreement, which committed each of the three of us to inform the other [and] to get approvals, and which said that the university would not take land off tax rolls except to meet educational needs. If we used land for any noneducational purposes, we would pay taxes on it. They wanted that in there, and I was willing to put it in.

"It took about a year and a half [until the council] went into effect. We met quarterly, and those meetings certainly were an important part of my sense of community. . . . We discussed everything, some things trivial, some not, parking, parks, housing, fraternities, any issue. . . . It's certainly better than not having that kind of communication. . . . The fact that it exists as a sounding board may in a curious way make its active use and its coming together less necessary, because you know you do have linkage."

O'Neil observed that the council structure has never been tested in a major crisis, like a natural disaster. "But I can't believe that communications lapses wouldn't be averted by the kinds of cooperation we have organized at many different levels. It forces police chiefs, planning directors, communications, transportation, and 911 people, all of them, to work together, all accountable to the group of executives who come together for periodic meetings."

"There has been a very conscious, deliberate effort," Dudley said, "in the last eight or nine years, starting when Bob O'Neil was president of the university, to change [the image of remoteness]. Part of it was to set up some structures, [such as] the planning and coordination council, . . . so they don't surprise each other, . . . and there is in fact a lot more open exchange of information. The university is working very hard in a lot of nontraditional ways to get people from the community into the university, to participate in university events. We now have a director of community relations that we didn't have a few years ago. It is an area that we know wasn't one of our strong points in the past."

UVa understands better than it ever has that it must live with both the promise and the risks of its exalted reputation. "This sounds very high-flown," said Dudley, "but it really is in the front of our minds: if something goes wrong, whether it's something we think we're at fault for, or even if it's not, we try to be direct. [We say] this is what we think went wrong, and this is what we're going to do about it. If we're going to have the visibility, we hope that we will also get visibility for our positive attitudes and our solid approaches to challenges."

CHAPTER 8

Never a Rose Garden

The Firing of Woody Hayes at The Ohio State University

One of the most abused words in the English language is *tragedy*, which is applied by every undereducated local television news reporter to every unfortunate car crash that kills a drunken teenager. What does that leave us to describe Oedipus or Lear? Or someone short of a king, one whose indisputable accomplishments and demonstrable humanity would make him a paradigm among men, except for inherent, uncontrollable flaws that bring contumely upon him. A football coach, perhaps, named Wayne Woodrow Hayes.

Woody Hayes served as head football coach at The Ohio State University (OSU) for 28 years. His Buckeye teams won 3 national championships and 13 Big Ten championships, and played in 11 bowl games, including 4 consecutive Rose Bowls. He was chosen national coach of the year twice and runner-up twice. He is in the college football Hall of Fame.

Hayes is well remembered for these achievements. But he is remembered, too, for a temper that flashed across television screens to millions of spectators and for punches aimed in the heat of struggle at intrusive cameramen and his own players. And he is remembered only too well for the last act of his illustrious coaching career. On the evening of December 29, 1978, in the final moments of the Gator Bowl game in Jacksonville, Florida, a Clemson University linebacker named Charley Bauman intercepted an Ohio State pass to assure the Buckeyes' defeat. As Bauman was driven out of bounds near the Ohio State bench, Hayes rushed at him and swung wildly. The scene was captured for the nation by ABC television and, of course, repeated countless times, that night and in the days to follow.

It was also repeated countless times the day Woody Hayes died, more than eight years later.

Those eight years "were the greatest years of his life," pronounced Richard Nixon, who flew to Columbus to eulogize Hayes at a memorial service March 17, 1987, and from a humanitarian perspective he may have been right. Eight hours after the Clemson eruption, Woody had been fired, and it was as if the steam had been released from a volcano. Relieved of the pressures to win—"I love to compete. That's the basis of life"—Hayes settled into an avuncular mode, teaching a bit of military history at the university, responding to voluminous correspondence, giving motivational speeches around the country, chatting amiably with frequent visitors to his tiny office in the Military Sciences building, and spending countless hours—quiet, unpublicized—cheering sick children and the dying elderly at Columbus hospitals. He pledged unwavering fealty to The Ohio State University, and he never once uttered words of recrimination about the president or the athletic director who had fired him. He also never apologized.

He could treat his players brutally, but, said George Stroud, sports editor of the Columbus Dispatch, "I've never found one that disliked Woody." "The man cared a great deal about people," said Archie Griffin, the only player ever to win the Heisman Trophy twice. "Woody was a loving man," said John Mount, who held four vice presidencies at the university. Then how to explain temper tantrums that a kindergarten teacher might punish and behavior unbefitting a role model for thousands of athletes and millions of citizens. Gordon Gee, Ohio State's current president and a former president of two other research universities with major football programs, said, "University presidents and other senior officials of the university, vice presidents and football coaches, are first and foremost role models. We have to live by the modeling that we set. . . . The only force that we ultimately have is a moral force. And if we invade that, or we fail to understand that, or if we break that covenant, then we no longer have the right to assert the public role that we've been cast in."

"I've always been a high-strung individual," Hayes once said, and more than once he admitted to Stroud that he had always had "a temper he found hard to control." So only a handful of Ohioans remember the hospital visits or how firm his friendship to Ohio State, and only serious sports fans remember the Rose Bowl triumphs, which were rarely replayed after his death. Rather, it is the contorted face, the snapping of markers on the field, and the ugly moment at the Gator Bowl that are remembered. In his prime, Woody Hayes was, along with the astronauts Neil Armstrong and John Glenn, the best-known Ohioan alive—and for better or worse he sometimes symbolized The Ohio State University, which is a finer university than many people give it credit for.

It was near midnight in Jacksonville when Woody Hayes lost control for the final time. Harold Enarson, the president of Ohio State, was sitting in the stands across the field from the Buckeyes bench, and, since he lacked the benefit of a television set, all he could see through the misty air was "some kind of altercation." When the game ended soon afterward, members of the Ohio State official party pushed their way through orange-clad Clemson celebrants and boarded chartered buses for the traffic-clogged, hour-plus trip to their lodgings at Ponte Vedra. There, Enarson suggested conversation and a night-cap to his colleagues and himself went outside to gather kindling to start a fire.

A few minutes later came a rap on the door, leading Enarson to joke that they must be making too much noise. Ohio State's vice president for university relations, Edwin M. Crawford, answered the door to find Hugh Hindman, the athletic director. Hindman asked to speak with the president outside; Enarson invited Crawford to join them. Hindman quickly discovered that the president did not know what had occurred, and, as Enarson remembers, "in a matter of fact, straightforward fashion, said that Coach Hayes had struck an opposing player. I said, 'Did you see it in person? Are you absolutely clear on what happened?,' and he said, 'Yes,' and I said, 'Well, that's just intolerable.' . . . We quickly agreed that he had to be fired and fired immediately. I figured this was a major scandal . . . and if we delayed, and then caved and fired him, that would be an intolerable situation. So you needed quick surgery."

Hindman went on to describe his discussion with Hayes: "I went to the dressing room after the game, and I told him that I felt he ought to resign, that we could not defend this kind of incident. And he refused to do it. I told him, I'm going to see the president, and tell him that this is what I plan to do: I'm going to give you until eight in the morning to think it over. I'll come to your room at 8 o'clock, and I hope you'll give me your resignation, so we don't have to fire you, because I don't want to do that."

Enarson and Hindman decided that the athletic director would report as soon as he had spoken to the coach the next morning. In the meantime, Ohio State's top administrators planned their forceful tactics, beginning with calls to the nine members of the university's board of trustees. A couple they woke up in Jacksonville, and a couple who had not attended the game they woke up in Columbus; the others were on a chartered plane headed home. "[The trustees] were saying, 'Well, there's no other course,'" Crawford recalled. "'But we hope you will give him a chance to resign and not have to fire him'. . . . There was nobody saying you ought to do something else."

Now in the middle of the night, Enarson and Crawford huddled over a public statement. "We developed two two-sentence statements," Crawford said. "One basically said, 'It is with great regret that we have accepted Coach Hayes's resignation.' There was another that said, 'Coach Hayes has declined to resign, and with great regret we've terminated him, effective immediately.'

We added a complimentary phrase about his long service to the university. . . . I spent the rest of the night thinking of media that I ought to contact once all of that was put into motion. The simplest way to do it, it seemed to me, was to call the AP [Associated Press]. . . . We wanted Saturday afternoon's papers to carry the fact that he'd been terminated, one way or the other. That was important, to show it was done while we were still in Jacksonville, that there wasn't any hesitation about it."

While the wheels were turning in the OSU hierarchy, George Stroud, who was then Ohio sports editor for the Associated Press, was finally getting to bed. Stroud had been on the sideline as the game ended, preparing to write a sidebar about Ohio State. Too far away to see the skirmish himself, he got details from some eyewitnesses and filed his story to the AP. After finishing his work, he stopped at the Gator Bowl hospitality room about 3 in the morning and noticed Nancy Hindman, the wife of the athletic director, her eyes red and swollen, as if she had been crying.

Stroud was awakened about 9 the next morning by a call from the AP office, telling him that an Ohio State official had just called with the information that Hayes had been dismissed. "I put on a sweater and slacks, no shoes, found out from Nancy where Hugh was, and ran down to the coffee shop, barefooted. [I saw] Hugh there, sitting at a table by himself, stirring his coffee. I asked if it was true. He said, 'Yeah.' This was a former Ohio State assistant coach, firing his former boss. I'll never forget what he said. 'This was the toughest thing I've had to do since I buried my father.'"

A couple of hours earlier, Enarson had awakened to await Hindman's call. "I did get antsy then, I really did," he remembered. "I was checking my watch every two or three minutes. The damn phone call was not coming through." Soon it came: Hindman said that he had confronted the coach, that Hayes had refused to resign, and that he had been terminated. No one knows for certain what occurred next, but apparently the coach called his longtime friend and biographer, Paul Hornung, then the sports editor of the *Dispatch*, to say that he had resigned. Hornung, back in Columbus, wrote the Hayes version for Saturday's paper. So the *Dispatch* was running a story that Hayes had resigned, while the AP, whose Columbus office adjoined the *Dispatch* newsroom, was reporting that he had been fired.

Later that day, two Ohio State charter flights left Jacksonville for Columbus, one carrying Hayes, his coaches, and the team, the other bringing home Enarson, the coaches' wives, and the rest of the official party. Anne Hayes, Woody's wife, sat alone, except when close friends would join her for a few moments; many of the assistant coaches' wives, knowing their husbands were almost certainly out of jobs, spent the flight in tears. When the team plane landed first, Hayes disappeared without a word. Enarson had scheduled a press conference at the Port Columbus Airport for 7 p.m., but a snowstorm diverted his plane to Pittsburgh; the official party reached Columbus in buses, bedraggled, about 2 the next morning. That left the Sunday papers with conflicting tales and recycled details on one of the biggest college football stories in decades.

At the moment Woody Hayes was punching the Clemson linebacker, one of the best football players he ever coached was watching the game in his motel room at a ski resort in Seven Springs, Pennsylvania. Daryl Sanders remembered saying, "Man, I can't believe it, the old man has finally gone over the edge. And the next morning, I said to my wife, 'We've got to leave, because no one will have the guts to talk to him, and he needs help right now.'" When the Sanders family returned Saturday to Columbus, where Daryl was a well-to-do Cadillac dealer, he called his friend Dan Heinlen, the longtime president of the influential Ohio State Alumni Association. Heinlen said no one had heard from Hayes since his return home, and people were worried. They agreed that someone should try to speak with him, and Heinlen suggested contacting Archie Griffin, twice the nation's outstanding college football player and one of Woody's favorite people. It would be hard for Hayes to refuse to talk if one of his white stars, Sanders, and one of his black stars, Griffin, arrived together. Griffin, who is now the associate athletic director at Ohio State, immediately agreed.

Sanders tells the story: "About 11 o'clock [Sunday] morning, we met in the parking lot of a strip mall on Lane Avenue about three blocks from Woody's house. We don't know what we're going into; we don't know if the old man's going to be in a rage, or so despondent. There were concerns about his mental condition. So Archie and I sat in the car together and prayed. We asked for guidance and help, and just to be a comfort to the old man, just to reach out to him.

"We went over to the house and knocked on the door. Woody answered the door himself. It took awhile [so] I think [Anne and Woody] looked at us through some other place. He stood there and looked at us. . . . He looked at me, he looked at Archie, and finally said, 'Come on in.' And we sat there in his living room for eight hours. We had no lunch. We didn't drink a glass of water. No dinner. It's dark out, and there's one little light that he ends up turning on, just so we're not totally in the dark. But I mean we were in the dark for about an hour. And he was just talking. We said, 'Yes, sir,' about three times. We didn't talk about the incident at all. We talked about life, experiences: 'Remember this, remember that.' It was almost like an old highlight discussion. We talked about things in life and politics. I talked to him about the Lord a little bit."

Sanders is not your run-of-the-mill former jock. The son of a Cleveland steel worker, he was already married with two children while at Ohio State, where he became an All-American tackle and a first-round draft choice of the

Detroit Lions. After four years as a starter, he quit pro football at 25 to take charge of sales-incentive programs for Chevrolet and Cadillac, and at 29 became executive vice president of a Fortune 500 marketing company. Soon he developed a lucrative new Cadillac franchise. Then, suddenly, he cashed in his chips because "God got hold of my life. I just had a sudden renewal of my faith." After five years of "training," Sanders founded his own church with 20 congregants not far from his old Cadillac dealership in Dublin, Ohio; his Zion Church has grown in a decade to 600 members with land and buildings worth $2 million. Handsome and silver-haired, Sanders conducts "a charismatic worship service, where people are expressive and slapping their hands, [demonstrating] that they're involved with God."

Sanders knows that big-time football has flirted with the unethical for decades. Forbidden by National Collegiate Athletic Association rules from holding a job during the academic year, he worked three jobs during the summer to help support his young family. "The reality is, someone gave me a car. The reality is, I sold my football tickets. And the reality is, I survived. I would think that over the last 30 years, at every school everybody has got some help." Still, he charges angrily that dishonesty and pressures on athletes have grown infinitely more intense. "It's an arbitrary, unrealistic world. I believe that Division I athletes are the most abused working class in America. . . . [When I played at Ohio State], we went to the weight room twice a winter. Now they're in the weight room five hours a day year round. They're doing these physical alterations to their body. There's a whole new level of steroids. . . . It's altering their behavior. [Coaches] tell them how great they're going to be. It's preying on these kids. . . . Kids [will] start dying in their 40s. Some kids, in their 30s, say, all that work and how much did I play. What did I get out of it?"

Woody Hayes worked in a different time, but those who knew him don't believe he would have played win-at-any-cost games at his players' expense. Big Ten athletic programs rarely violated academic standards during the Hayes era, said one of his proteges, Bo Schembechler, then the University of Michigan football coach, at a memorial to Hayes, because Woody "set the tone" of "integrity." Anyone who violated the rules would "have to face the old man." His closest associates, players, and assistant coaches, in George Stroud's words, "saw another side of Woody. . . . Woody really wanted to be portrayed [in the media] as a mean old coach. . . . We're always looking for the negatives, for the dissidents, but I never found one. He really cared about how [his players] did in the classroom, too. He really got on them to do their studies."

Archie Griffin remembered getting "a little teary-eyed" when he learned of Hayes's firing. "Not only that he was a great football coach," Griffin said, "but he cared about people." As the winner of the Heisman Trophy his junior year,

Griffin was in demand for appearances all over the country even though he still carried a full academic load. "One time [Hayes] called me into his office. He knew I was out, going everywhere, doing everything. He said, 'Archie, you've got to watch all that stuff you're doing right now. Because it could make you soft.' He lowered his voice and repeated, 'Because it could make you soft.' I got the point."

Anyone close to Ohio State football knew the Hayes temper. On the closed practice field, his impatience with imperfection verged on the ludicrous. Not content with hurling his trademark baseball caps to the ground and stomping on them, he took to tearing up the caps. When he discovered that he couldn't tear a normal baseball cap, he had his equipment men cut the caps slightly so that they could be ripped apart. He was known to fling his wristwatch to the ground and step on it. He would punch himself in the face, sometimes cutting himself with his ring. In bitterly cold weather, he would work in a tee-shirt, his arms turning blue, to demonstrate the power of discipline, mind over matter. Studying game films, he might hurl the projector if he didn't like what he saw.

Although he repeatedly struck his players, they accepted the treatment as Woody's effort to make them better. "There was just such a passion in this guy, and he would express it," Sanders said. "He hit me once in the stomach. He didn't hurt me and he didn't hit me to hurt me. He was driving his point home as a teacher." Griffin tells similar stories. "In practice, he'd hit you, hard, on the shoulder pad. Shoot, it didn't hurt, you had pads on. . . . At the time it might hurt your ego a little bit in front of the team. But [after practice] you'd have to pass his door. He'd pull you in and tell you why he did what he did. The next day you'd go out, and do something halfway decent; he'd stop practice and show everybody what you did, but he'd build it up to make it seem like the best thing since sliced bread."

Next to his players, Hayes cared most about Ohio State, said John Mount. He particularly remembered Hayes's response that painful day in 1960 when the faculty senate stunned the sports world by voting to refuse a Rose Bowl invitation for the Big Ten champion Buckeyes. Students staged a nasty protest at the corner of 15th and High, which edged toward the violent. Hayes and some of his stars got up on a truck bed to calm the students down. Who got hurt most, the players asked rhetorically. We did, and we're accepting it. "That was the kind of person Woody was," Mount said, "putting The Ohio State University first in his mind." Ruth Mount, John Mount's wife and a former dean of students at the university, remembered gratefully Hayes's assistance when students protested the Vietnam War. "Woody's philosophy was to reach out into the community in lots of ways," she said. "Anything he and his football team could do to make life easier on campus, he would do it. When there were demonstrations on High Street or on the Oval, he and his young men would frequently go out and be among the crowd. Of course students knew him by sight . . . and [they] paid attention to him."

Hayes's ugly temper attracted attention partly because of his contentious relationship with the press: "A newspaperman never won a game for us," he liked to say. In 1958, during the annual preseason visit by a group of sports-writers from major newspapers in the Midwest, he threw them off the practice field because he didn't like the way practice was going. A year later, after an Ohio State loss in the Rose Bowl to the University of Southern California, two California sportswriters accused Hayes of throwing punches at them, which led to a rebuke from the ethics committee of the American Football Coaches Association. In 1973, the *Los Angeles Times* brought assault charges against Hayes after he pushed a camera into the face of a *Times* photographer before the Rose Bowl game. Hayes said the photographer had intruded into the Buckeyes' huddle, and charges were dropped in a Pasadena court. In 1977, he knocked down an ABC cameraman who in his judgment had ventured too close to the Buckeyes bench. That brought him a year's probation from the Big Ten, which expired only six weeks before the Clemson episode.

But there were displays of childish anger aimed not just at journalists. In 1971, in the final minutes of a loss to Michigan on national television, Hayes threw a tantrum after what he thought was an erroneous call by the officials and broke a sideline down-marker over his knee. Not once did he apologize.

It was after the Michigan tirade that President Enarson decided he must confront the coach. "I asked him to come in and see me. The night before, I lay there sorting out what I was going to say. I had, I think, six or seven points. They weren't prosecutorial. I just wanted to have a friendly talk, and I wanted him to understand that this kind of behavior was damaging to the university. So I asked him a series of questions, like, do you realize the importance the public at large attaches to Ohio State football and to your performance. Yes, he knows. I went through the questions. It was a very courteous conversation. He listened to me patiently, and he said, 'Prexy, I love this university.' I said, 'Woody, I know you do. Don't do anything that hurts us.' And he said something to the effect, 'Do you think I meant to do this?' That stunned me. I didn't know what to make of that. . . . He didn't say, gosh, gee whiz, I blew it. I think he was incapable of saying that, [but] the thrust of the conversation was [that he didn't] want to embarrass the university. . . . He was so, 'obsessed' is the only word, with football that he didn't have an adequate sense of perspective."

Gordon Gee, who served as president at West Virginia University and the University of Colorado before moving to Ohio State, has thought a lot about the relationship between a president and his marquee coaches. "[It is] not only an important question, but in many ways an imperative question, because probably at institutions [like this], two or possibly three people receive more publicity than they should—the football coach, the men's basketball coach, and the university president. Therefore, we are in the public eye and public life to an extraordinary sense. I often had to explain this to Bill McCartney [the former football coach at the University of Colorado, who resigned to organize a Christian fundamentalist program for men], who is a very dear friend. Bill marched to a different tune, and every once in awhile I had to go over and gently sit down with him, and say, 'Bill, you know, you and I basically lost our First Amendment rights when we took on these roles. That's not right. It's not the way it should be, but that's the nature of public life and the world that we're in'. . . .

"I think it's very important that the president of the university have a personal relationship with those people within the institution that have such high visibility, so that in good times you can enjoy each other, and in bad times you have the credibility to tell them that they can't do something. And if they do do it, you'll cut them off at the knees. And they will believe you and respect you for saying that. . . .

"If you're viewed as being anti-athletics, not supporting the mission of the athletic program . . . I think that you lose a lot of opportunity to be a significant force for positive change, which is an absolutely essential ingredient, particularly in the 1990s, of running a college athletic program. . . . I have a very strong athletic director, I have an enormously capable vice president for student affairs, who has responsibility for athletics but who I work very closely with, and together we have a very clear philosophy about how we are going to manage the athletic program. . . . I make it very clear to the athletic coaches and other people that we represent the university [and] we represent it with the kind of dignity and class that we should. . . . [N]o one is above that, and if they think they are, they won't work here very long. Period. . . . I think you have to have standards, and if you have standards for yourself and for everyone except for the football coach and the basketball coach, then you are in the wrong business. You just have to establish that up front. There are a number of coaches in this country who would not work for me, because I wouldn't have them."

Mount, a longtime friend of Hayes, attributes some of his problems on campus to faculty jealousy of his visibility. "[Some] in the academic world, wanting to have academics lifted to the highest level, were jealous of the fact that a person in athletics would bring recognition of an institution. . . . In my view, in terms of an institution, we need to lift up as many good things as we can, and it's the combination of all of them." What's the harm "if out of that comes a personality, like a Woody Hayes."

His visibility and volatility caused some anxious moments after his dismissal for the administrators in Bricker Hall. For some weeks, Hayes made no public statements or appearances, then consented to speak to the annual luncheon of the Columbus Chamber of Commerce. He received roaring standing ovations when he entered the ballroom of the Neil House, when he was introduced, and when he completed his remarks. True to his nature, Hayes uttered not one word of criticism of the university and not one word of apology for his actions. The closest he came was an expression of regret that several of his assistant coaches were still out of work.

Then Hayes settled into his quiet new life: a few classes to teach; a lot of banquets to attend; well-received motivational speeches—all over Ohio, a national 4-H Club convention in Oklahoma City, a conference of physicians in San Diego, and hospital visits to the infirm and the dying. Once he was hospitalized himself for an operation, and as he recuperated, he looked pale and lacked energy. Upon his readmission to the university medical center, it was discovered that doctors had left a sponge inside his body. In today's world, for many people, that could have meant a multimillion dollar lawsuit. Woody Hayes just told the doctors, "Well, everybody makes mistakes."

Everyone agrees that Hayes cared not a whit about money. He never earned as much as $50,000 annually at Ohio State and had only one additional source of income, a postgame television show during the season that paid $1,000 a week. He lived in a white frame house with green shutters in a modest section of Upper Arlington, the city's old-line prestige suburb, close enough to campus that he could walk to work. (His widow still lives there.) With his future in doubt after the firing, Hayes's friends worried about his ability to support himself. "After I left Woody [that first night]," Sanders said, "I thought, the old man has no idea about the business side of this thing. I wrote down a list of 15 questions and called him. 'Think about what you want the university to do.'" Hayes finally met with Enarson, which led to an office at the university, a secretary, and a rank as professor emeritus. But he received only the standard financial severance package and no bonus representing special service to the institution.

Before long, the university was honoring him. The athletic training building was named the Woody Hayes Facility, and the street separating Ohio Stadium and St. John Arena was renamed Woody Hayes Drive. Ohio State also welcomed him back in a particularly symbolic way. Before every home football game, the extraordinary Buckeye band forms a script Ohio—it is modestly billed as "the most famous band formation in the world"—with a tuba player prancing to midfield to "dot the i" in *Ohio*. Before a game in 1983, Woody Hayes was escorted on the field to dot the *i*, and the roar of greeting shook the concrete of the old gray horseshoe.

But the best was still to come. In March 1986, the university he loved paid Hayes a tribute beyond his imagining: He was awarded an honorary doctorate and was asked to give the principal address at Ohio State's winter commencement. As Hayes stepped to the lectern, tears welling in his eyes, he could barely speak. "I am so grateful, so appreciative," he began. "Today is the greatest day of my life." An avid military historian, he spoke of battles won and battles lost. And he invoked his favorite message, inspired by Ralph Waldo Emerson: No one can pay back those who have helped them, so everyone is duty-bound to help those who follow, to "pay forward."

A year later, March 12, 1987, Hayes was dead. Hundreds of former players and coaches returned for his funeral service, at which his friend Richard Nixon gave the principal eulogy. Nixon recalled his first meeting with Hayes at a party at the home of Senator John Bricker after an Ohio State football game. "I wanted to talk football," sports fan Nixon said, "and he wanted to talk foreign policy. You know Woody. We talked foreign policy." A few days later, thousands filed into Ohio Stadium on a chilly late-winter afternoon for an outdoor public memorial. Among the dozen speakers was Bo Schembechler, who had played for Hayes and served as his assistant before going on to head coaching positions at Miami University and the University of Michigan, where he had over the years frequently surpassed the master. Woody was "the greatest football coach the [Big Ten] conference ever had," Schembechler pronounced. "People were always saying he was more than a coach. He wasn't more than a coach. He just set a different standard for coaching."

An argument offered by those who remember Hayes lovingly is that the university acted too hastily in firing him. "There was a graceful way to do this," Sanders contended, "and they did not grace it. There was no need to react in such a fashion." What would have been graceful? "I think a man who's given 28 years of his life, . . . there's [got to be] some dignity. You don't have to do it at 6 o'clock the next morning." Sanders, though, thinks Ohio State has failed the dignity test "time after time. This university has fired every football coach since Paul Brown left . . . every basketball coach . . . and they have never done these things right."

John Mount, who has been associated with Ohio State for nearly six decades from his days as an activist student to his retirement as vice president and now alumni volunteer, wishes events had played differently, but he understands the dilemma faced by the president and the athletic director. "In my view, we should not make decisions at the spur of the moment like that. There is due process. But Woody made it very difficult to have that due process. . . . Hugh [Hindman] was deeply hurt by the way Woody responded to Hugh's trying to be helpful and making the best of the situation. Woody was his own enemy." Mount thinks an immediate suspension would have been appropriate. "I believe that [if there had been a suspension], during the process of the months ahead, there would have been a resignation," he said, conceding that he is indulging in hindsight. As is commonplace in circumstances like this, he also blames the media. "The media all hitting the president, what choice would the president have [except] to say that Woody's no longer our coach."

Given Hayes's reputation, Enarson's position was, and is, that rapid action was essential. He worried about the national embarrassment to the university if it did not act promptly, and he worried, too, about the possible growth of support for Hayes if the matter dragged on, embittering the state. "It didn't take much imagination to know the counter pressures that would be building up. There would be very powerful people saying, 'You know, we could work our way out of this, let's don't do anything drastic.' . . . This was something, one of those fairly rare occasions, when a person in a leadership position simply has to act very, very quickly, hoping that one has read the entire situation and acted appropriately. I've never doubted for one moment that I acted appropriately, not one moment."

George Stroud of the *Dispatch* considers the outcome inevitable. "It was no great shock in this community that [Woody] did the thing, and that the university finally reacted by firing Woody. There were times in the past before this incident that people thought he should have been fired, whether they be staff, whether they be faculty, or whether they be fans of the university. There was a cross-section here of people who thought he had survived some incidents he shouldn't have survived. It was almost like a cat with nine lives, the coach who survived nine incidents." But finally the administration had to act. "You can't hit an opposing player. They didn't have any choice."

Enarson believes that most Ohioans understood that. For all the attention football got, it wasn't the coach who caused the president the most grief during his tenure, but a group of doctors. An official Ohio State history observed that some people considered it not one university but four: University of Intercollegiate Athletics, University of Medical Affairs, University of Agriculture, and "all the rest, which was what the president actually ran." Almost alone among university medical teaching faculties nationally, Ohio State's physicians kept for themselves all of the tens of millions of dollars in patient fees they collected, even though they benefitted from university facilities, equipment, and prestige. Several attempts had been made before Enarson's term to encourage the physicians to contribute to the general welfare of the university, always without success. When Enarson attempted to install a "medical-practice plan" that would force the physicians to share their wealth, Ohio State's doctors argued that they had been recruited without such a plan and the money they made was no one's business but theirs.

The OSU history called it "one of the most brutal and most costly power struggles in the University's history," and concluded that it became "something of a personal vendetta by the doctors against Enarson." The president invited the doctors to establish a practice plan of their own liking, but they refused to give a mite. After a draft had been approved by the board of trustees, 139 doctors filed a federal class-action suit alleging that the proposed plan violated their rights to privacy, income and property, due process, and equal protection under the law. The federal court was only one of their negotiating weapons. The doctors, of course, were treating the governor, various trustees, and various state legislators, and had their ears, so to speak, under the most intimate conditions. Enarson ultimately forged a compromise that brought the university and Ohio's taxpayers some relief. But he paid dearly, and he knew it. "I had the fight of my life with the physicians in the medical school," he said. "It was a brutal fight. I couldn't believe the way in which they did a number on me." The board of trustees unanimously backed him in private, but "when the chips were down, and we were in Federal District Court, the board caved, and negotiated a settlement."

"It's a huge, complicated enterprise," said Enarson, reflecting on his presidency at Ohio State, "which commanded every ounce of energy and wit that I had. It consumed me day and night; it was an unending responsibility. . . .There are times when real courage is required. For the most part, presidents survive when they stand up. You can't do it stupidly. You've got to build your support. . . . I'm not sure that all crises in human affairs can be avoided. The president has to move within some framework of acceptability. There are any number of ways in which one can stumble. One can offend powerful trustees. You deal with a variety of constituents. You use up your credits. You are legally responsible for the enterprise. And the things that can go wrong are legion."

Looking back from a rustic retirement home in Boulder, Colorado, Enarson thinks his resignation in 1981 was appropriate. "I had run out of steam in a variety of ways. I was more tired than I realized after I left. . . . They gave me a year's leave of absence and a truck." (They also gave him the title of president-emeritus and named a building after him.)

Enarson has long been acknowledged as one of the nation's leading authorities on higher-education administration. But he admits that he was not prepared for the place of football at Ohio State, as exemplified by one experience he still recalls vividly. The morning following a losing Rose Bowl game, after most of the official party had departed, he and his wife, Audrey, took a walk through the luxuriant grounds of the Huntington Hotel in Pasadena. "As we came back, there were two or three reporters; I didn't know any of them. It was a little bit like those lions on the Serrangetti Plain, dozing, and they look up and say to themselves, 'Huh! That's a zebra coming close here; it's a zebra!' and they say, 'Well, let's go see him.' So they stop me, and they kept, I thought, harassing me. 'Woody's not doing any talking now,' they said. 'Look, fellows'—the devil got my tongue—'Look, after all, it's only a game.' It was a dismissive comment; it certainly was not a comment that I reflected on." The next morning in the *Dispatch* came the shocked headline,

"Enarson Says It's Only a Game." When he got home the president received several calls of protest, including one person who told him football was "the heart and soul" of Ohio State.

Like a number of other good universities, Ohio State is at once blessed and cursed by the prominence of its athletic program. Sports tends to distract attention from the 16 graduate programs that rank among the top 25 in their fields nationally, and undergraduate academic standards that have moved from open to increasingly selective admissions. On the other hand, sports brings together alumni and many other Ohioans in enthusiastic support of the university. Dan Heinlen, chief executive of the alumni association, builds many of his alumni education programs around football weekends. "We use athletics to advance the interests of the university," Heinlen said. "Football is part of the culture at Ohio State. We've never not had it."

As the state's flagship institution, Ohio State may have no choice but to provide athletic entertainment at the highest level. As Malcolm Barroway, executive director of university relations, pointed out, the city of Columbus, Ohio's capital, has no major league sports teams within a hundred mile radius, the closest being Cincinnati, Cleveland, Pittsburgh, and Indianapolis. "In Columbus, Ohio State is the franchise." George Stroud felt the impact during national and international assignments for the Associated Press. "Whether I would be in Edmonton, Canada, or Caracas, Venezuela, or San Juan, Puerto Rico, the first question I always got, wherever I went, was, 'How's Woody doing?' They associated Columbus, Ohio, with Ohio State and Woody Hayes."

Some still do, two decades after his dismissal and a decade after his death. In the fall of 1995, with Ohio State scheduled to play the University of Notre Dame, the much-anticipated first meeting of these traditional football powers in 60 years, a long preseason *New York Times* interview with Notre Dame coach Lou Holtz was devoted almost entirely to his experiences as an assistant to Hayes. "Everybody complained about him on the staff," Holtz said. "But all of us coached just like him." Four months later, in the *New York Times* coverage of Ohio State's game in the Citrus Bowl, this was the lead: "It was the sort of day Woody Hayes would have loved. Dank. Hammering rain. A soaked field, perfect for three yards and a clod of mud. Old Woody, the legendary Ohio State coach . . . " It is perhaps fitting for Woody Hayes that so many people now remember him more warmly that he deserves, and so many others remember him more coldly than he deserves. But then he never promised a rose garden, just a Rose Bowl.

CHAPTER 9

A Water Buffalo Is More Than an Animal

The Judicial System on Trial at the University of Pennsylvania

The university's judicial system wasn't set up in a way that would allow it to handle this case effectively given the glare of publicity that came. The university's system was designed to operate in a community that was almost like a family. . . . Penn is not the first university to have found that when the national press comes, the lengthy, and polite, and judicious, and gracious procedures that we have don't work very well.

Sheldon Hackney, president-emeritus
University of Pennsylvania

The spring of 1993 promised to be celebratory at the University of Pennsylvania. Sheldon Hackney, whose progressively more successful presidency was concluding after 13 years, looked toward a tribute-laden transition. The university's capital campaign surpassed expectations as it rose to $1.2 billion. The spirit of a chapter completed, another about to open, freshened the tree-shaded red-brick and gray-stone campus, startlingly tranquil amidst the urbanism of West Philadelphia.

Before the academic year ended, three unrelated sets of circumstances had combined to inflict on Hackney some of the worst anguish of his professional life and to challenge some of Penn's most cherished promises and processes. The first—the "water buffalo" case—stretched to bursting the university's meticulously constructed student judicial system. The second—the *Daily Pennsylvanian* protest—challenged the university's proud commitments to racial understanding and free speech. The third, the action that knotted the first two together and flung them beyond the campus to a national audience, was the nomination of President Hackney by President Bill Clinton to become chairman of the National Endowment for the Humanities (NEH).

Of all the cases discussed in this book, Penn's is the most difficult to grasp. Most of the cases are subject to differing recollections. With Penn, it is not merely that participants' recollections are contradictory; it is that the flashpoints of conflict were so emotionally charged that the participants cannot be sure what they themselves said and did. It is impossible, I believe, to know precisely what happened.

It is not difficult, however, to conclude that an uncountable number of errors in judgment, mistakes of omission and commission, occurred during the course of events that followed the flashpoints. Nearly all these mistakes were made by well-meaning people, trying to do the right thing, trying to follow the rules. A few were made by angry, self-serving people. Either way, the university got into trouble largely because it paid so much attention to "process" that it forgot about how human beings behave when they are upset. Or, to put it another way, it forgot common sense.

The first of these trying circumstances began late in the evening of January 13, 1993, with five black women celebrating the 80th anniversary of their sorority outside a high-rise dormitory. By no means the most important fact about this matter, but illustrative of the difficulty in reconstructing it, is what exactly the women were doing. As one of the protagonists, a white freshman, Eden Jacobowitz, described the scene, the women were engaged in "loud stomping, shouting, and chanting." As one of the women, Ayanna Taylor, put it, "My sorority sisters and I went out to Superblock to sing songs, not to stomp, shout, or chant." Who is right? Who will ever know?

Before long, men in the dorms were shouting down to them to be quiet and leave, but the women didn't leave. When the shouts, from many men in many windows, grew nastier and occasionally racially charged (the area was lighted well enough so that the women were seen to be black), the sorority women called university police, who entered the dorm with them to try to identify the taunters. Every resident denied participation save one, Jacobowitz, whose room was on the sixth floor. He said that he had been trying to write a paper and had finally yelled, "Shut up, you water buffalos! If you want to party, there's a zoo a mile from here."

The women insisted, however, that they had heard Jacobowitz shout "black water buffalos." He denied saying "black." The women might have thought they heard "black water buffalos" when they hadn't. It was night, noisy, confusing, difficult to identify individuals shouting from dorm windows, and the women certainly were hearing racial insults of one kind or another. On the other hand, Jacobowitz might have added the word "black" without thinking. No one—including those most concerned, I suggest—will ever know.*

Although the water buffalo episode occurred January 13, it was known only to a few people until late April, for reasons that are part of this story. But before continuing the water buffalo slog through the university judicial process, I need to describe the *Daily Pennsylvanian* or *"DP"* affair. It is critical to emphasize timing here: The *DP* clash began early in the morning of April 15, 1993—three months after the water buffalo episode took place but two weeks before it became public; further, it occurred only days after Hackney's nomination, and well before he had to face confirmation hearings, for the chairmanship of the NEH.

That spring night, a group of students calling themselves "The Black Community" stole nearly all 14,000 copies of the independently run student newspaper, the *Daily Pennsylvanian*, which contained what they considered a racist opinion column. Next to trash containers and dumpsters where they junked the papers, they posted signs protesting "institutional racism," by the *DP*, in particular, and the administration, in general. Among the places from which the *DP* was stolen was the university's important anthropological museum, which had been the site of several recent thefts of artifacts. As the students fled the museum carrying dark plastic garbage bags, the contents of which could not be known to anyone else, several of the protesters were chased and caught by a museum staffer and university policemen. The staffer and officers later said they asked the protesters for student identification but were refused. The protesters said they were assaulted, handcuffed, and detained at university police headquarters. It is impossible now to know who said what first or second, and who did what to whom in those harried moments.

In contrast to the water buffalo episode, which oozed through the student judicial system, the *DP* theft exploded on campus. Many students picked up copies from the dumpsters and the *DP* managed to reprint 6,000 copies of the April 15 issue, including Gregory P. Pavlik's opinion column, which argued that "reasoned discourse on this campus is largely nonexistent." Pavlik had regularly insulted black students at Penn in columns that even a sympathetic reader, the syndicated columnist George Will, characterized as "often extreme and heavy-handed."

A sample follows: "Penn's administration, and its ceaseless pandering, is getting a bit tiring. . . . Could someone have caught on to our dirty little secret,

---

*The level of comprehension might be further illustrated by a comment later in the process. A staffer in the student life office told Jacobowitz that he must have intended a racial slur, since he called the women water buffalos, which are "fat, black, African beasts." In fact, water buffalos are gray draft animals, native to South Asia.

that admissions standards are thrown out the window . . . when it comes to the sensitive subject of race? . . . Of course, the thinly veiled attempts at mind control that masquerade as campaigns against 'intolerance' were primarily the object of [a letter to Pavlik from an administrator]. Wouldn't want anyone to think independently and revive the dark ideas of merit, hard work, and individual achievement."

Earlier in the semester, an official complaint of racial harassment had been filed against Pavlik, and a letter to the *DP* protesting his work had been signed by 202 black students and faculty. It read in part: "We have always given the newspaper the benefit of the doubt, and assumed the staff was ignorant, not intentionally prejudiced. However, we cannot fathom how Pavlik's articles can be published with the obvious understanding that he intends to demean and discredit. . . . We no longer believe the excuse that a publication's writers are entitled to extensive creative license beyond control."

Call it "creative license" or "freedom of the press," editors of the *Daily Pennsylvanian* responded angrily to the thefts. In an editorial the next day, they contended that the black protesters had "illegally muffled" open expression and "crossed the fine line between lawful and unlawful expression." Because of its freedom-of-the-press ramifications so dear to self-referential journalists, the *DP* case quickly inspired national stories on thefts of student newspapers— "Bonfire of the Profanities" in the *Los Angeles Times* and "A Trash Course in Free Speech" in the *Washington Post*.

When much of the campus recoiled at the theft of the papers, black leaders perceived yet another affront. A statement signed by the chairpersons of the African American Association said: "We deplore the actions of campus security . . . who chased, detained, arrested, handcuffed and assaulted students who were exercising their right to protest. . . . [B]e assured that these African American students were exercising their First Amendment rights to protest, and they are entitled to no less protection than those who protest by burning flags, burning draft cards, or disrupting publication of a newspaper due to a labor dispute."

The *DP*'s defenders, on the other hand, were particularly incensed by an official statement from President Hackney that at first glance appeared to equate the theft of the papers with the principle of free speech. "This is an instance in which two groups important to the University community, valued members of Penn's minority community and students exercising their right to freedom of expression, and two important University values, diversity and open expression, seem to be in conflict. . . . There can be no compromise regarding the First Amendment right of an independent publication to express whatever views it chooses. At the same time, there can be no ignoring the pain that expression may cause. . . . Penn must be both a diverse and welcoming community for all its members and one in which freedom of expression is the supreme common value. As a free forum for ideas, the University must be open to all and open to all ideas or it is not free."

While pleading for "peaceful coexistence," Hackney reiterated university policy that condemned the theft of the papers: "Though I understand that those involved in last week's protest against the *DP* may have thought they were exercising their own rights of free expression, I want to make it clear that neither I nor the University of Pennsylvania condone the confiscation of the *Daily Pennsylvanian*."

That position proved not to be firm enough, as Hackney recalled during our conversation in his spacious NEH office at the elaborate Old Post Office Building: "The day the papers were seized it bubbled all through the day; there were people running, there were confrontations, there were mass meetings, there was a tremendous amount of pressure. So that night, and the next morning, I wrote a statement, and it is not surprising that it was neither the most felicitous statement that I have ever written nor maybe the most designed to avoid any misinterpretation.

"It tried to recognize the situation that the black students were reacting against. And I thought they had a good bit of justice in their complaints against the *DP*. So I said something about values in conflict. Then I went on immediately to say that on a university campus it's clear which value is paramount. It has to be free speech. But the *Wall Street Journal* simply took that one section and kept repeating it. And people on campus said, 'Gee, I wish you'd been more clear. I wish you'd said they were wrong to take the papers.' Well, that was a judicial offense and there was a process that should occur."

Obviously race held an important place in both the water buffalo and the *DP* episodes. Here was a great university committed to diversity, an intellectual island bordered by the churning sea of West Philadelphia. "It's important always to keep in mind that this institution is an urban institution," said one longtime observer of the university. "It has not always been seen as a friend of the neighboring community, which is by and large black."

Sheldon Hackney, a native Alabamian and a historian, wanted to change that relationship. By encouraging minority enrollment in the university, of course, but, more, by dispatching significant resources into the neighborhood. "Sheldon has been very committed to helping Philadelphia," an outside authority on higher education said. "Penn spends millions of dollars a year on community activities, summer programs, outreach programs, with thousands of student and faculty volunteers. The money Sheldon committed to urban resuscitation is extraordinary, and his commitment is very real and very powerful. A real Southern, best-of-the-South commitment, a Southern liberal."

Yet even for people marching toward similar goals, the path was seldom smooth. For example, the mayor's scholarships. In 1882, in exchange for increasing its land holdings, Penn agreed to provide 50 yearly scholarships for students from the public schools of Philadelphia; in 1910, in exchange for more land, the number rose to 75, and in 1977, another land deal raised the total to 125, four-year, full-tuition scholarships.

Almost out of nowhere came a lawsuit against the university in 1992, contending that the agreement meant 125 scholarships *per year*, for a total of 500 over four years, not 125 scholarships spread among students over four years. The university argued that guaranteeing the larger total would tie its hands on admissions and that the lower figure was after all not a ceiling but a floor under the number of Philadelphia students. Supported by the mayor and the city solicitor, Penn won, but not until it had faced embarrassing protests from neighborhood groups, shouting at city hall hearings, and posturing from politicians in Philadelphia and the state capital in Harrisburg.

Hackney said he knew the water buffalo episode was being watched closely in West Philadelphia, but he was less worried about problems in the outside community than about conflict on campus. "Race is a volatile issue on every campus and in American society, and this was a racial incident. I was worried about things exploding on campus. We got beaten up by the right wing. But if I had done something differently, I would have been beaten up by the left wing."

When the water buffalo event occurred in mid-January, it could have passed as a commonplace student shouting match, unknown to the Penn community except for the few students who heard the ruckus and quickly forgot about it, unreported in the press. The five women, however, filed official racial harassment charges against Eden Jacobowitz, dropping the case into Penn's Byzantine student judicial system. Perhaps other entities could figure out a system as complicated, but surely a university, with its anxiety about fairness and its willingness to talk endlessly about anything, is a likely place for a process as baffling as the one Penn concocted.

Let me attempt to explain the process—more or less briefly—hopeful that the reader's eyes will not glaze over. (The explanation that follows applies to the time of the water buffalo case; the system has changed since then in some particulars.) Within the framework of the student judicial charter, there is a full-time judicial inquiry officer (JIO) with 9 to 5 hours and a secretary. A case is most likely to be brought to the JIO by a student or faculty member—known as the "complainant." The JIO investigates quietly, and if she (in this case, the officer was a woman) considers the accusation valid, negotiates with the person charged—known as the "respondent"—toward an appropriate sanction. For example, a charge of public drunkenness might lead to required enrollment in an alcohol-awareness program.

The JIO concluded that Jacobowitz had violated the university's racial harassment policy, so she proposed to him, informally, a set of sanctions, including a promise to apologize, to conduct a racial sensitivity seminar in his building, and to serve dormitory probation. When she sent him a written copy of the sanctions, however, the JIO had, in Jacobowitz's term, "upped the ante." He now was asked to sign an admission of guilt and accept a notation of guilt on his transcript until his junior year. It was alleged—and denied—that the JIO had been told to add those sanctions by her superiors in the student life office, which some faculty at Penn thought of as the central force of "political correctness" on campus.

Since Jacobowitz considered this a "crime I had not committed," he balked at the sanctions and claimed his right to invoke a "hearing panel" (complainants can also ask for a hearing panel if they find the sanctions too lenient). At this point an ad hoc judicial administrator (JA), usually a respected faculty member, assembles a panel to render judgment from an existing roster of volunteers. The JIO, having been first an investigator, then a judge, becomes a prosecutor before the hearing panel.

If the panel rules against the respondent, the vice provost for student life imposes whatever sanctions have been recommended and decides for how long the sanctions may be retained on the student's transcript. (It should be noted that the system provides no role for the president of the university or the provost, to whom these staffers report, or for the general counsel, who is the authority on legal affairs. These top officers may occasionally play unofficial roles in routine judicial matters. In the water buffalo case, however, their actions were significant.)

All this activity takes place with no publicity, presumably to avoid embarrassment to the parties. At one time the entire system was confidential; now statistics are issued that include categories of cases (fake ID, propulsion of object, excessive noise) and dispositions (more than half of complaints withdrawn), so that the community knows in general about the punishments rendered for certain types of infractions. The serious minds that created this system did not think all the way through the question of privacy. Complainants were not allowed to speak publicly about their case, so that respondents would not be identified and perhaps humiliated. Yet no such stricture applied to respondents, since it was assumed that they would not want the charges known. Thus, in this case, the women, playing by the rules, could not discuss it; Jacobowitz, also playing by the rules, could discuss it.

"This is maybe the important point: the procedure did not imagine a political case," Hackney said. "It imagined a case of regular discipline— plagiarism, misbehavior, rowdiness in the hallways, noise, maybe even an assault or theft; things in which the defendant would not want it known that he was being accused of anything. But here we had a political case, in which the defense was a political defense: basically 'I'm a victim of PC.'"

Outside lawyers are barred from these campus proceedings, but both complainants and respondents are entitled to the services of a faculty advisor. The five black students lost their first advisor, a black woman civil-rights specialist, who left the university during the proceedings; so they had to begin again, this time with a white woman anthropologist who headed the women's studies program. Jacobowitz's first advisor, a white woman, also withdrew, which turned him to Professor Alan C. Kors, a respected scholar and vibrant teacher, whose entry into the case changed it monumentally. Complex and unpredictable, Kors is a Republican who was one of the founders of the National Association of Scholars; he decries the religious right and chaired the academic-freedom committee of the American Civil Liberties Union of Greater Philadelphia; he thinks of himself as a libertarian. He is prominent on campus and well connected with the national media.

As soon as Professor Kors decided that the case against Jacobowitz was foolish and unfair, he bypassed the scrupulously drawn rules of Penn's judicial system and entered into several weeks of behind-the-scenes efforts to settle it. He talked privately in his home with Howard Bromberg, the judicial adminis-trator, a meeting that both men considered a practical step toward reaching a solution but that clearly violated the system since the women complainants and their advisor knew nothing about it. The negotiations, however, faltered at a seemingly insuperable barrier: Because of a ludicrous oversight, the judicial charter contained no provision to dismiss a charge after it had been validated by the JIO, no matter how fragile it might be.

Kors apparently alerted the Philadelphia branch of the ACLU, which threatened to seek a restraining order barring a university hearing on the charge against Jacobowitz. At that, Penn's general counsel undertook quiet negotiations with the ACLU to fend off outside forces, including state and federal courts. This may have been a good faith effort by university lawyers, but it violated Penn's own rules; not only did the ACLU not belong in the campus negotiations, but there was no role under the student judicial charter for the general counsel's office, which appears to have been involved at any number of levels.

Kors also went right to the top, calling Hackney, whom he tried to convince to end the case by fiat. "There were a lot of people mad at him, but I think from his point of view he behaved correctly throughout this matter," Hackney said. "He did call and say, there is this case brewing, charges have been brought, and I, Alan Kors, think that it's an injustice and you should call it off. And if you don't—these were not his exact words—if you don't, I'm going to go public with it, and I'm going to cause a lot of trouble. I knew he could cause a lot of trouble. He had been active in the National Association of Scholars and had been widely quoted and was therefore someone that the *Wall Street Journal* would be likely to listen to."

It was about this time that Penn's associate vice president for university relations, Carol Farnsworth, first heard about the water buffalo case. She called Hackney's office and eventually received a copy of a letter Jacobowitz had written to the president, which he had copied to several journalists, including George Will and Dorothy Rabinowitz of the *Wall Street Journal.* "Given who this letter was sent to," Farnsworth said, "I knew there was going to be a great big mess hit the fan fairly soon. If you can comprehend the significance of these four or five names, you'd better do something, because these were arch-conservative writers and columnists. The reality of what was going to happen was so clear. Yet there was no response, or, 'Well, yes, we know it's going to happen, but after all, these are our rules, and this is the right way to go.'"

The *Wall Street Journal* editorial page—widely recognized as the most influential voice of conservatism in American journalism—listened. On April 26, it assaulted the university in an editorial headlined, "Buffaloed at Penn," calling Jacobowitz "the latest victim of the ideological fervor known as political correctness" and the episode "one of the more Kafkaesque chapters in the ongoing campus follies." That pretty much took care of the no-publicity goal.

No one is supposed to know who writes any of the unsigned *Journal* editorials, but leading universities have become a particular target for one of the editorial writers, Dorothy Rabinowitz, whom one journalist who knows her calls an "ideological terrorist." Soon after the *DP* event, Hackney was advised to telephone her to explain his statement about it. Although he had appeared to equate diversity and free speech in one section, he reminded Rabinowitz that he had gone on to state, unequivocally, that free speech was the paramount value. "That conversation," Hackney told me with a small smile, "was so traumatic that I can almost remember it word for word." It also did no good. "It was something the *Wall Street Journal* just distorted. They caricatured me. That suited their purpose. They didn't care about me. They wanted a demon, which they could use to represent 'political correctness' and then they could flail the demon. If they have to distort the truth, that's what they will do. I do think they purposely distorted the truth."

Still, Hackney clung to the process. "The problem was that the president and the provost are not in the judicial process. For me to intervene would have been an extra-constitutional act, and it would have thrown the campus into a huge tizzy. Even later, friends and advisors urged me to say that although the president is not supposed to do this, it is so terrible that I'm intervening and calling it off. That would have been terrible. It would have involved the university in a huge and divisive squabble with who knows what sorts of activities on campus."

Hackney thought Jacobowitz would prevail before the panel, but the judicial system couldn't get its act together all winter and spring. "The JIO was busy, and then the JA, who was supposed to gather the committee, was a retired professor who sort of couldn't get everybody to agree to appear at the same time and the same place. This was an enormously contentious issue, so people were posing, and posturing, and jostling. There were some individual errors of judgment, but the system was set up to allow for that." The hearing was twice postponed, once by each side. When it was rescheduled for the summer, Jacobowitz protested that the score of witnesses he had recruited would be unavailable, so it was finally reset for May 14, near the close of the academic year. This was four months after the episode took place, a month after the still-simmering newspaper theft controversy, shortly before Hackney's NEH confirmation hearing.

Meanwhile, Kors had persuaded the judicial administrator that despite the charter, the May 14 hearing should deal with the possible dismissal of charges against Jacobowitz. As if that weren't enough, the JA didn't tell the five women or their advisor about the change in agenda, so that they came to the hearing prepared to argue the substance of the charges, not the question of dismissal. After a four-hour, secret session, the panel rejected Jacobowitz's request for dismissal, but postponed a hearing on the actual charges until the fall semester. It also "requested" that both sides "respect the confidentiality" of the proceedings—confidentiality in a case that had already been the subject of editorials and letters to the editor in the *Wall Street Journal,* of countless news stories and opinion columns in newspapers across the nation, and of threatened lawsuits.

To call that request naive is kind, and its nonsensicalness was instantly demonstrated. First, the five women called a press conference to announce that they were withdrawing their complaint from "a judicial process which has failed us miserably." They attacked Jacobowitz's efforts to "try this grievance among students in the national media." Because "we honored the university's confidentiality policy which precludes us from publicly responding, the coverage of this case, thus far, has been slanted in favor of the respondent." They were "victimized" on January 13, they said, then further by the media, and finally by the university judicial process.

It was here, finally, that the women's specific accusations were made public. They said someone had yelled, "Shut up you *black* [emphasis added] water buffalos," and "Go back to the zoo where you belong." Further, they said others had used "the 'N' word and sexually demeaning words" and "a word used to describe a female dog." It is not hard to believe that men in the high-rise dorm had yelled "nigger" and "bitch" and more; but no one, including Jacobowitz, was ever identified or specifically accused of doing so.

The only person ever accused held his own press conference at ACLU headquarters. Agreeing that "other people were yelling out of their windows all these really inflammatory words," Jacobowitz again denied that he had used the word "black" and stated his zoo reference as, "if you're looking for a party, there's a zoo a mile from here." The executive director of the Pennsylvania ACLU, Deborah Leavy, said, "the real problem is the hate-speech code; and until Penn gets rid of the hate-speech code, every student at Penn can fear going through what Eden went through, and that is too much punishment and too much chilling of speech. It has no place in an academic community."

The Penn professor who advised the women students, anthropologist Peggy Sanday, saw it differently. "This case should not be confused with issues of free speech or political correctness. Free speech and political correctness have to do with ideas, not with offensive conduct interfering with the rights of others." Everyone believes in the free exchange of ideas, she said, but "this case shows that we cannot agree on where fighting words end and free speech begins. Until we can determine the fine line between the two, the current all-out verbal warfare and abusive atmosphere that plagues so many of our campuses will continue."

M. J. Warrender, a thoughtful graduate student who served on an official board of inquiry into the episode, reflected with sadness on these different views. "Even though there was little disagreement as to what took place, everyone had a different perception as to what that action meant. The complainants had a completely different perception about what they considered racial harassment than Eden and his roommates, who heard all this noise outside and felt they were being harassed because they were trying to study and sleep; so they just started yelling things out the window. They were living separate realities. It's what one of my professors calls 'the garbage-can effect'— you bring to a situation all of your past hurts, all of your unresolved issues, and dump them as if in a garbage can."

After the other statements following the May 14 hearing, Hackney issued his own—notable for its wishful thinking. Calling the case "a painful experience for everyone involved in it and for the university as a whole," he said he was "thankful that it is over."

Not quite. First, the university commissioned a board of inquiry to tote up the errors in the process. This eventually produced modifications in the student judicial system. Then it created a Commission on Strengthening the Community to deal with such issues as conduct, campus environment, and communication, which led to revisions of Penn's speech code. Still, nothing could wipe clean the residue of unpleasant memories, as events of the next year demonstrated.

A few days later, however, good cheer prevailed as Hackney presided over his final commencement at Penn, with Hillary Rodham Clinton as principal speaker. Both the retiring president and his wife, Lucy Durr Hackney, received honorary degrees. (Sheldon Hackney and Bill Clinton met through their wives, both lawyers and trustees of the Children's Defense Fund.) "We were frightened that commencement would be turned into a sort of water buffalo and *DP* protest," one top Penn administrator said. "But nobody booed. No one wore little water buffalo things on their hats. There was great applause for Sheldon."

Sent off from Penn with warm appreciation for his leadership, Hackney faced his next test at NEH confirmation hearings that summer. Armed with clips from the *Journal* editorial page, conservatives on the Senate Labor and Human Resources Committee pushed him hard on the issues of speech codes and political correctness. "I resent bitterly being victimized by slander, by slogan," Hackney snapped back. "I am not just a cardboard figure. I am someone who has spent his career defending free speech, and I will do that at the NEH as well." One remarkable touch was the appearance in Washington of Jacobowitz, a 19-year-old college freshman who, believing that his act of calling some college women water buffalos qualified him as a pundit, had the hubris to call a press conference to oppose Hackney's confirmation. Hackney was confirmed by a Senate vote of 76-23, the negative votes traceable almost completely to the *DP* and water buffalo cases.

Back at Penn, the board of inquiry—three professors, one graduate student, and one undergraduate—labored for nearly a year, averaging a meeting a week, spending hundreds of volunteer hours interviewing and discussing. Their reward was contumely. "There was so much upheaval over our report," said Warrender, who delayed her thesis to serve the university, "we kind of just threw up our hands and said we don't want to do this anymore. We did what we were supposed to do and we spent two semesters doing it. After that experience, I was so disgusted with university politics I just wanted out."

Noting that it had not been asked to rule on "the issue of guilt or innocence of the respondent," the board found much to fault in the judicial procedure. It criticized the judicial inquiry officer for increasing the proposed sanctions against Jacobowitz after their original agreement, stating, "[T]he act of elevating the proposed penalties, at any point, is coercive [and] erodes the good faith required for success." It condemned the unofficial negotiations between Kors and the judicial administrator, the Jacobowitz publicity campaign, and the intervention of outside organizations such as the ACLU. It pointed up holes in the judicial charter and recommended changes, such as speeding the appointment of hearing panels, better preparing faculty advisors, increasing emphasis on mediation, and creating a system to review the actions of the JIO. It also concluded that "serious deviations" from proper procedure justified the "complainants' condemnation of the process and their withdrawal from it."

The report inflamed Kors, who responded caustically in a letter to the *Almanac*, Penn's remarkably candid faculty-staff newsletter. His opening sentence referred to the board as "distinguished but uninformed," and unloaded a series of accusations against a variety of university authorities. The board "views the media and the ACLU in the manner that the state of Mississippi in the 1960s viewed what it termed 'outside agitators,'" Kors continued. It "may prefer a set of mechanisms in which powerless innocent people must defend themselves against Kafkaesque charges in the shadows of collusive injustice, but, universities in their self-image excepted, this remains America. . . . As I had said to Sheldon Hackney [and others], if you are going to lynch this kid, you are going to have to do it in the sunshine, with the world watching." Kors concluded with references to the "vile, repugnant, wicked dishonesty of this affair" and the "catastrophic incompetence" of the panel.

Invited by the *Almanac* to respond, Professor Jacob Abel, who chaired the board of inquiry, began: "One needs a taste for irony to get by in academic life. I may be the only member of the faculty who has been excoriated by both Houston Baker [an outspoken, leftist black professor] and Alan Kors—a distinction but not one to be particularly relished." Kors's criticisms, Abel said, "really can be summarized by saying that the five of us didn't do what he wanted us to do." Abel said the ACLU should have gone to court, as it threatened to do, instead of mucking in the structured university proceedings. It was in the courts that Penn's counsel "and the ACLU should have met— wide out in the open rather than in a back room deal ratified by a fax and kept secret from the complainants." Kors and the ACLU chose the wrong strategy, "one that did not bring the real issues into the sunlight but rather brought Professor Kors into the limelight. Ironically, Mr. Jacobowitz was a victim of that error as well."

The letters to the *Almanac* continued for weeks. In early May, a long missive from Jacobowitz reargued his case and defended his advisor Kors; it was followed by opposite arguments in letters from two of the women, from Kors again, then Abel again. Three weeks later, Kors viciously escalated the conflict: "Professor Abel continues to misinform the Penn community, for reasons beyond honesty, integrity, and decency. It truly is a moral scandal!" This ad hominem assault on a faculty colleague was published May 24, 1994, a year to the day after Hackney pronounced the water buffalo affair "over."

The *DP* episode of the previous spring had reached a conclusion somewhat more rapidly, but with comparable bitterness. In this matter, the university tiptoed across racial eggshells by commissioning three different ad hoc studies. The first, an "independent review panel" charged with examining events on the night of the thefts, reported in the summer that it had found fault on all sides. The panel said, for example, that the black students should have shown their student identification when asked to do so; it did not comment on the absence of common sense inherent in identifying oneself while committing a theft. It also said that if the black students intended the thefts as a form of protest, they should have alerted official university "open expression monitors." Yes, Penn had raised protest to an art form by designating Open Expression Monitors to oversee it; the panel did not explain how the protesters were supposed to steal the papers if they alerted university monitors in advance. (One might ask: Is Open Expression Monitor an oxymoron?)

The university police and the five-foot, four-inch museum staffer who had chased down the students came off worse. The police thought they were only doing their jobs, stopping thefts and asking for student ID; but they were supposed to understand immediately, while chasing thieves in the middle of a hectic night, that several emergency calls around campus indicated an organized protest. A number of them were reprimanded. One supervisor and one officer received a "letter of counseling," two officers received "oral warnings," another officer was suspended without pay for three days for his use of a baton. The staffer who thought he was protecting the museum received a "letter of counseling."

The second report came in the fall from a professor appointed as a special judicial inquiry officer—presumably this case was too hot for the regular JIO. He was responsible for deciding whether the protesters had violated the student charter, and if so, what punishment they should receive. He noted that since 1987, when a faculty member had confiscated some *DPs*, the official faculty-administration handbook held that: "The confiscation of publications on campus is inconsistent with the University's policies and procedures, and with the ideals of the University. . . . [Those responsible] should expect to be held accountable." But the students shouldn't have been expected to know that stealing newspapers was irresponsible, the professor said, since that restriction did not appear in the student handbook.

Still, he found the "confiscation . . . even as an act of protest" violated university policy. He also found the community "in need of healing," that students seemed willing to talk to each other, and that the administration was committed to dealing with future "institutional lapses." He recommended that students be told that stealing publications is unacceptable and "constructive dialogue" be encouraged. What about the students he found to have committed a "violation?" Nothing. "There is no need for further judicial or disciplinary action," he declared. The acting president of the university, Claire Fagin, announced her approval of this decision.

The third report, delivered the next year, offered new protocols for university police training, arrest procedures, and use of force.

The Commission on Strengthening the Community (part of the water buffalo fallout) issued a 20,000-word report in the spring of 1994. It recommended that "student speech as such should not be the basis of disciplinary action. . . . [R]ecent and painful experience at this University suggests that the entire enterprise of attempting to discipline student-to-student speech deflects attention from the underlying problems. The message is wrong for offender and offended alike, and the process is likely to open more wounds than it heals." The commission also recommended that "[t]he process or processes used to resolve allegations of minor student misconduct should be less formal and most expeditious." Without authority over the independent student newspaper, the commission suggested, "We urge the *Daily Pennsylvanian* to consider making use of the services of an ombudsman, which is a common journalistic practice."

A month later, the university abandoned the rules under which Jacobowitz had been charged in favor of a new speech code, which stated, "The university condemns hate speech, epithets, and racial, ethnic, sexual, and religious slurs. However, the content of student speech or expression is not by itself a basis for disciplinary action. Student speech may be subject to discipline when it violates applicable laws or university regulations or policies." A university spokeswoman explained that the code "simply means speech that breaks the law will be punished. If you say, 'You're fat, I'm going to kill you,' that's against federal law. If you say that at this university, you're going to be punished."

A committee of students and faculty had debated for weeks before striking a provision that could have left speech more easily punishable: "[P]atterns of student speech or expression may constitute conduct." But Jacobowitz, who had completed his sophomore year, was not pleased. "There's a new speech code that says absolutely nothing," he declared. "The university is just paying lip service to alumni who are up in arms about the way the university has treated students over the past year." The *Daily Pennsylvanian*, however, was mollified: "Anything that allows for true freedom of speech is something we support."

In retrospect, Hackney is still "not sure what the press office could have done" to ease the pain of these two events, but he does regret not having a news professional in his inner circle. Farnsworth, the chief public affairs officer, reported to the vice president and secretary of the university, Barbara Stephens, who had "very good judgment" in Hackney's estimation but little news experience and a strict sense of hierarchy that kept Farnsworth from reaching the president as often as she thought necessary.

One tale in particular illustrates how far out of the loop Penn's news service was. One day in March 1993 (two months after the water buffalo episode occurred and while behind-the-scenes negotiations were taking place), an ACLU representative was meeting with Barbara Beck, director of news and public affairs, on an unrelated matter. He casually mentioned the water buffalo story, which he knew about and assumed she did, too. "I had no idea what he was talking about," Beck said, "and I thought, that's an incredible story; it couldn't possibly have happened here. I told him, I think you must mean Penn State." Beck went to her boss, Farnsworth, who said she didn't know either; that is when Farnsworth called the president's office and procured the letter Jacobowitz had already sent to journalists.

Beck remembered a variety of issues in which the news office was called upon to write public statements without being close enough to the decision makers to know what to say. "Even when advice was given from this office on how to handle a situation, it was not taken," she said, "or the advice was asked for after the situation broke. We had to put out the fire." "When there was a crisis," Farnsworth said, "there would be a meeting called, and it would inevitably be late in the day, or the morning after the episode, so by now it was almost a whole business day later. There would be all these people assembled to discuss the problem and decide what to do, which was by then much too late for any good media placement of what we were doing."

The two episodes in the spring of 1993 did lead to the formulation of a modest crisis communications plan, but not to an increase in Farnsworth's authority. The next year she left to become vice chancellor for university relations at the University of Denver, reporting directly to the chancellor. And the news service appeared not to be a high priority for Penn's new president, Judith Rodin, who took nearly two years to fill the top job.

In the spring of 1996, Rodin chose Kenneth Wildes, who had spent 15 years at Northwestern University, a decade under well-regarded President Arnold Weber. The critical negotiating point, in Wildes's estimation, was the reporting line: He answers directly to the president, with the title director of university communications. "Reporting to the president is the only way to go," Wildes said. "I would not have come unless Judith Rodin was prepared to make that change." He considers his next most crucial relationships to be with the offices of legal affairs and student affairs.

Wildes sees three principal elements of his role: national visibility, strategic planning in public affairs, and crisis and issues management. For the first two he likes to convene what amounts to focus groups with deans and department heads, partly to find out what audiences and issues are their priorities, and also because they frequently have unrealistic expectations about what the news service can accomplish. The academic administrators must determine "what is the responsibility of university relations and what the schools have to do on their own, because clearly there are some things schools have to do on their own." He also resists "the temptation to say we will service equally every academic area of the institution, because we can't unless there are vast resources."

The key to crisis management—Wildes shares this view with Farnsworth and most other news officers—is preparation. At Northwestern, "we created a working group as soon as a crisis was apparent, whether it had broken out or not." If important enough, it was chaired by the president himself; the general counsel and chief news officer were always part of it, and other administrators as their areas were concerned. In one egregious struggle with animal rights activists, the university working group met on and off for six and a half years. Shorter-lived was a group prepared to signal swiftly Northwestern's continued commitment to a successful athletic program when it appeared that football coach Gary Barnett might jump ship in early 1996 after leading the Wildcats to the most glorious season in their history. The group disbanded when Barnett signed a long-term contract.

Sheldon Hackney appreciates now more than he did then the value of getting in front of a news event. "Colleges and universities ought to be aware of the framing of anything that becomes a public issue. The way it is framed originally is crucial, because that's the way the public will perceive it. There's a ripple effect, and newspapers 2,000 miles away are writing stories because they read it on the Associated Press wire, or they read it in the *Wall Street Journal,* and they basically accept the premise of the first story."

Hackney has also come to believe that changed circumstances demand that college presidents become adept in managing public affairs. "What is happening in America in general is that things are played out much more in the public arena. That is an arena that responds to symbols and to a set of rules that most of us don't know. Increasingly, public relations is a fundamental part of the job. You can't get things done unless you, and your organization, are somehow good at explaining in public your side of the story, doing that in ways that are extremely skillful. There are other people who are going to manipulate the symbols and the news, so college presidents have to be much better at that than we have tended to be."

The water buffalo and *DP* cases at Penn burned both its student judicial system and its public affairs apparatus. The labyrinthine judicial process grew from an effort to treat modern-day students in an appropriately formal manner while shielding them with old-fashioned *in loco parentis* from the outside world's legal system. The news operation relied on old-fashioned academic controls of information when it needed crisp professionalism to cope with the outside world's increasing attention. Penn was caught in a time warp.

AFTERWORD

Doing the Right Things
Thoughts on Improving Public Affairs Programs in Colleges and Universities

T his book is not intended as a formal text. It contains no set of black-letter rules, no hard *do's* and *don't's*, no checklists for beginners to turn to when crisis strikes. In an academic sense, I think of it more like a law-school casebook: *This is what happened, and this is how and why it happened. Now, think about it, think about what you might have done to change the outcome, think about what you would do if faced with similar circumstances. Let's discuss it.*

CO-OPT THE PRESS

Telling their stories, for colleges and universities, means both touting the good and explaining the uncomfortable. Over the years, in talks to groups of university news officers, I have frequently offered a particular suggestion to which many respond, "I could never get my president to agree to that," or "They would never let us do that." My suggestion is that in times of crisis universities should be as open with the media as they possibly can. And be open as quickly as possible. Instead of being unavailable, or trying to withhold information, administrators should be ready to speak with reporters, and news officers should assist them in gathering information. For example, if certain faculty members disagree with the administration on a particular issue, let reporters know who they are.

Obviously, this policy has risks. But the recommendation is not intended to make journalists' lives easier, let alone embarrass the institution. It is designed to do no more than take advantage of circumstances and human nature. First, reporters will almost always find on their own most of the people they want to interview, and most of the information they want. And if the university doesn't tell its side of the story—in as detailed a way as possible and as rapidly as possible—reporters are more likely to get its side wrong, or get someone else's version of what purports to be its side. Second, however difficult it is for some to accept, journalists are human beings. If someone cooperates with them, is helpful to them, they are far more likely to write an understanding piece this time and treat the person in a more positive light in the future. In short, the recommendation is to co-opt the press.

SEIZE OPPORTUNITIES

Colleges and universities often fail to consider the most obvious public relations steps. For instance, why have they allowed the benchmark year for measuring tuition increases to be 1980, a time when the rate of inflation was beginning to fall and tuition was only beginning to catch up with huge jumps in the cost of living? Why not 1975, when the rate of inflation was increasing in double digits and tuition did not come close to matching it? And why have institutions not made clearer that increases in "administration" result largely from government requirements and student-comfort demands?

Universities have understood for years the importance of having strong development offices. They have learned more recently the value of good admissions officers, who by necessity have become marketing experts. Yet fewer institutions have grasped the importance of building a powerful public affairs office, staffed with skilled, experienced, well-remunerated professionals. Skilled news officers can tell an institution's story in the best ways and protect it in times of crises, with the added benefit of helping administrators and faculty understand how news media work.

CONSISTENT THEMES

In evaluating universities that have struggled through crises, a number of themes appear consistent. Administrators usually claim that by objective standards, they suffered relatively little. The private universities can show that fund raising remained steady, even in the face of embarrassing news, and public institutions seldom received blunt financial punishment from legislators or donors. Most institutions did not appear to have slipped in numbers of freshman applications or yield rate. On a research level, little faculty exodus occurred, and grants from government and private sources held up. All those elements are affected by many things, crisis being just one. Yet statistics tell only part of the story. Reflecting on the big picture, administrators and faculty responded as if they were thinking out loud, and the conclusions at almost every institution were similar: "Did we suffer? By the numbers, perhaps not too much. But was it damaging to morale and painful for how we thought of ourselves, and how our friends thought about us? Yes, it was."

Several institutions examined here survived gracefully. Brown, Queens, and Ohio State faced hugely different public affairs crises: prostitution by senior women living off-campus; an independent student newspaper dealing with an outsider's anti-Semitic propaganda; and the firing of a football coach who was the best-known public figure in the state. But they certainly had one thing in common: They cooperated with the media. Brown did it by confronting the press, even shaming the mainstream press, while answering every reporter's questions. Queens did it by maintaining lines of communication to its internal and external Jewish constituencies and co-opting the redoubtable 60 Minutes. Ohio State did it by informing its trustees and planning its media posture moments after the decision had been made and before the dismissal had occurred.

Stanford, Utah, and Virginia represented a different kind of problem: issues that were large and essentially beyond institutional control. Stanford, historically one of the most open universities, had the bad luck to be undergoing an upheaval in its news operation when the crisis erupted and perhaps the bad judgment to have pushed the indirect-cost envelope too far. But the issue once opened was so consequential, so potentially far-reaching, and so caught up in Washington politics that almost nothing could have avoided the embarrassment the university suffered.

Administrators at Utah, which like Stanford has long had a nationally respected public affairs office, clearly focused too much on tempting financial prospects and because of that paid too much attention to outside lawyers unappreciative of academic culture. But the university also found itself caught in a brutal fight between turf-guarding chemists and physicists over a cold-fusion issue big enough to affect the future of the planet, so that it could do little more than repeat its bona fides and trust that its long-term record would restore its honor. Virginia, ensnared by its fame, ambitious police officers, and racially fueled town-gown conflict, found itself a "poster child" for a national war against drugs. It could not cope with the press immediately after the raids on fraternities because law enforcement officials from Charlottesville to Washington controlled not only the flow of events but the flow of information.

South Carolina was a special case because the university, the capital city, even the whole state had been hypnotized by a smoothie president who harnessed institutional fame to his own. It was essential to his style that only he and his closest confidants dispensed information, so that an enervated public relations operation could barely pick up the pieces for an embarrassed university when the con game fell apart. Georgia was victimized by misjudgments at the highest levels of its administration, caused by a startling lack of understanding about the importance of public opinion in a trial that turned on the honor of the football program, and by a fundamental distrust of the media as messenger. The university's opponents understood that the real battle would be fought in the court of public opinion. At Penn, the administration wanted to maintain silence about the "water buffalo" case for the most honorable of reasons: to protect the privacy of students and to follow the university's scrupulously drawn rules of conduct. But it appeared to have little confidence in its news officers, who were never close to the decision-making process, and when events exploded in the press, they were incapable either of advising or of stemming the flood of unpleasant attention.

IN THE LOOP

One theme that emerges from many of the studies is that a university causes needless trouble for itself when someone skilled and experienced in dealing with the news media is not "in the loop"—that is, does not know everything important occurring at the institution. Ordinarily this would be the chief news officer. But it doesn't actually have to be a person so designated if a higher-level official with appropriate skills and experience is close enough to the president. Unless the president is accustomed to dealing comfortably with the press, and sometimes even then, someone else in her or his confidence must be familiar with events or circumstances bubbling through the institution, even when there is no immediate prospect that they will boil and splatter. This means that the news officer (or equivalent) must be present at regular meetings of the president's top advisors. If there are two such regular meetings, one administrative, for executive staff, and another more academic that includes deans, the news officer ought to attend both. She or he should serve as an early warning system.

The importance of access can be compared to the White House. When the president's press secretary is a respected advisor and privy to policy decisions, the press is usually mollified, and the president will look at least as good to the public as he deserves. James Haggerty and Dwight Eisenhower formed one such pair. When the press secretary doesn't know what is really going on— Ron Ziegler with Richard Nixon—bad conditions become worse. Bill Clinton's first press secretary, DeeDee Meyers, was frequently uninformed, which frustrated both her and the media; when Michael D. McCurry demanded and received high-level access as a condition of taking the job, both sides benefitted.

CHARACTER AND ABILITY

This relationship requires, of course, that the president of the university trust the character and ability of her or his chief public affairs officer. Character, as demonstrated by loyalty both to the institution and the president, and discretion when entrusted with the most confidential information. Ability, as demonstrated externally by the news officer's exchanges with the media—how he or she persuades reporters to respect the institution and understand the difficulties inherent in its decisions—and internally by the soundness of the advice he or she provides, in long-range planning and under emergency conditions. Both character and ability are enhanced by experience—as a journalist, or within higher education, preferably both. To attract people like this requires paying them substantial salaries. If the public affairs office is treated as a junior billet, with junior people earning junior incomes, the quality of their work will probably be commensurate with their standing.

COMMAND DECISIONS

Many presidents don't appreciate the value of a skillful public affairs officer and news staff. They have frequently come to their positions through the ranks of academe, having spent little time dealing with the media and having absorbed their profession's standard biases: Journalists are not to be trusted; they are at best sloppy and unknowledgeable, at worst out to get you. Some of these feelings may be valid—journalists are skilled and honorable at only about the same rate as people in other educated professions. But the fact is that universities today must spread much of their message through the media, like it or not, so they had better understand how to spread it as smoothly as possible.

The importance of the position should lead top administrators to focus more precisely on the selection of chief public affairs officers than they often do. The appointments should be made not at some intermediate level but only with the direct participation of the president or at the least the president's chief deputy. Chemistry counts; presidents should get along with their press envoys. The chief executive must have confidence not just in the ability of the person to supervise the routine work of the news operation but in that person's strength in the face of crisis. As one president said of her choice, "I needed someone who wouldn't fall apart when things got tough."

A VARIETY OF MODELS

No one can prescribe a perfect model for university communications. Organization varies, the rank in the administrative hierarchy of the chief public information officer varies, and the name assigned to the information office varies. Neither the organization pattern, the chief officer's rank, nor the departmental name is a certain guide to the influence of the information operation on the institution and its executive officers. The name of the department, for example, may be the office of university relations, or public relations, or news, or news services, or public affairs, or public information. The person who supervises it may hold the title of vice president (or vice chancellor), associate or assistant vice president, or director. The public information function may operate as a semiautonomous entity or be part of the development division. The chief information officer may report directly to the president or have a dotted-line relationship to the president or report to the president through a vice president. The organization and reporting lines vary depending on the overall structure of the institution, such as whether it has a medical school.

Obviously there are exceptions. At the University of Virginia, the chief news officer, Louise Dudley, reports to Executive Vice President Leonard Sandridge, who supervises all the workings of the institution except academic affairs. Dudley doesn't attend cabinet meetings, but, in Sandridge's words, "except for the boring parts" she learns what goes on at those meetings. This organization pattern works because President John Casteen III has confidence in Sandridge, who has confidence in Dudley. But it wouldn't be surprising to see it change with new top executives.

The lesson from Virginia is that relationships between people can transcend organizational structure. It may not be essential for the news director to attend top-level meetings, as long as certain criteria are met: The vice president who supervises public information is close to the president; the vice president (and the president) are unusually attuned to public affairs, and the vice president and the news director communicate closely—the vice president keeping the news director well informed and the news director informing the vice president about information he or she may have learned in dealing with the media.

THE PRESIDENTIAL PRESENCE

Clearly some presidents are better prepared to deal with the press than others. A few like Rita Bornstein of Rollins College have come directly from university development divisions. Edward T. Foote II, president of the University of Miami, was a newspaper reporter before attending law school and entering academe. Vartan Gregorian, who was president of Brown University before accepting the presidency of the Carnegie Corporation of New York, had established himself as one of New York City's most visible public figures during his earlier tenure as president of the New York Public Library, fraternizing with the media capital's most prominent journalists not just professionally but socially.

Gregorian inherited at Brown one of the nation's best higher-education public-affairs officers in Robert A. Reichley, who had served as the university's major spokesman under the cautious and media-distrustful Howard Swearer. Reichley, who was also responsible for alumni relations and special events, could speak confidently to the public because he was closely informed about critical matters within the institution. The balance changed under Gregorian, who was as comfortable in the media spotlight as any university president in the country. Gregorian and Reichley needed a different kind of relationship, and both were smart enough to develop one.

As president at Stanford, Donald Kennedy was a man accustomed to media pressure from his days as a high-level administrator in Washington. He reveled in dealing with the public at any level. He encouraged a news operation long renowned for its openness and spoke often and candidly—perhaps too often and too candidly—about consequential issues concerning Stanford, in particular, and higher education, in general. But there are public figures and public figures. James D. Holderman at South Carolina was a most visible president, yet he absorbed so much statewide attention that his university played a supporting role. Given Holderman's style, the structure of the public information office at South Carolina became irrelevant.

Confidence played a big role in the successful organizational structures at Ohio State and Queens. Both presidents, Harold Enarson and Shirley Strum Kenny, understood the significance of media relations and both were comfortable dealing with the press. At the same time, they had vice presidents, Edwin M. Crawford and Ceil Cleveland, whom they trusted with the whole gamut of external relations, including news. Thus, although the news directors usually dealt with the presidents through the vice presidents, there was no disconnection, either in planning or in crisis situations.

INFORM AND TEACH

In recent years the public has become increasingly impatient with institutions of higher education. So it is useful, I believe, for college and university trustees, administrators, and faculty to understand better how their behavior and their decisions are communicated to their external constituencies. By examining crises that some institutions have undergone in the past, others may benefit in the future. I hope that this book not only informs but teaches.

One thing more. I have tried to tell these stories in human terms. I have tried to empathize with these leaders, in their times of crises, just as I hope readers will.

A NOTE ABOUT
SOURCES

This book relies on two principal categories of primary sources: personal interviews and contemporaneous newspaper and magazine accounts. (A third category could be my experiences as a journalist who followed the events as they occurred; informal but important.)

The significant events in all but one of the case studies took place between 1986 and 1993 (the exception is Ohio State, in which one of the two pivotal events occurred in late 1978, the other in early 1986). Thus, they are well remembered by the leading players, nearly all of whom I interviewed personally. These events are well remembered not merely because of proximity in time but because they were so important to the people involved (and often unnerving). As one of the interviewees said about a particular moment, "That conversation was so traumatic that I can almost remember it word for word."

I conducted nearly 100 major formal interviews. Myself; no researcher did any. Except for two or three telephone conversations, every interview was face to face. All are on tape and were transcribed by me personally, creating nearly 800 single-spaced pages of text. This may seem like inefficient use of time (transcriptions generally take four or five times longer to produce than the interviews themselves), but it was done for two reasons: first, to capture every useful word, even if it meant rerunning a tape a half-dozen times (in contrast to professional transcriptions, full of "indecipherable," "passage not understood," or statements that were plainly misunderstood); and second, to help me recall the scene as no transcript could. The setting for almost every interview was the respective campus. I visited every one, spending several days, sometimes during several visits, which gave me a sense of place and the opportunity to speak informally with many people.

Almost everyone was willing to speak on the record. Some asked to go on "background" or off the record occasionally, on certain subjects. A few sources asked that they not be identified at all (see those noted below). Only three people who could have contributed significantly to the book declined to be interviewed.

Separate citations for individual quotations are not included. In most cases, this is plainly unnecessary; the speaker's name accompanies the quotation. If the name is not included, the source is usually apparent. In some cases, the speaker did not want his name used. Similarly, separate citations are not used for the basic details in the studies, for example, a criminal sentence after a drug raid, or the result of a football game. Nearly always, such information came from contemporaneous newspaper or magazine reports. It seemed to be repetitious to cite the same publications over and over again. Names of the publications are given below and sometimes cited in the text.

All tape recordings and all transcripts of interviews are in my files. All news stories used as sources are also in my files.

Interviews were carried out over a period of more than two years, mostly in the summers of 1994, 1995, and 1996. Not surprisingly, many of the subjects have changed professional positions from the time of the interview to this writing (and no doubt others will up to publication of this book). They are identified by title at the time of the interview. (In a few instances, in the text, new positions are noted.)

All these cases were thoroughly covered in newspapers and magazines at the time they occurred. As might be expected under deadline pressure, some of the facts were reported inaccurately, and some misunderstandings and incorrect judgments found their way into the stories. I have attempted to correct those faults. But the stories gave essential details and a framework for the new interviews. Most of the news stories were provided by the institutions themselves, which usually kept careful records; some came from newspaper libraries. Information on every case also came from the *Chronicle of Higher Education*, gathered in 1994 by Charles Ornstein, who was serving as an intern. My thanks for the cooperation of the top editors at the *Chronicle*. Altogether, I read more than 1,000 newspaper and magazine stories.

Sources and interviews for each case follow.

CHAPTER 1: STANFORD UNIVERSITY

As the five volumes of press clippings in the office of Larry Horton, the director of community and government relations, suggest, the indirect cost episode was one of the most widely covered higher education stories in years. Horton provided important material, including videotapes of the Dingell subcommittee hearing and the *20/20* program concerning Stanford, and Terry Shepard, director of university communication, provided a great deal. Bob Beyers, former director of the News Service and still a chronicler of matters Stanford, shared his cache of information about the university collected over the years.

The many important Stanford interviews include

Bruce Anderson—former Editor, *Stanford* magazine

Bob Beyers—former Director, Stanford News Service

Bob Cohn—Editor, *Stanford* Magazine

Doug Foster—Director, Stanford News Service

Larry Horton—Director of Community and Government Relations, Stanford

Donald Kennedy—former President, Stanford

Robert Rosenzweig—former President, Association of American Universities; former Vice President for University Relations, Stanford

Terry Shepard—Director of University Communication, Stanford

William Stone—President, Stanford Alumni Association

Three sources asked not to be named.

CHAPTER 2: UNIVERSITY OF UTAH

Thousands of newspaper and magazine stories written about the cold-fusion episode were collected by the Office of University Communications in two three-inch-thick looseleaf notebooks and provided by Director Pamela W. Fogle.

The many detailed and candid interview subjects include

James C. Bapis—Science Writer, University News Service, Utah

Pamela W. Fogle—Director, University Communications, Utah

Raymond A. Haeckel—Executive Director, Government and Community Relations; former Director of Public Relations, Utah

Richard Koehn—Vice President for Research, Utah

Chase Peterson—former President, Utah

Hugo Rossi—Professor of Mathematics, former Dean of College of Science, Utah

Arthur K. Smith—President, Utah

One source asked not to be named.

CHAPTER 3: UNIVERSITY OF GEORGIA

Details of the events surrounding Jan Kemp's lawsuit, in particular the trial, were gathered from newspapers that covered them thoroughly. They were, primarily, the *Atlanta Constitution*, the *Atlanta Journal*, the *Athens Daily News*, the *Athens Banner Herald*, and the *Macon Telegraph*. I inspected most of these stories in the University of Georgia library archives; the library provided photocopies of those I thought most pertinent. (The Office of Legal Affairs at the university assigned a junior lawyer to screen all these 10-year-old stories before I was allowed to see them, even though I was accompanied at the time by the director of the Office of Public Information. This was the only institution to do so.)

Much of the discussion in this chapter is based on long and exceptionally candid interviews with those most closely concerned with the case. They include

Lee Anderson—widow of Robert Anderson, former Vice President for Research, UGA

Ralph Beaird—former Dean of Law, UGA

Scott Cutlip—former Dean of Journalism, UGA

Fred Davison—President, National Science Center Foundation, Augusta, Georgia; former President, UGA

Vince Dooley—Athletic Director, former head football coach, UGA

Donald Eastman—Vice President for Development and University Relations, UGA

Hue Henry—Athens lawyer, counsel to Jan Kemp

Tom Jackson—Director of Public Information, UGA

Jane V. Kidd—educational consultant, Athens; former member of the Office of Public Relations, UGA

Charles Knapp—President, UGA

Tom Landrum—Special Assistant to the President, former Director of Public Relations, UGA

Virginia Trotter—former Vice President for Academic Affairs, UGA

Barry Wood—Director of Public Affairs and Special Assistant to the President, National Science Center Foundation; former Director of Public Relations, UGA

Two sources asked not to be named.

CHAPTER 4: QUEENS COLLEGE

The written material for this chapter came primarily from two sources. Andrew Wallenstein shared information on the Queens College episode that he had collected for his personal files. Bradley Smith shared his extensive files on his dealings with college newspapers, including the aftermath of ads placed, as well as other personal material.

The important interviews include

Ron Cannava—Director of Public Relations, Queens

Ceil Cleveland—Vice President for University Affairs, University at Stony Brook; former Vice President for Institutional Relations, Queens

Chris Ferraro—former Managing Editor, *The Quad*, Queens

Edward T. Foote II—President, University of Miami

Shirley Strum Kenny—President, University at Stony Brook; former President, Queens
Bradley Smith—writer; affiliate, Institute of Historical Review
Andrew Wallenstein—former Editor, *The Quad*, Queens

CHAPTER 5: UNIVERSITY OF SOUTH CAROLINA

Much of the general material about James D. Holderman's presidency and its aftermath came from newspaper accounts in the *Charlotte Observer* and the *State* of Columbia. I am indebted to the chief librarians of the newspapers, Sara Klemmer of the *Observer* and Dargan Richards of the *State*, for their assistance.

The bulk of the material on which my analysis was based comes from interviews with people close to the events. They include
David Beasley—Governor of South Carolina
Peter Becker—Professor of History, USC
Henry Eichel—Columbia correspondent, the *Charlotte Observer*
Gunther Holst—Professor of German Literature, USC
Russell McKinney—Director of University Affairs, USC
John Monk—Washington, D. C., correspondent, the *Charlotte Observer*
Cheryl Perkins—Columbia lawyer, who with her husband, Paul, brought the Freedom of Information Act suit that led to the opening of the Holderman records
Paul Perkins—Columbia lawyer (see Cheryl Perkins, above)
Fred Sheheen—Executive Director, South Carolina Commission on Higher Education
Arthur Smith—President, University of Utah; former Provost, USC
Gil Thelen—Executive Editor, the *State*, Columbia
Ginny Wolfe—Press Secretary to Governor Beasley
Two sources asked not to be named.

CHAPTER 6: BROWN UNIVERSITY

Details about the arrest of the two Brown students and the Providence businessman and the subsequent police and judicial proceedings, as well as profiles of the students, came from contemporaneous newspaper and magazine accounts. Details about other Brown events and well-known students also came from contemporaneous news and feature stories. A large part of this material is in the files of the Brown University News Service, which allowed me to read and copy it. Most of the information comes from interviews. They include
Eric Broudy—Associate Vice President, Brown

Vartan Gregorian—President, Brown
Robert A. Reichley—Executive Vice President, Brown
Richard S. Tamurini—Deputy Chief of Police of Providence; former head of
    the department's plainclothes unit
One police official and one other source asked not to be named.

CHAPTER 7: THE UNIVERSITY OF VIRGINIA

The University of Virginia News Service provided copies of the hundreds of
news stories written about the drug raids and their aftermath, primarily in
newspapers in Charlottesville, Richmond, Washington, D.C., and New York.
Louise Dudley, director of university relations, also made available valuable
university material, such as guides, histories, and the contract governing
Contracted Independent Organizations.

   Important interviews about the university and the raids include
Staige Blackford—Editor, *Virginia Quarterly Review*
John DeKoven (Deke) Bowen—Chief of Police, Charlottesville
Robert Canevari—Dean of Students, UVa
John T. Casteen III—President, UVa
Louise Dudley—Director of University Relations, UVa
William Fishback—Senior Advisor to the President and Lecturer in English;
    former Associate Vice President for University Relations, UVa
Robert M. O'Neil — President, Thomas Jefferson Center for the Protection of
    Free Expression, Charlottesville, Virginia; former President, UVa
Mike Sheffield — Chief of University Police, UVa
Leonard Sandridge — Executive Vice President, UVa
James Mingle — General Counsel to the University (Special Assistant Attor-
    ney-General of Virginia), UVa

CHAPTER 8: THE OHIO STATE UNIVERSITY

Two books were important to preparation of this chapter—*Beyond Winning:
The Timeless Wisdom of Great Philosopher Coaches,* by Gary M. Walton, and
*The Enarson Years, 1972–1981; Volume 9 of the History of The Ohio State
University,* by Paul Underwood. News stories about events surrounding Woody
Hayes's firing and his death were provided primarily by George Stroud, sports
editor of the *Dispatch* in Columbus, and Malcolm Baroway, executive director
of university relations at Ohio State. Two helpful videotapes contain compila-
tions of significant events in Hayes's life, such as the Clemson game, his Ohio
State commencement speech, and various interviews with him, as well as his

funeral service and a university memorial service. They were provided by John Mount, retired vice president of Ohio State.

Interviews furnished the most important information in the chapter. They include

Malcolm Baroway—Executive Director of University Relations, OSU

Edwin M. Crawford—consultant to the Council for Advancement and Support of Education; former Vice President for University Relations, OSU

Harold L. Enarson—former President, OSU

Gordon Gee—President, OSU

Archie Griffin—Associate Director of Athletics, OSU

Dan Heinlen—President of the Alumni Association, OSU

John Mount—former Vice President, OSU

Ruth Mount—former Dean of Students, OSU

Daryl Sanders—minister; former football player, OSU

George Stroud—Sports Editor, the *Dispatch,* Columbus

CHAPTER 9: UNIVERSITY OF PENNSYLVANIA

The *Almanac,* the faculty-staff newsletter at the University of Pennsylvania, is the most candid internal publication I have seen on any campus. In the water buffalo and the *Daily Pennsylvanian* cases, it not only published verbatim every official statement and report but letters in response to those statements and letters in response to the letters; thus it was a trove of material that in most other cases needed to be collected from several sources. Karen Grimes, its editor, provided many issues of the *Almanac* and other guidance to campus administration. The *Pennsylvania Gazette,* one of the nation's finest university magazines, covered the water buffalo and *DP* cases as it did other issues of interest to Penn alumni and friends—informatively and interestingly. Anthony Lyle, who was then its editor, provided the useful material.

Contemporary news stories, largely from newspapers in Philadelphia, Washington, D.C., and New York, and issues of the *Daily Pennsylvanian,* the independent student newspaper and itself a part of this case, were provided by the university Office of News and Public Affairs.

Interviews include

Barbara Beck—Acting Director, News and Public Affairs, Penn

Carol Farnsworth—Vice Chancellor for University Relations, University of Denver; former Associate Vice President for University Relations, Penn

Karen Grimes—Editor, *Almanac,* Penn

Sheldon Hackney—Chairman, National Endowment for the Humanities; former President, Penn

George Keller—analyst of American higher education; former director of the
    higher education program, Graduate School of Education, Penn
Marshall Ledger—Editor, *Penn Medicine* magazine
Anthony Lyle—Editor, *Pennsylvania Gazette*
M. J. Warrender—graduate student in higher education, Penn; member of the
    commission investigating procedure in the water buffalo case
Kenneth Wildes—Director of University Communications, Penn
Three sources asked not to be named.

INDEX

by Michele B. Graye

Note: A small *n* following a page number refers to a footnote.